EARLY TUDOR GOVERNMENT
HENRY VII

EARLY TUDOR GOVERNMENT
HENRY VII

BY

KENNETH PICKTHORN

1967

OCTAGON BOOKS, INC.
New York

First published 1934 by Cambridge University Press

Reprinted 1967
by permission of the Cambridge University Press

OCTAGON BOOKS, INC.
175 FIFTH AVENUE
NEW YORK, N. Y. 10010

LIBRARY OF CONGRESS CATALOG CARD NUMBER: 67-18780

Printed in U.S.A. by
NOBLE OFFSET PRINTERS, INC.
NEW YORK 3, N. Y.

PREFACE

Some years ago I began to write a one-volume Constitutional History from 1485. The opening chapters grew longer and longer, partly from a desire to make the starting-point as firm as possible, partly from the necessity of working rather short spells at rather long intervals, and the consequent tendency to elaborate the comparatively detailed. The original intention was soon abandoned, and an attempt undertaken to describe the condition of government and its development under the first two Tudors. Beginning in the middle of the history of English government, I felt bound to try first to indicate the circumstances of a particular generation, and this could hardly be done otherwise than analytically; but I tried to be fairly chronological from the first, and on reaching Henry VIII to make the order mainly that of time rather than that of the topics into which governmental history might be analysed.

I hope that the footnotes indicate all direct obligations to books, and that with the help of the list on pages 183–6 the books may be easily found in catalogues and bibliographies. My personal debts are so many that an enumeration of some of them may look like pretention, but it is possible to owe much without having much to show.

Anything more than the slightest schoolboy interest in constitutional history I owe to the immense good fortune of having been as an undergraduate taught by Mr D. A. Winstanley and Mr G. T. Lapsley, Fellows of Trinity College. Without the late Sir Geoffrey Butler, Fellow and Librarian of Corpus Christi College and Burgess for the University, courage to embark upon a long book would have been lacking. Nor would it have held out but for the kindness of the Regius Professor, of the late Dr J. R. Tanner, Fellow of St John's College, of Professor C. H. Williams of Sidney Sussex College and King's College, London, each of whom read some early portions of the book in the first draft and saved it some errors, as did also Sir William Holdsworth, Vinerian Professor of English Law in the University of Oxford.

Professor A. F. Pollard and Professor A. P. Newton, both of London University, and Professor P. H. Winfield of the University of Cambridge, very kindly and helpfully answered questions which I put to them.

I am very grateful also to the authorities and officials of the British Museum and of the Cambridge University Library, especially to Mr Arthur Ellis, superintendent of the Reading Room, and to Mr Pink of Room Theta, each of whom did much for me which I had no right to expect.

KENNETH PICKTHORN

Cambridge

July 1934

CONTENTS

CHAPTER I

HENRY'S RESOURCES, *pp.* 1–27

CHAPTER II

COUNCIL, *pp.* 28–50

CHAPTER III

JUDGES, JUSTICES OF PEACE, FORCE, JURIES, *pp.* 51–88

Contents

CHAPTER IV

PARLIAMENT, *pp.* 89–131

CHAPTER V

LAW AND STATUTE, KING AND CROWN,
pp. 132–166

Contents

CHAPTER VI

VILLEINS AND CLERICS, *pp.* 167–82

LIST OF AUTHORITIES, *pp.* 183–6

INDEX, *pp.* 187–92

CHAPTER I

HENRY'S RESOURCES

IT is an English habit to assume when any question of government arises that there must be an answer to the question already on record. Much good has been attributed, some of it justly, to this habit; some evil also is due to it, and especially a tendency to believe that every modern definition and articulation of political ideas and institutions had an existence, or at least a manifestation, in every earlier epoch, at any rate since the Middle Ages and the Feudal System came to an end in 1485. It is comparatively easy to remember that king, lords, commons, exchequer, privy council, quarter sessions, liberty, have now meanings different from those they bore at the end of the fifteenth century; it is much more difficult to convince the mind that the relations between these public institutions were not then the same as they are now, nor even of the same kind; not merely that they were undefined, but that they were still for the most part conceived as existing on a plane where technical definition was not to be thought of, though ruling principles ought to be plain. The rules of government resembled rather the rules of conversation than those of bridge: the relations between its various organs were more like those between the members of a family than like those between the officers of a limited liability company: the idea of it was the distribution of justice according to the ancient good customs, not the administration of a state according to the provisions of a sovereign constitution or a sovereign legislature.

It is clear, therefore, that the study of Tudor government cannot be begun with a principle (as the study of Victorian government might be begun with parliamentary sovereignty) nor with a comprehensive document (as the study of the government of the United States might be begun with the American Constitution). For any period of English history it is well to study institutions before seeking a constitution, for the Tudor period it is quite absolutely necessary: and the most active and decisive institution, as it had always been the most elevated and the most central, was the kingship: it was also the most ancient and the most conspicuous, and might be expected to have come nearest to definition: yet the kingship in 1485 was still so far from definition that it was by no means certain how the title to it was transmitted or how a challenge of the crown could be tested.

On 22 August 1485 Henry VII was king of England because he had defeated and killed Richard III the day before: he was king when he died on 21 April 1509 because during those twenty-four years he had suppressed every rival, if necessary with sword or axe: but such a tenure does not amount to a legal or constitutional title. There was no doubt that the lawful king at any given moment was the next heir of the last lawful king for whom an heir could be found. But there was no certainty what constituted heirship for this purpose, and in 1485 there was no certainty who had been the last lawful king. Nor was there any tribunal authorised to settle these preliminary questions. The highest tribunal within the realm was parliament, and the highest outside was the papal curia: it could hardly be asserted, it could in no sort of way be either proved or assumed, that pope or parliament had the right to lay down rules for the English succession or to apply the rules in a particular case; though certainly recognition from either of those authorities would be of great and incalculable assistance to any monarch whose inheritance had not been beyond dispute.

In 1460 the duke of York had put into the parliament chamber his claim[1] to be the true king (although Henry VI was then in the thirty-ninth year of his reign, and the sixty-first year of his dynasty) on the ground that he was, through his mother and grandmother, heir-general to Edward III. The lords spiritual and temporal (or such as were present, for most seem to have stayed away)[2] decided that "inasmuch as every person high or low, suing to this high Court of Parliament, of right must be heard...the said writing should be read and heard, not to be answered without the King's commandment, for so much as

---

[1] *Rot. Parl.* v, p. 375.
[2] W. Worcester, 484, quoted in J. Gairdner, *Paston Letters*, I, p. 191 (library edition, 1904).

the matter is so high, and of so great weight and poise". Next day, the duke pressing for an answer, they were unanimous that "the matter was so high and of such weight, that it was not to any of the King's Subjects to enter into communication thereof, without his high commandment agreement and assent had thereto"; to secure which they went at once to the king's presence, and the king told them to search for every possible objection against the duke's claim and title.

On this the lords sent for the king's justices and delivered to them the duke's claim, that they might find out all such objections: but they answered[1] that

they were the King's Justices, and have to determine such matters as come before them in the law, between party and party, and in such matters as be between party and party they may not be of Counsel; and sith this matter was between the King and the said Duke of York as two parties, and also it hath not been accustomed to call the Justices to Counseill in such matters, and in especial the matter was so high, and touched the King's high estate and regalie, which is above the law and passed their learning, wherefor they durst not enter into any communication thereof, for it pertained to the Lords of the King's blood, and th'apparage of this his land, to have communication and meddle in such matters; and therefore they humbly besought all the Lords, to have them utterly excused of any advice or Counsel, by them to be given in that matter.

The lords next applied to the king's serjeants and attorney, but with no better result, for they replied that "sith the said matter was so high that it passed the learning of the Justices, it must needs exceed their learning, and also they durst not enter any communication in that matter". To whom it was answered that they were the king's particular counsellors, and paid as such; and to that they replied that "they were the King's counsellors in the law, in such things as were under his authority or by commission, but this matter was above his authority, wherein they might not meddle".

Lacking expert advice, the lords themselves then formulated five objections to the Yorkist claim—the oaths which they had taken: great

[1] *R.P.* v, p. 376.

and notable acts of parliament of divers of the king's progenitors: divers entails made to the heirs-male as for the crown of England, as it may appear by divers chronicles and parliaments: the fact that the duke bore the arms of Edmund Langley and not of Lionel duke of Clarence: Henry IV's claim that he was right inheritor to Henry III. To these objections the duke replied[1] as best he could, and in especial that "the divers entails made to the heirs-male as for the crown of England" were in truth reduced to one made in the parliament of 6 Henry IV,[2] and that Harry of Derby's claim to inherit from Henry III was only to colour and shadow fraudulently his violent usurpation.[2] Finally, at the suggestion of the chancellor, the lords agreed to a compromise by which Henry VI was to remain king for life but to be succeeded by York and his heirs.

The arguments on both sides and the results are not here of the first importance: what is of the first importance is the failure of all concerned to find any indisputable rule or any indisputable judge of the succession, and beyond this failure, the assumption of all concerned that the succession was a matter above human authority. On the day on which Richard III was alive and was dead the finding of an available authority had become much more difficult still, for there was now no king in being and no parliament in being (and how can a parliament come into being unless a king calls it?), and the Lancastrian case was more than ever complicated by the doubtful legitimacy of the Beauforts, and the Yorkist case by the sex of Elizabeth, and both by attainder.

If Henry VII had not an indubitable hereditary right, neither had any one else, and the kingdom he won by the sword did not possess and could not provide itself with any constitutional means of deciding in such a situation who ought to be king: nor was it supposed, least of all by Henry, that it was for any earthly power to make rules for the

---

[1] *R.P.* v, p. 377; and cf. York's argument that his oath of allegiance was a spiritual matter, about which he would answer before any competent spiritual judge.

[2] 6 H. IV c. 2. Cf. *R.P.* v, p. 377. "And if he might have obtained and rejoiced (enjoyed) the said Crowns, &c. by title of inheritance, descent or succession, he neither needed nor would have desired or made them to be granted to him in such wise, as they be by the said Act".

descent of kingship. *Deus facit haeredem*, and the divine control is especially exclusive and essential in the case of kings.

So, though Elizabeth should have been crowned if the crown descended to heirs-general, and Warwick[1] if it descended to heirs-male, yet it was possible for Henry to maintain that as the nearest kinsman to Henry VI on the side of Henry IV he was entitled to the throne, and that is what he did maintain.[2] Henry did not go into any detail about his hereditary claim, perhaps on the sound general principle that the less a man bases himself on argument the less he can be proved wrong, perhaps from his consciousness that one of the first results of any technical argumentation on the point must be to bring to public notice the clause *excepta dignitate regali* in Henry IV's confirmation of the Beauforts' legitimacy.[3] Nevertheless, Henry could assume without absurdity, and did assume with success, that he was king by right of inheritance, and that the God of battles had made his right plain at Bosworth. Henry knew very well that one of the instruments employed by the God of battles was his promise to marry Elizabeth of York, and he knew also that his right, however divine, could not be too firmly certified. When Richard III was slain and Stanley picked the crown out of a bush and put it on Henry's head, Henry was king of a kingdom where there was so little public law, so little constitutional definition, that the very succession to the kingship had never been fixed. He did not intend that defect to be supplied by act of parliament or by archiepiscopal unction or by papal bull or by dynastic treaty; but he was very willing that any or all of these agencies should register and affirm the just title of inheritance and true judgment of God by which he had come to the throne.

Henry was the Lancastrian claimant whose success had brought to an end a century of dynastic strife. It is always remembered, generally in a quite false sense, that the Lancastrian champion was especially

---

[1] Elizabeth was daughter of Edward IV, and Warwick son of Edward's brother Clarence.

[2] W. Stubbs, *Medieval and Modern History*, p. 344.

[3] Cf. J. Gairdner, *Letters and Papers of Richard III and Henry VII*, II, p. xxx: who adds that perhaps Henry did not know, as his cousin of Buckingham did, that the exception had been foisted in by Henry IV and was of very dubious validity.

bound to parliament: it should not be forgotten that the traditions of his house inclined him to take high views of kingship no less than of parliaments. English kings had always borne two characters: they were the principal feudal personages in a society which consisted largely and conspicuously of feudal arrangements, and to that they owed most of their definable rights and practicable powers. They were also sacred and national personages, and though there was a shorter inventory of assets to be written down under this head and no item was very definite, yet the sum of the items was infinite, and the obligations, so onerous a part of the feudal bargain, were here practically inconsiderable: practically inconsiderable, for the debts were to the Deity and to the people and the credit was long.

It is not strange, then, that our kings always preferred their regal to their feudal capacity and that they were always eager to emphasise its sacred character. Peter of Blois[1] said of Henry II *sanctus enim et christus Domini*, and since Henry's time English kings[2] habitually performed miraculous cures, a power which early in its manifestations began to be considered as an hereditarily transmitted privilege of the royal race. Then, there was intimately and essentially connected with the gift of miracle-working, the holy unction[3] which a king received

---

[1] Marc Bloch, *Les Rois Thaumaturges, passim*, and especially pp. 45, 54, 68, 82, 135, 141, 186, 205, 210, 215, 336.

[2] Edward the Confessor also had this power: Bloch, p. 45.

[3] Bloch, pp. 66, 68, 74, 135, 141, 207. Cf. also J. Wickham Legg, *The Sacring of the English Kings* (1894), pp. 3–8, especially his reference to Wm. Lyndewode, *Provinciale*, lib. iii, tit. 2 (Oxford, 1679), p. 126, "Quod rex unctus non sit mere persona laica, sed mixta", unlike the chancellor, e.g., who may some day be a layman (p. 125): the anointing was limited to England, France, Jerusalem, Sicily, and towards the end of the Middle Ages Scotland: there were twenty-two kings in Christendom who were neither crowned nor anointed, and only England and France had the right to the "chrisma". Legg says also (p. 3) that of the three swords borne before the king at his coronation one shows his claim to spiritual jurisdiction, and that this ceremony can be traced back to Richard I (the three swords were borne before Henry VII, *Rutland Papers*, pp. 5–11). And note especially that Lyndewode's point is that the king for all his unction cannot by any length of prescription acquire "Jure suo potestatem circa spiritualia, videlicet circa ea quae pertinent ad Regimen Ecclesiasticum, et ministrationem Sacramentorum et Sacramentalium; necnon circa Ecclesiasticae Jurisdictionis exercitium". [The title which he is here glossing is that against clerks keeping concubines in their houses or visiting prostitutes with scandal.] Cf. also the so-called Anonymous of York and

at his coronation and which conveyed to him a peculiar consecration and something of the priestly character: not all of the priestly character, not as much in England as in France, nor anything very definable, but still something of the priestly character and certainly something very sacred.

It was here that the Lancastrians had succeeded in effectively increasing royal pretensions. The ceremony of unction began in England towards the end of the eighth century, probably in imitation of the rite with which Pippin the Short's usurpation was sanctified. From the end of the ninth century the legend was believed in France that the oil[1] for the royal unction had been brought down from heaven by a dove at the baptism of Clovis. It was clearly desirable that the kings of England, whether or not they had indeed borrowed the rite from France, should be anointed with oil of not less lofty origin than the oil at Reims. Accordingly, Edward II sought to obtain from John XXII authorisation for the use of a phial of oil alleged to have been presented for the purpose by the Blessed Virgin to St Thomas of Canterbury. Edward failed, but Henry IV was anointed with this

his very regalist, anti-papal, views: see on him Z. N. Brooke, *The English Church and the Papacy*, p. 160. "His views were as extreme on the one side as were the papal on the other, and to neither would the normal bishop adhere. He remains therefore isolated. However, I think the normal English bishop at the beginning of the twelfth century would have inclined to his standpoint more readily than to Anselm's. They still believed it to be their duty to obey the royal commands, and Anselm's refusal to do so undoubtedly shocked many of them. Belief in the sacred character of the kingly office was not confined to this anonymous clerk...." Cf. also H. Spelman, at the end of the *Larger Treatise concerning Tithes* (1st pubd. 1646), pp. 147 ff. in his *English Works* (1727), especially p. 148 "anointed also by the Bishops with the Oil of Priesthood"; p. 149 "touching their Unction, the very Books of the Law do testify to be done, to make them capable of Spiritual Jurisdiction", only four monarchies had it, and how and why; p. 150, Edward the Confessor's Church at Westminster "granted and confirmed" by Nicholas II "a Place of Regal Constitution"—"In which Words I note, first, that the Kings of *England* in those ancient Days, being before their Coronation merely Lay-Persons, were by their Consecration made *candidate Ecclesiasticae Potestatis....* For to what other purpose was Consecration....?"
[1] Or rather cream, *chrisma*, olive oil and balm mixed: cf. Legg, p. 5: it was especially a vehicle for the infusion of the Holy Ghost, pp. 5–7 (cf. *Rutland Papers*, p. 15 for the singing of *Veni Creator Spiritus* and praying *Te invocamus* before the unction): Legg, p. 8, shows how much the royal sacring resembled an episcopal consecration.

miraculous oil and succeeded in adding to its legend the belief that the first king so distinguished would reconquer Normandy and Aquitaine: all his successors used the same oil, till James I refused.[1]

Nor was this the only way in which the house of Lancaster emphasised the sacred character of kingship and the extent to which it escaped the laws and courts of men. If the transmission of kingship is altogether to escape human control, the insistence upon unction, which might make priestly intervention seem indispensable, requires some qualification. Now, as long ago as Edward I (and ever since) kings had dated their regnal years from earlier than the days of their coronation and unction. The Lancastrians went further.[2] Henry V and Henry VI each dated his reign from the morrow of his father's death, and the accession of Henry VI to the realm of France was proclaimed by his heralds over the tomb in which Charles V had just been placed. And Fortescue, the great Lancastrian publicist and our principal authority for what it is rather rash to call the constitutional ideas of the fifteenth century, explained that though the unction was necessary to the king's curative power yet it was efficacious only when applied to the proper person, to the king legitimate by blood. Otherwise the unction no more conveyed the royal character than ordination would make a woman a priest (said Fortescue),[3] or than baptism would make a penguin a Christian.[4] And Fortescue adds that the right to be king, the fitness to receive the unction, cannot be transferred by the people of England or by anything less than a "disposition of God...known openly by manifest, certain, and authentic revelation". Nevertheless, the sentimental value of

---

[1] Bloch, p. 241: but Legg says that though Elizabeth was the last to use the Latin service for her coronation and unction, the Stuart kings were anointed with a pure cream, p. 7.

[2] J. E. W. Wallis, *English Regnal Years*, p. 22, and Bloch, pp. 219, 223. Cf. p. 16, n. a. Rather oddly, the Yorkists were in this respect rather less legitimist: Edward IV dated his reign not from his father's death 30 Dec. 1460 (although his father had been spoken of by the commons as king of right) but from his own recognition 4 March 1461 (on the other hand, he took no count in his regnal years of Henry VI's restoration 9 Oct. 1470–14 April 1471): Richard III reckoned from 26 June 1483, not from his brother's death on April 9 nor from his nephews' on June 22.

[3] *Works* (ed. Lord Clermont), pp. 85 f.

[4] Anatole France, *l'Ile des Pingouins*. Cf. the sixteenth-century problem about the mouse that ate the consecrated wafer, cf. *Henry VIII*, p. 516, n. 4.

unction remained considerable, as may be seen from Henry VII's scruples about his treatment of Lambert Simnel, who had undergone the ceremony of coronation at Dublin: "They say", reported Raimondo de Soncino, the Milanese envoy, "that His Majesty, out of respect for the sacred unction, wants to make a priest of him".[1]

It is not intended to suggest that the view of kingship indicated in the above paragraphs was the only possible view at the end of the Middle Ages, nor even that it is the whole of one view: but it is necessary to insist that if the Tudors were inclined by the previous history of their party and dynasty, and driven by the inexorable necessities of their situation, to some acknowledgment of parliament and to some courting of their subjects, yet at the same time their dynasty and party inclined them no less to make the highest claims for their royalty and to refuse all admissions that it was derived from any human source. And while in twentieth-century sentiment about politics the first impulse is usually to ascribe almost a monopoly of mystical force and theological virtue to the people, in fifteenth- and sixteenth-century feeling, on the contrary, if there was any claimant to such monopoly it was the king: and political thinking, at any rate among English politicians, had till then exacted so little definition that there was not even any fixed and clear method of telling who was king, although the king's claims were loftier than those of any modern government, outside Russia, and his action was indispensable to every legal and social act.

The primary business of any government is to maintain itself: for fifteen years the primary business of Henry VII's government was to maintain itself against dynastic dangers, and even after that it was always apprehensive of such dangers. By the end of the century—with the capture of Warbeck,[2] the quieting of Ireland,[3] enhanced prestige abroad, the defeat of the Cornishmen at Blackheath[4]—the danger had

[1] *Mil. Cal.* I, 325, 16 Sept. 1497, quoted in Pollard, *Reign of Henry VII from Contemporary Sources*, I, 163.
[2] End of 1497.
[3] By the end of 1495: cf. A. Conway, *Henry VII's Relations with Scotland and Ireland*, p. 88 and earlier.
[4] June 1497. Add the execution of Warwick, Nov. 1499: and the return of Suffolk to England and to court about then: and the negotiations for marrying Mary Tudor to James IV, Sept. 1499 to Jan. 1502.

ceased to be imminent: but even then the Spanish ambassador was too optimistic when he wrote that "not a doubtful drop of royal blood remains in this kingdom, except the true blood of the king and queen".[1] Suffolk (son of Edward IV's sister Elizabeth) still represented the White Rose and the government could still be scared of him[2] until (and even after) it got him into the Tower in 1506.

It is not known[3] certainly that Henry assumed the title of king before his victory, but he acted as king on Bosworth field and ever after: that very evening he exercised a royal right by knighting eleven of his followers:[4] and according to Bacon[5] "the king presently that very day being the two and twentieth of August,[6] assumed the title of King in his own name without mention of the Lady Elizabeth at all, or any relation thereunto. In which course he ever after persisted: which did spin him a thread of many seditions and troubles". Very soon after the battle, almost certainly the next day,[7] he sent out a circular letter which began, "Henry by the grace of God, king of England and of France, prince of Wales and Lord of Ireland".

[1] "...above all, that of the lord prince Arthur", *L. and P.* I, p. 113; C. H. Williams, *England under the Early Tudors*, p. 54.
[2] C. L. Kingsford, *Chronicles of London*, p. 233. On 5 March 1503 he and his supporters were solemnly cursed at Paul's Cross with bell, book, and candle, Kingsford, p. 259. For other evidence of the importance of the dynastic factor, cf. Williams, p. 129.
[3] J. Gairdner, *Henry VII*, p. 31: cf. Gairdner's *Paston Letters*, III, no. 883 (edn. 1900), where is Richard III's proclamation (23. 6. 1485) denouncing Henry Tudor's "ambitiousness and insatiable covetousness which encroacheth and usurped upon him the name and title of royal estate of this realm of England": cf. also Hall's account of Henry's harangue before the battle (ed. H. Ellis, 1809), e.g. "such as by murder and untruth committed against their own king and lineage yea against their Prince and sovereign Lord, have disinherited me and you and wrongfully detain and usurp our lawful patrimony and inheritance. For he that calleth himself king keepeth from me the Crown and regiment of this noble realm and country contrary to all justice and equity". Cf. also Bernard André (ed. Gairdner, Rolls Series), pp. 26, 30.
[4] Gairdner, *Henry VII*, p. 29.
[5] Bacon is here following the contemporary authorities, Bernard André and Polydore Vergil, II, p. 1434 (edn. 1603); Bacon's *Works* (ed. Spedding), VI, p. 31.
[6] It is usually said that he reckoned his reign from Aug. 21, but according to A. F. Pollard, *Inst. Hist. Res. Bul.* VII, p. 3, the grounds for this assertion have never been properly investigated. Cf. p. 8 above.
[7] A. F. Pollard, *Reign of Henry VII from Contemporary Sources*, I, p. 11, where the letter is printed from Halliwell's *Letters of the Kings of England*, I, p. 169.

As soon as the battle was over Henry had arranged for securing the persons of the two possible Yorkist claimants, Elizabeth and Warwick. By 27 August 1485 he was in London, joyously and solemnly received as king and studiously bedecking himself with all the marks of the royal dignity. On September 6 he began [1] the long series of grants rewarding his supporters, not awaiting the decision of any court before he used for this purpose the property of those who had fought on the wrong side. Nine days later he summoned a parliament to meet on November 7. On September 24 he issued [2] a general pardon (with a few exceptions) to those in arms against him in the north, their services being needed against the Scots. On September 29 the king wrote [3] to his escheator for Hereford and Wales that the bishop-elect of St David's had contented him about the words prejudicial to his crown in the papal bull of preferment and that therefore the escheator was in every way to treat him as bishop. A fortnight later he directed the sheriff of Surrey and Sussex to proclaim the recently concluded truce with Charles of France. In the middle of October he was instructing [4] sheriffs, mayors, bailiffs, constables, and all other officers, ministers, liegemen, and subjects to prepare themselves against the ancient enemy Scotland and against rebels and traitors: towards the end of the month he created two peerages, [5] and on the thirtieth he was crowned. [6]

---

[1] Wm. Campbell, *Materials Illustrative of the Reign of Henry VII*, I, pp. 6f.; Polydore Vergil, II, pp. 1434 f.
[2] Robt. R. Steele, *Tudor and Stuart Proclamations*, no. 1.
[3] Rymer's *Foedera*, tom. XII, pp. 275, 277.
[4] See the quotations from Campbell and from the Rutland MSS. in Pollard's *Reign of Henry VII*, I, pp. 19–20.
[5] Campbell, I, pp. 100, 102.
[6] And the archbishop of Canterbury was first (according to the *Device for the Coronation* preserved in the *Rutland Papers*, ed. Wm. Jerdan for the Camden Society 1842, p. 13) to present him to the people, saying: "Sirs, I here present H. [true] and rightful, and undoubted, inheritor by the laws of God and man to the crown and royal dignity of England...elect, chosen, and required by all three estates of the same land to take upon him the said crown...will ye, sirs, at this time give your wills and assents to the same coronation, inunction, and coronation?" and they were to shout "Yea. Yea. Yea. So be it. King Henry! King Henry!" (My spelling.) And before the actual anointing and crowning he was to be asked by the archbishop "Will ye grant, and keep, to the people of England, the laws and customs to them as of old rightful and devout kings granted", especially those of the Confessor: he was to promise: then he was to make a series of special promises—

All this time the king had been most busily engaged in taking over the control and recasting the personnel of administration. Parliament met on November 7, when the commons were instructed to elect a speaker and were given lists of the persons appointed by the king to act as receivers and triers of petitions:[1] two days later the speaker was presented to the king, who "with his own mouth" showed to the commons "his coming to the Right and Crown of England to be as much by just Title of inheritance as by the true judgment of God in granting to him Victory over his enemy in the Field", and that every one should enjoy their lands and goods except offenders against his Royal Majesty "who were to be punished according to their demerits in the Court of the present Parliament".

In the early days of his stay in London after Bosworth the victor had "assembled his counsel and other principal persons [says Bacon],[2] in the presence of whom he did renew again his promise to marry with the Lady Elizabeth". Gairdner makes this much more modern and specific when he writes that the king "summoned a Council, in which the fulfilment of his promise to marry Elizabeth was the principal subject of discussion, and it is said the day was even named". The council was an institution[3] now some centuries old, and it was able to act both as an administrative board and director of policy and as a court of law and equity: but if it was a recognised institution it was not a corporation, its membership had no sort of fixity, and it could take no initiative without royal authorisation. Henry VII could hold a council as Haroun al Raschid a divan or George V a conversation. The men attended whom the king summoned and the resultant action was

peace and concord to the church, the clergy, and the people: "equal and rightful justice in all your dooms and judgments, and discretion, with mercy and truth": "the rightful laws and customs to be holden, and . . . such laws as to the worship of God shall be chosen by your people by you to be strengthened and defended": to all bishops and abbots and their churches "the privilege of the law canôn, and of holy church, and due law and rightfulness, and us and them defend": and "I Henry, King of England was to promise and then to swear upon the sacraments".

[1] *R.P.* VI, pp. 267, 268.
[2] *Works* (ed. Spedding), VI, p. 33: cf. Polydore Vergil, II, pp. 1434–5; Bernard André, pp. 36, 37; Jas. Gairdner, *Henry VII*, p. 34. Whether Bacon wrote *counsel* with a *c* or an *s*, an *e* or an *i*, a capital or a small initial, makes no matter.
[3] Cf. p. 28 below.

what the king decided. When a king died, at any rate when an usurping king was slain, the council being the king's and the late king being no more, there was no council.[1] There would in any particular case be some men whom the new king was bound to summon, but this was an obligation of political expediency, not of legal necessity and hardly of constitutional propriety: it was besides (as will be seen) an obligation which bound Henry VII singularly little: and in any case no man was a councillor till the king summoned him. Henry's councillors were not even chosen from a class particularly marked out to advise the king, still less from persons who had previously exercised that function, so that Henry's holding of a council did not imply a confirmation of his royalty by recognition, even in the sense in which it would be a recognition of leadership if, for instance, a politician signing his name as "leader of the Liberal party" were to circularise Liberal personages with an invitation to a party meeting and if they actually attended. In short, no affirmation of Henry's title was made by anybody more representative than the Common Council of London[2] until, after his coronation, his first parliament was called, by which time he had already, as has been shown above, performed every sort of royal act.

But, though Henry thus assumed, very deliberately and very effectively, that he was king by divine right and needed no further authorisation before doing anything that any king might do, yet even Henry himself had nothing like a logically complete picture of his position: not merely that he found it best to be vague about the channels by which royalty had descended upon him, but also that he had not the

---

[1] Or, in so far as the old council did act (and therefore exist) it was merely to execute (by virtue of the old reign) the formalities by which a new reign (and therefore council) could get going. But the development of an organisation for sealing was making possible a government with a royal mainspring even when the royal person was impotent: the infant Richard II, unlike Henry III but like Edward III, "from his accession was provided with a great seal, privy seal, and signet; documents of every sort were issued by his witness and authority, and no regency was formally established", T. F. Tout, *Chapters in Medieval Administrative History*, III, p. 323: cf. also p. 326 for council's reluctance to act more than was necessary in these circumstances: after the infant king had been crowned, his council elected by the magnates was, "to make its position more formal,...appointed by patent and sworn in the king's presence". Cf. *Henry VIII*, p. 538.
[2] 31 Aug. 1485; Campbell, I, p. 4.

indisputableness either of prescription or of principle to support his choice of a date for the beginning of his regality.[1] When the news of the defeat and death of Richard III reached York, the council of that city put it on record that "King Richard, late mercifully reigning upon us, was through grete treason of the Duke of Norfolk and many other... pitiously slane and murdered, to the grete hevynesse of this City":[2] and on the supposition that a short interregnum would be recognised, a council meeting was dated *vacata regali potestate*.[3] Nor was this feeling confined to Richard's natural partisans at York: on parliament's recognition of the claim that Henry was king before Bosworth, the prior of Croyland commented, "O God! what security are our kings to have henceforth, that in the day of battle they may not be deserted by their subjects?"[4] Yet Henry himself did not make the full legitimist claim as, for instance, Charles II was to do when he dated his reign from the moment of his father's death. Henry began his regnal year from the day before Bosworth,[5] and treated as traitors the men who had fought against him when he was a pretender: wherever it was necessary in public documents to allude to Richard III it was always as "king in deed, but not of right": but Edward IV was habitually qualified as "that most noble prince king Edward",[6] although on Lancastrian principles he was as unmistakable if not as foul an usurper as Richard, and, after all, if Henry was king one day before Bosworth, why not ten days, or a hundred, or a thousand?

If, then, in 1485 the legal or constitutional identification of the wearer of the crown was so little provided for, although no one could or can doubt that the crown was then in every way the chief legal and

---

[1] Cf. pp. 8, 9 n. 4 above.
[2] R. Davies, *Extracts from Municipal Records*, p. 218, quoted in Pollard, *Reign of Henry VII*, I, p. 17.
[3] Drake, *Eboracum*, p. 120, quoted in Jas. Gairdner, *L. and P.* II, p. xxxi.
[4] Gairdner, *L. and P.* II, p. xxxi: and cf. below, p. 151.
[5] Every king before Edward I reckoned his regnal year from his coronation: Edward from the proclamation of his succession four days after his father's death: Edward VI and each subsequent monarch (except the two Maries, each of whom reckoned from the date of recognition) counted as his first day the day of his predecessor's death: cf. J. E. W. Wallis, *English Regnal Years and Titles*, pp. 20, 22, 23.
[6] Cf. e.g. Campbell, I, p. 524.

political institution in England, it is not surprising that the crown's rights and duties, powers and obligations, lacked definiteness and precision. But besides rights and powers, which if they had the advantage of being unlimited had also the disadvantage of being indefinite, Henry VII possessed also great resources of a more material kind. The two conditions which enabled him to establish his dynasty and to revive the efficiency of the kingship were the strength and independence of his financial position and the coincidence between the objects of his policy and the needs of his subjects. Of these topics, the second can hardly be isolated and specified, at least at the beginning of a study of the period: but the salient features of the first can be indicated,[1] and perhaps nothing else could show so clearly the distinguishing characteristics of Henry VII's government.

In fifteenth-century theory there was no doubt that the king should live of his own, in other words, that he should meet all his expenses out of his fee-farms, feudal receipts, profits of justice, purveyance, customs, and estates acquired by heritage or forfeiture: taxation, the raising by parliamentary authority of additional sums for royal purposes, should be an expedient only for great and rare emergencies, such as rebellion or invasion. In fifteenth-century experience, the ordinary revenues had become insufficient for the needs of government and the consequent necessity of frequent recourse to parliamentary taxation had done much to produce that governmental weakness which was the characteristic vice of the age, and the avoidance of which was the dominant idea of the next age. The husbanding of the king's "own" income so that he might very seldom need to ask his subjects for a share of theirs was therefore the principal political problem with which Henry was confronted, and his method and success in dealing with it were during his reign the decisive factors in the relations between the crown and other governmental institutions.

As has been shown above, Henry after his victory at Bosworth waited for no further authorisation before doing all sorts of things which only

---

[1] Thanks especially to Prof. F. C. Dietz, *English Government Finance*, 1485–1558 (Illinois, 1920), and A. P. Newton, "The King's Chamber under the Early Tudors", *E.H.R.* XXXII, p. 248.

a king could do, and among such things was the exercise of royal rights of property and patronage. On 6 September 1485 he granted to William Grene the office of bailiff of Wyldgolet during pleasure and keeper of the park there,[1] and thereafter the stream of royal expenditure was never interrupted, though it was very carefully regulated by Henry's own prudence. His rights over his patrimony, a patrimony which included the crown and all that went with it, were confirmed by the opinion of the judges[2] in the matter of attainder. The question arose in this way: many of Henry's supporters, like Henry himself, lay under attaint, and of these many not a few wished to sit in parliament: the judges held that they should not sit until parliament had decided their cases. Then there was obviously a further question—if these people attainted for adherence to the Lancastrian claim were thereby incapacitated until they should have received a parliamentary purification, what was the position of the Lancastrian claimant himself? The judges resolved unanimously that the king could not stand in need of such rehabilitation, that the very fact of being king discharged him from any alleged attaint.

So Henry Tudor by the mere fact of being Henry Tudor was king and was entitled to every kind of right to which any of his predecessors had been entitled; and, as a result of the last century's history with its feudal agglomerations and its series of forfeitures, these rights were in fact worth more to him than they had been to any other monarch since the Conqueror. His first parliament assured to the crown the duchy of Cornwall, the earldom of Richmond, and other lands: it attainted a number of great proprietors, whose lands were thereby forfeited to the crown: it resumed to the crown all the lands of the duchy of Lancaster which Richard III had ever possessed, or Edward IV at any time after March 3 in his first year: and all the lands possessed on 21 October 1455 by Henry VI as king of England, prince of Wales, duke of Cornwall and Lancaster, and earl of Chester. There were important exceptions to these resumptions and there were restorations to persons attainted under

[1] Campbell, I, p. 6.
[2] Quoted by A. F. Pollard, *Reign of Henry VII*, II, p. 10 from the *Year Book* (edn. 1679), 1 H. VII, p. 4. Cf. p. 151, n. 3 below.

Richard III, but the balance in Henry's favour was great: the income from land in his first year was £13,633, whereas in the last year of Edward IV it had been only £6471.[1]

Nor was this all, for in the course of the reign there were numerous and important additions to the royal lands by way of forfeiture, escheat, and resumption; the property of Sir William Stanley, for instance, yielded the king over £1000 a year, that of the duchess of York £1200:[2] and even more fruitful than new additions were improvements in management. Parliament at the time of the great resumption in 1486 had assigned annually £7723 to the cost of the household and wardrobe: the surplus from the crown estates proper after meeting these costs and all the expense of administration was, in 1491, £3764. 18s. 7d.: it rose continually, and in 1504 it was £24,145. 4s. 10d.[3] Similarly, the treasurer of the chamber received from the chancellor of the duchy of Lancaster in 1488, £666. 13s. 4d. and in 1508, £6566, all clear surplus from the Lancaster estates.

As estates were better managed, so feudal profits were more punctually exacted. The mayor and bailiffs of Leicester were commanded to see that the king's shops and ovens were properly frequented:[4] commissions were issued to summon all earls, barons, and knights, to enquire how many archers each was bound to find, and take the musters:[5] proclamations frequently enjoined knighthood upon all men with lands worth £40 a year:[6] *inquisitiones post mortem* and suit of livery were vivified and supervised to make sure that no land held directly from the king was allowed to slip out of that relation, depriving

---

[1] For this paragraph see Dietz, p. 21, especially his quotations from *R.P.* VI, pp. 271 ff. When Henry married Elizabeth of York, he acquired the rights in Ireland of the heiress of the De Burgos and Mortimers, became earl of Ulster and lord of Connaught, Trim and Leix, though those dignities were mainly nominal, cf. Conway, p. 130.

[2] Dietz, p. 25.

[3] Dietz, p. 27.

[4] Campbell, II, p. 369, 26 Nov. 1488.

[5] Campbell, II, p. 384, 23 Dec. 1488.

[6] E.g. Campbell, II, p. 76, 14 Dec. 1486, and Jas. Gairdner, *L. and P.* II, p. 379. Knighthood involved not only fees but also military service. These royal rights were confirmed by statutes 11 H. VII c. 18 and 19 H. VII c. 1, and especially enforced by Empson.

him of his profitable rights of wardship, marriage, and escheat. With how much success all this machinery was handled may be roughly guessed from the figures of income from wards' lands, which rose from £353 in 1487 and £343 in 1491 pretty steadily to £6163 in 1507. The king's right to enjoy the temporalities of bishops and abbots could not be exploited to the same extent, but it was exploited in the same sort of way.[1] Then there was a considerable revenue from the hire of royal ships, from treasure trove, from the sale of alum, and from a great variety of sources, most of them as innocent as these, but some of them less so, like the grants of pardons, the sale of offices, and the promise of the royal favour in pending suits. The most famous of these miscellaneous resources is the exaction of fines, and though there seems to be no evidence for the traditional wholesale re-enforcement of old feudal laws, Henry certainly did keep a very careful and effective eye upon fines as a branch of income.[2]

All this was the king's "own"; it was true that the attainders and resumptions which gave all this some of its peculiar value for Henry VII were parliamentary acts, but they were acts in which the initiative came from the king and in which the consent of the houses was so much matter of course that it did not need to be bargained for, and they were acts which registered the transfer to the king not of income but of capital. Henry had also by mere right of his accession the ancient customs[3]—the customs strictly so-called, *magna and parva custuma*—and his first parliament gave him for life the customs, subsidies of tonnage and poundage and of wool, woolfells, and leather. This revenue

---

[1] Dietz, p. 31.

[2] *Justitia magnum emolumentum* was a medieval maxim not forgotten in the sixteenth century. When Edward VI's councillors were "divided into several Commissions and Charges", the first was for hearing suits, the second for calling of forfeits, the third "for the State", the fourth for watching the revenues and expenses of the courts and "for the Debts", the fifth "for the Bulwarks": cf. J. R. Tanner, *Tudor Constitutional Documents* (2nd edition, 1930), p. 222. Cf. also Henry VII's use of recognisances: e.g. in 1504 Willoughby de Broke's recognisance that he owes £500 not to be demanded as long as he keeps the peace with Sir T. Brandon, Williams, p. 176, quoting from the Close Roll. In 1498 the special commission for dealing with the Devon and Cornwall rebels collected £8810. 16s. 8d., cf. p. 55, n. 1 below.

[3] Cf. S. Dowell, *History of Taxation*, I, pp. 74–81.

was originally intended for the defence of the realm, especially at sea, but in fact Henry was able to use it as he pleased, and it may be treated as part of his secure and uncontrolled income:[1] this resource also he thoroughly exploited.

He improved by treaty commercial relations with Denmark, Iceland, Norway, the Netherlands, and the Mediterranean: he lent money to English and Italian merchants without interest but on condition that their trading benefited the customs by certain amounts: he cut down exemptions and tightened up administration,[2] especially by way of improving the valuation of customable goods: all to such effect that this branch of the revenue, which in the three years of Edward V and Richard III had fallen to little over £20,000 a year, in the first ten years of Henry VII averaged nearly £33,000, and during the rest of his reign increased to over £40,000. In general, Henry VII's stewardship was so prosperous that the total receipts at the exchequer from all regularly recurring sources, which had been about £52,000 a year at the beginning of his reign, in the last few years averaged £142,000.[3]

It is clear, then, that the crown at the beginning of the sixteenth century enjoyed that sort of independence of other organs of government which monarchs most desire and seldomest attain, financial independence, and the means by which that independence was enjoyed are clear enough also. If the figures that have been quoted above fail to give an accurate or complete or plain exposition of the subject,[4] at least it is beyond doubt that the source of income there indicated did suffice for Henry's needs, and that under his skilful and fortunate management

---

[1] Dietz, p. 11, n. 1: and cf. p. 18 above.
[2] And reduced the monopoly rights of the Merchant Adventurers, and made protective legislation more effective, either to exclude foreigners or to get advantages from them: cf. L. F. Salzmann, *English Trade in the Middle Ages*, p. 342. Cf. Dowell, I, p. 178 for the special duty imposed in 1590 on malmsey imported by foreigners, in retaliation for tariff discrimination against Englishmen by the Venetian masters of Crete.
[3] Dietz, pp. 12, 24, 25, 86: N. W. B. Gras, *Quarterly Journal of Economics*, XXVI, pp. 766 ff.: and E. F. Churchill, *Law Quarterly Review*, XLII, pp. 81 ff.
[4] I do not always find it possible to reconcile Prof. Dietz's figures with each other, e.g. those on page 25 and those on page 80 of his book: but perhaps the fault is mine, and anyway my argument is not essentially affected.

the sources were developing faster than the needs. Another way of showing the strength of Henry's financial position and its relation to other constitutional factors is to indicate the occasions when he found it worth while to take money that had to be asked for.

Like every other pretender, he began his reign in debt: he owed money in Paris, in Brittany he owed more than 10,000 crowns, he had to get the royal jewels out of pawn, where Richard III had placed them, and he had to pay some of Richard's debts. To meet urgent necessities the king contracted short-term loans with various ecclesiastical dignitaries, with the merchants of the Staple at Calais, with the City of London: all of these loans were punctually repaid, and it is to be noted that the city had lent only £2000 though asked for £4000: willingness to lend increased with experience of Henry's fidelity to contract.[1]

Towards the end of 1486 Henry had recourse to another sort of loan, a forced loan this time, commissioners being sent into the counties to arrange for contributions, which averaged only twenty shillings each: the same method was used again in 1489, but in these early years of the reign, when Henry still found borrowing necessary, he raised much greater amounts by ordinary arrangement with big lenders than by these compulsory means: all his loans were repaid.

The first thing Henry's first parliament did, on the day after it met, was when the commons appeared before the king in full parliament and, with the assent of the lords, granted him tonnage and poundage for life, for the defence of the realm "and in especial for the safeguard and keeping of the sea".[2] This was permanent and indirect: the first direct and occasional parliamentary tax was not granted till two years later, when, after Simnel's defeat at Stoke, for "the hasty and necessary defence of the realm", there were granted two fifteenths and tenths and a poll-tax on resident aliens: both convocations had already voted one tenth of the value of benefices. In January 1489 a still larger sum was granted, for the popular object of preventing the absorption of Brittany by France, £100,000, of which three quarters was to be supplied by

---

[1] Gairdner, *Henry VII*, p. 149.
[2] *R.P.* VI, p. 268: and cf. p. 18 above.

the laity and one quarter by the clergy: it was to be raised by a ten per cent income-tax and

a levy of one and eightpence on every ten marks worth of goods above ten marks. The assessment[1] was to be made by royal commissioners, and the collectors were to be appointed by them. In other words, it was to be raised as a national tax and not as a local rate for national purposes like the fifteenth and tenth. . . ..Although a failure, the tax of 1489 is of interest as the first on realty and personalty conjoined which was actually levied.[2] It was in fact the first of the Tudor subsidies on land and goods.[3]

In the autumn it appeared that the laity had paid only £27,000 and the deficiency was in large part made good by the grant of a fifteenth and tenth.[4] The truth is (and though it may be expounded later it must be mentioned here) that the obtaining of parliamentary consent was at this time very far from being the sole, or even the main, difficulty in the way of collecting taxes: although the fifteenth-century Englishman was not as sure as his modern descendant of parliament's right not to

[1] For the fifteenth and tenth the amount to be paid by each township had got stereotyped, and it did not matter to the crown how the assessments were made inside each township. Cf. Dowell, III, p. 69, fifteenth and tenth compounded for since 1334 at £39,000, which tended to diminish by allowances to decayed towns.
[2] In the parliament of 1404 there had been a suggestion of raising 1s. in the pound on clear income from land worth £1 and more, and 1s. for every £20's worth of chattels from those who had no land or houses. (*Annales Henrici IV*, J. de Troke-lowe, p. 379: according to the next page this very modern parliament granted the king £12,000 "de subsidio antedicto, expendendarum pro suae arbitrio voluntatis".) Tait thinks this a more equitable distribution than any attempted in practice till once or twice in the time of Henry VIII and again under Charles II and William and Mary. In 1411 there was a land tax. Under Henry VI there was a graduated tax on income from offices, annuities, rent-charges, and land: after 1450 the fifteenth and tenth again became the sole direct tax: in 1463 there was an unsuccessful attempt to bring land as well as goods under contribution and to recover from those assessed at more than ten marks the £6000 regularly deducted for exemptions: in 1472 there was an unsuccessful proposal to meet war expenses by an income-tax of 10 per cent.
[3] Jas. Tait, *Taxation in Salford Hundred* (Chetham Soc. vol. LXXXIII), p. xxiv: cf. *R.P.* VI, pp. 421 ff. for the grant of January 1489.
[4] *R.P.* VI, p. 438. There had even been forcible resistance, in the course of which the fourth earl of Northumberland was slain, cf. Holinshed, III, p. 492: cf. p. 35 below.

make money grants,[1] yet his objection to actually paying money was not
altogether removed by the mere fact of parliamentary grant:[2] and then,
the machinery for assessment and collection was very ineffective: as
the chronicler puts it in connection with this subsidy of ten thousand
archers (the £100,000 voted in 1489), "there was graunted unto the
king towards the defence of Brytayn (Brittany)...the Xth penny of
men's lands and goods movable; but it was so favourably set by the
commissioners that it amounted nothing so much in money as men
deemed it would have done".[3]

In July 1491 Henry made the patriotism of his subjects even more
remunerative. His policy with regard to Brittany having been stultified
by the marriage of that duchy's ruler with Charles VIII, he resolved to
make use of his claim to the French throne. For this purpose he did
not hesitate to exact a benevolence: and that a sufficiency of his subjects
agreed with him in thinking these means justified by their anti-French
end was shown when parliament met and voted two fifteenths and
tenths, with the promise of a third if the army should stay abroad more
than eight months. On a later occasion parliament was more explicit
in its approval of a benevolence: in 1495, says Bacon,[4]

although the parliament consisted of the first and second nobility,
together with principal citizens and townsmen [i.e. just the classes on
whom a benevolence would fall] yet worthily and justly respecting

---

[1] Cf. Chief Baron Fray in 1441—"the law which binds the king to defend his
people, also binds the people to grant of their goods to him in aid of that defence":
Y.B. 19 H. VI, Pasch. no. 1, quoted by T. F. T. Plucknett in R. W. Seton-Watson's
Tudor Studies, p. 165. And cf. J. Fortescue, *Governance of England*, ch. 8, "Wherefore since every realm is bound to sustain its king, yet much more be we bound
thereto, upon whom our king reigneth by so favourable laws as is before declared".
[2] Cf. the Northumberland rising of 1489 and the Cornish rising of 1497.
[3] Kingsford, *Chronicles*, p. 194.
[4] *Henry VII*, ed. J. R. Lumby, Cambridge, 1876, p. 92: of course, Bacon is not
much of an authority for the composition and motives of parliament in 1495, and
he would be willing enough to show how obliging and self-sacrificing parliament
had been in the old days. But no doubt his account is substantially correct, if
allowance be made for a little flattery: cf. p. 71 below. The statute authorising
collection of the arrears of the benevolence is 11 H. VII c. 10. Cf. with Bacon's
remarks, Erasmus's view of taxation by estates: 1 March 1517, writing to More from
Antwerp, "Large sums are demanded of the people, and immediate payment. It
has been allowed by the nobles and clergy, that is, by those who will not have to
pay it", *L. and P.* H. VIII, II, pt. 2, no. 2974.

more the people, whose deputies they were, than their own private persons, and finding by the lord Chancellor's speech the King's inclination that way: they considered that commissioners should go forth for the gathering and levying of a benevolence from the more able sort.

In 1491 the king had not intended his military operations to be very expensive, and after a promenade rather than a campaign he accepted a peace by which Charles acknowledged a debt of 745,000 écus d'or, to be paid off at the rate of 50,000 francs (£5000) annually. The benevolence[1] alone seems to have just about covered the cost of the expedition, so that the clerical grant, parliamentary grant, and French pension were all pure profit.

Henry did even better out of the Scottish war of 1496. He called a great council, including certain burgesses and merchants, which granted £120,000:[2] then parliament[3] voted two fifteenths and tenths and also an aid and subsidy to come to the same amount less £12,000, this vote being not altogether in addition to that of the council but partly in confirmation of it: the clergy of Canterbury granted £40,000, although they had voted a tenth the year before: the whole supply for the occasion may be reckoned at something like £160,000. The expense seems to have come to £58,863, the rest was profit, and more than the rest, because the cost includes the suppression of the Cornish rebellion and the defeat of Warbeck, whereas in effect these two achievements almost paid for themselves, so heavy were the fines imposed upon the Cornishmen[4] and upon Warbeck's adherents.

In 1504 there was no military excuse for requesting supply, but the king was entitled to two reasonable aids, for knighting Arthur[5] and

[1] For the appointment of commissioners to collect this, see *Cal. Pat. Rolls*, 1485–94, p. 366, quoted by Williams, p. 156.
[2] Cf. Kingsford, *Chronicles*, p. 211. For Henry's letter asking for a loan in accordance with the decision of this council, see *Christchurch Letters* (Camden Soc.), p. 62, referred to by Williams, p. 40.
[3] Which met on 16 Jan. 1496/7.
[4] They had not seen why people living so far south should contribute to any expedition against the Scots, which they reckoned in any case a matter for the military class, knights and landholders.
[5] Though Arthur had been knighted more than fifteen years before, and had been dead for two years. Cf. Busch, p. 284.

marrying Margaret:[1] the commons[2] would not face enquiry into the titles of their lands and the charges upon them, and offered a payment of £40,000 in lieu of the aids: Henry had demanded, according to Roper,[3]

about three fifteenths....At the last debating whereof Thomas More made such arguments and reasons there against, that the King's demands were thereby overthrown. So that one of the King's privy chamber, named Master Tyler, being present thereat, brought word to the King out of the Parliament house, that a beardless boy had disappointed all his purpose. Whereupon the King conceiving great indignation towards him could not be satisfied until he had some way revenged it. And forasmuch as he nothing having, nothing could lose, his grace devised a causeless quarrel against his Father, keeping him in the Tower until he had made him pay to him an hundred pounds fine.

And one way and another More was so distressed that "had not the king soon after died, he was determined to have gone over sea". So Roper reported, but Roper wrote about fifty years after the alleged events, and Henry had certainly not been "disappointed of all his purpose": the session ended with "a show of polite accommodation... the Commons offered £40,000, and the king took only £30,000".[4]

Altogether, in the twenty-four years of Henry's reign there were only six occasions on which it was found necessary to accept any kind of extraordinary supply[5] from parliament, and even then *necessary* is too big a word. As has been seen, the king's general habit was to ask his subjects for money only when they might be reckoned as eager to give as he to receive, and his skill was to put all or almost all that they did give into reserve: accordingly, his surplus was mounting up all the time.

Already before the end of 1489 the Treasurer of the Chamber had a balance of £5000 on the last two years' accounts: in 1490 short-term loans ceased: in 1492 Henry began spending money on jewels, which

[1] To James IV of Scotland, two years before.
[2] *R.P.* VI, pp. 532–42.
[3] *Life of More*, ed. J. R. Lumby, p. vii (my spelling).
[4] W. Busch, *England under the Tudors*, I, p. 285.
[5] The second was to bring the first up to what it had been estimated at, and from 1492 to 1509 there were only two.

was one way of hoarding, and before his death he had put aside at least £128,441 in this way. It was after the Scotch war (1496) that Henry was above all necessity of borrowing, that his surplus was considerable and continually increasing, and that he was famed as not only the wisest of kings but the richest also. Besides his building, his purchase of jewels, and his other capital expenditure, he was able also to lend at least £260,000 to the Archduke Philip and his son, and large sums to other people. The king was living well within his means.[1]

And they were the king's means. The obligation to use tonnage and poundage for defence had never been much more than nominal and had become rather less: Henry, like Edward IV in 1482, made a merit of lightening the burden of purveyance[2] by enacting in parliament[3] the assignment to the Household of various revenues amounting to some £14,000, but this was neither in intention nor in effect an experiment in appropriation as a device for the parliamentary control of the king's expenditure: it did not make him spend a penny on anything he did not want to pay for.

The king had another financial power in his ancient and undoubted rights of exemption. Not only could he dispense with feudal and quasi-feudal dues, as when he dispensed York[4] from payment of £60 out of the £160 of its ferm, but also he could exempt from national taxation, as by adding to subsidy acts provisions exempting impoverished towns[5] or by releasing his servants from fiscal demands: apparently not before Stuart times was objection taken on the ground that in such matters to favour some was in effect to tax others. In cases, indeed, where the tax-payer was likely to be even more sensitive to the exemption of other people than over direct taxation, Henry VII was able to make separate arrangements on his own authority, as when in February 1488, reciting first parliament's vote of tonnage and poundage and the subsidy on wool, he proceeded to grant specially favourable terms to the merchants

---

[1] For the above seven paragraphs cf. Dietz, pp. 51–8, 78, 79, 85.
[2] Forced buying of supplies for the king and court.
[3] *R.P.* VI, p. 299: cf. Newton in *Tudor Studies*, p. 235.
[4] Campbell, I, p. 462: cf. a similar case at Northampton, II, p. 349.
[5] Cf. E. F. Churchill, "The Crown and its Servants", *Law Quarterly Review*, XLII, pp. 82, 91, 93, 94.

of Venice, Genoa, Florence, and Lucca.[1] And besides the diminishing financial profits of obsolescent feudal arrangements, the crown had also a still subsisting capacity to create new feudal arrangements, as by the grant to John Trelawney in December 1487 of a market each week and a fair each year, toll and team, court leet, frank-pledge, assize of bread and ale, infanghthef, and utfanghthef.[2]

Nor, at that time, did "the crown" mean anything fictitious, but it did indeed mean the man who wore the crown: this was especially true in the fiscal sphere, and Henry VII did a great deal to make it more true.

In this reinforcement of royalty his principal methods were personal attention and the substitution of the King's Chamber and the Court of General Surveyors[3] for the Exchequer, which, in its two branches of Receipt and Account, had been hitherto the main financial machine of England. Already Edward IV, and still more Richard III, had seen the advantage of getting fiscal administration into hands easily controllable by the crown. This was accomplished by Henry:[4] the Treasurer of the King's Chamber was in every sense the king's servant,[5] unhampered by a prescribed routine and offering a loyalty which his master did not have to share with any great dignitary or traditional corporation: to him instead of to the Under-Treasurer of the Exchequer were now to be paid the new revenues, and as the reign went on an increasing number of the old ones also—all new land revenues and some old ones (including those

[1] Campbell, II, p. 245.
[2] Campbell, II, p. 248.
[3] For all that is here said of these institutions cf. Dietz, pp. 60–72: for earlier history of the Chamber, cf. T. F. Tout, *Chapters in Medieval Administrative History*, esp. I, pp. 28, 84, 231, 286, 297; II, pp. 31, 156, 257, 337, 355; III, pp. 52, 173; IV, pp. 212, 227, 467.
[4] Like many of his achievements, this one had been foreshadowed under the Yorkists: cf. Newton in "The King's Chamber under the Early Tudors", *E.H.R.* XXXII, pp. 350–2. And as important as any formal method was his almost daily practice of checking his accounts with his own hands.
[5] Appointed by word of mouth and dismissible in the same way: cf. Newton in "The King's Chamber under the Early Tudors", *E.H.R.* XXXII, pp. 351, 353. In the first years of Henry VII's time he was directed entirely by the king's word of mouth, later by sign manual or occasionally signet bill; Newton, p. 368. He often lent from the king's more private coffers, to the Cofferer, to whom the Exchequer transferred the amounts assigned, by tallies on the receivers of particular revenues, which tallies were by no means always quickly convertible into cash, cf. Newton in *Tudor Studies*, pp. 236–7.

of the duchy of Lancaster above the amount appropriated to the Household), benevolences and forced loans, fines and compositions,[1] the French pension, money raised by recognisance and obligation, butlerage and prisage, and in the later years clerical and lay subsidies: some of them, it is true, by way of assignment[2] from the Exchequer, but most of them not. At the same time, to supplant the Exchequer of Account, there was developed an institution which early came to be called the Court of General Surveyors, and this court, with no origin or support but the king's will, became much more important than the Exchequer of Account. The exchequer officials naturally endeavoured to stop this transfer of functions, instituting processes against fiscal officials who had ceased to present their accounts to them, but Henry VII was able to thwart these efforts by instructing his attorney-general[3] to take such processes into his own hands, and by prohibiting them for the future. His son found it worth while to fortify the new court with statutory authority.[4]

[1] After 1487, cf. Newton, p. 363: and p. 364 for the magnitude of the sums dealt with by Heron.

[2] In 1495 (*R.P.* VI, pp. 497–502) the receivers of the assigned revenues were to pay them to the treasurer *or* cofferer of the household, which meant in practice the latter: increase in importance of chamber accounting and of the treasurer of the chamber to high water mark in the early years of Henry VIII, cf. Newton in *Tudor Studies*, p. 235.

[3] And by his treasurer of the chamber, John Heron, also chamberlain of the exchequer, supervisor of customs in the port of London, clerk of the jewel house, clerk of the hanaper of the chancery, keeper of the king's writs: Newton, pp. 356, 357.

[4] The first such act was 1 H. VIII c. 3 (cf. *Henry VIII*, p. 51), which marks "the full measure of the growth of the treasurership of the chamber under Henry VII from an office of merely court importance into the general receivership of the king's revenues": Newton, p. 356, which also explains how at the same time the lord treasurership became a purely honorific office.

CHAPTER II

COUNCIL

To explain fully what the kingship was which Henry VII wielded it would be necessary to write all the history of England before his accession. Its most characteristic features seem to be the prevalent idea of it as something belonging to Henry, like the birthright to Esau, or greenness to grass; and the large effectiveness of it, resulting from financial independence.

In any government managed under the forms of monarchy the king must have advisers and assistants, and among the primary questions, therefore, about any such government are these—who are his advisers? how much liberty has he in the choosing of them? in removing them? in accepting or rejecting their advice? The first institution of a monarchy is a council.[1] But it does not follow that every king has always had a council possessed of every attribute which the word evokes in the twentieth century, a conciliar body of which the composition is fixed and something less than arbitrarily alterable, and of which the action requires some minimum of attendance and agreement. Here, indeed, is the crux of the question how much the king in his own head settles policy and directs administration: what rules, if any, controlled Henry's dealings with his council?

The composition of the council was what mattered most in this connection, and it was entirely in Henry's hands. What members the council was composed of at any particular date in his reign no one can now exactly tell, nor even then could be sure except by seeing with his own eyes the faces of the persons actually present. The nearest thing to a shibboleth for distinguishing men who were councillors from men who were not was the council oath,[2] and this test was not infallible.

[1] Cf. p. 12 above.
[2] J. F. Baldwin, *The King's Council*, p. 346. The oath was already some two and a half centuries old: by Henry VII's time it had settled down to its permanent form, of which these were the essential clauses: "Ye shall as ferfurth as your connyng and discretion suffiseth, trewely, justely, and evenly counseille and advyse the Kyng

It was possible, no doubt, in Henry VII's reign to make a list of the men who had taken this oath, and such lists showed how the council was composed, but their evidence was not exhaustive: the king was not by any means compelled to summon to any particular meeting all or any specified section of those who had been sworn:[1] and besides being at liberty to act on advice from any one he pleased even though unknown to every organ and official of government, he might also summon to council meetings persons who had not been sworn, as is proved by the swearing of three lords on one occasion which was certainly not the first of their attendance.[2] Councillors might be formally admitted, and even allotted a regular annuity,[3] but they might not, and even if they were they did not thereby acquire any professional security of tenure or expectation of being heard.

The council had always been the body of men whom the king summoned because he thought their advice would be useful. Henry had more real freedom than any, or almost any, of his predecessors in exercising his judgment on this point. Naturally, a successful pretender was not bound by the appointments of his usurping predecessor. The only one of the great families to which he had any obligation was the Stanleys, and they were very far from being able to provide a king-maker or mayor of the palace: indeed, Sir William Stanley was the only councillor whom Henry ever removed.[4] The grandees could be excluded from the council, and the few that were admitted could be

in all materes to be comoned, treted and demened in the Kyng's Counseille, or by you as the King's Counseiller, and generally in all thinges that may be to the Kynge's worship proufit, and behove...And ye shall kepe secrete the Kynge's Counseill, and all that shall be comuned by way of Counseille in the same...".

[1] A. Conway, p. 229, says she has collected the names of 146 who attended one or more council meetings besides 22 who did not: but it was only a very small proportion (like Savage, Bray, and Lovell, whom she names) who attended more than very occasionally.

[2] B.M. Add. MSS. fol. 113, quoted Baldwin, p. 436: cf. also E. R. Turner, *The Privy Council*, 1603–1784, e.g. p. 52.

[3] In Henry VIII's time, e.g. T. Nevill councellor vice E. Dudley, during good behaviour £66. 13s. 4d. (*L. and P.* II (1), no. 2736, p. 874). In 1519 Sir Robt. Wyngfeld was similarly remunerated (III, no. 417). In 1518 T. More got £100 (II, no. 4247), and so did Robt. Southwell in 1540 (xv, no. 436/56).

[4] J. Gairdner, *Henry VII*, p. 210, William Stanley was beheaded as an accomplice of Warbeck.

kept in due order. If some great offices were nominally left to them, their duties and powers were really transferred to deputies and substitutes who were absolutely the king's men, as has been seen already with regard to finance. There were plenty of competent men, lay and clerical, who had gained experience in affairs abroad or under Edward IV and who were willing to serve the king without presuming to have a policy of their own. Men all of whose importance arose from the royal service were always the majority of Henry's council,[1] and it is not too much to say that in his time councillors were the king's superior servants diversified with a few harmless noblemen, and that he sent for such of them as he wanted when he wanted them, listened to their advice when he had asked for it, and did what he liked with it when he had heard it. His councillors were certainly too numerous to have been an efficient consultative body, and it appears alike from probability, from contemporary evidence, and from respectable tradition that Henry's intimate and trusted advisers were very few[2] and their influence on policy slight and indirect.

Henry's consultations were, then, at his own choice and unrestricted by forms: nevertheless his council was not altogether without formality, continuity, and self-consciousness. As has been seen, it was a sworn body.[3] It had (like earlier councils) a clerk, who was certainly acting by 5 December 1485, and who, on 4 March 1486, was appointed as

---

[1] D. M. Gladish, *The Tudor Privy Council*, pp. 10 ff. and Baldwin, p. 436. Many of them were clerics: note especially John Morton archbishop of Canterbury (of whom the collector of Peter's Pence reported on 5 Oct. 1488 to Innocent VIII that he was "prime minister, well adequate to everything, excellently deserving of the Apostolic See and of his Holiness, and worthy of honour", *S.P. Ven.* I, p. 535) and Rd. Fox (bishop successively of Exeter, Bath, Durham, Winchester), and also e.g. T. Savage bishop of Rochester, and H. Deane bishop of Bangor, and towards the end of the reign Wolsey. Cf. pp. 174, 181 below.

[2] *Sp. Cal.* I, p. 439, 5 Oct. 1507, and Wm. Paulet marquis of Winchester to Queen Elizabeth, in Hy. Ellis, *Original Letters*, 3rd series, III, p. 370, both quoted in *E.H.R.* XXXVII, p. 343, by A. F. Pollard. Cf. *Sp. Cal.* I, no. 204, pp. 160 and 162, July 1498 and no. 268, p. 223, June 1500, and Hall's *Chronicle* (ed. 1809), p. 424, all quoted by Gladish, p. 13. Miss Conway, p. 229, examined forty-six meetings and found the usual attendance from six to ten: the ordinary proportion would be four or five of the inner ring, two or three experts on the principal item of the agenda, and a couple of lawyers.

[3] But not altogether: cf. the last paragraph but one.

from the previous September 30:[1] part of his duty was to keep some sort of record.[2]

Besides the clerkship there was before the end of Henry VII's reign,[3] and has been intermittently ever since, another conciliar office, the presidency; whatever functions the lord president had, and it is by no means clear that he had any, they proved singularly dispensable.[4] More may be said of him later, but here he is evidence for two propositions: first, the existence of his office is an argument that the council had a considerable and increasing formality; secondly, his appointment by royal word of mouth, without any patent or seal[5] or any definition of duties, is an instance how absolutely royal the council was, and how easily the king could manipulate its formalities.

The numerous functions of the council cannot be described with brevity and precision: its general function can be fairly stated in a few words—to enable the king to do what he ought; not to decide what the king ought to do. The council had no competence which did not arise from the exercise of the royal prerogative,[6] it could do nothing that the king did not want it to do, and had no existence apart from him. It might meet in a place where the king was not, but his presence was always assumed[7] and the resultant action was his action. The council had a variety of styles and manifestations. In the first place, the council might be *great*: a *magnum concilium* was a meeting with a special summons and unusual solemnity of a council as numerous as possible

---

[1] Campbell, *Materials Illustrative of the Reign of Henry VII*, I, pp. 195, 338. Baldwin and Gladish both say he was appointed on Sept. 30 and refer to Campbell, I, p. 154, but I can find nothing relevant on that page.

[2] The extracts from the *Liber Intrationum* which survive were made for purposes of controversy and include a good many references to the early years of Henry VII and to occasions when the king was present: cf. A. F. Pollard and C. H. Williams in *Bul. Inst. Hist. Res.* v, pp. 23 ff.

[3] About 1496: Baldwin, p. 445, quotes from J. Caesar, *Auncient State Authoritie and Proceedings of the Court of Requests* (1597), p. 14, *Coram Presidente Consilii domini Regis* in 1497.

[4] Cf. Pollard in the *E.H.R.* xxxvii, pp. 351 ff.: the office was vacant from 1558 to 1679.

[5] There was no council seat till about 1566 (*E.H.R.* xliii, p. 190).

[6] Cf. T. F. Tout, *Chapters in Medieval Administrative History*, I, p .11; II, p. 147; III, pp. 466, 467; v, p. 63; and Baldwin, *The King's Council*, p. 385.

[7] Cf. p. 41 below.

and afforced with such an indefinite number of extraordinary attendants as seemed useful for the occasion. It was a *magnum concilium* which made the king the grant to meet the crisis of 1496, and besides this, it is possible to reckon four or five other *magna concilia*[1] in Henry VII's reign: they were occasionally summoned by Henry VIII also, and once by Charles I. But the usefulness of such special assemblies between a normal council and a parliament was dubious and dwindling: great councils may be considered to have become by the sixteenth century a matter of not much more than antiquarian interest.

If in dealing with the first Tudor there is not much that need be said here about Great Councils, about The Privy Council it is safest not to speak at all till the time comes to deal with the government of his son. Specially private meetings of the king's advisers must always have been occasionally necessary, and there must always have been an inner circle of advisers: moreover, the council was sometimes called *concilium privatum*, and it may be fair in dealing with Henry VII's reign to speak of his more confidential servants as serving "in his inner council",[2] but it is still premature at that date to make a distinction more than descriptive between council and Privy Council. A council might be specially privy as it might be specially great, but there was as yet no Privy Council. *Privy* was the description of an occasion, not the title of an institution.

The council was indeed already showing a fissiparous tendency, a tendency to split, if not into separate institutions, at least into several instruments of government: but the labels by which the divergent manifestations are to be recognised are less definitive than descriptive and are adverbial rather than adjectival—"in the Star Chamber", "in the White Hall",[3] "ubicunque fuerit", rather than "Great", "privatum", "ordinarium".

There had been from time to time potentially two branches of the council, the one attending the king wherever he might be, often

---

[1] Robt. R. Steele, *Catalogue of Tudor and Stuart Proclamations*, I, p. lxxvi.
[2] Cf. A. P. Newton in "The King's Chamber under the Early Tudors", *E.H.R.* XXXII, p. 357, where he is talking of John Heron, one of Henry's chief financial assistants.
[3] For poor men's causes: cf. I. S. Leadam, *Select Cases in the Court of Requests*.

designated by some such phrase as "about the king's person", the other remaining at London or Westminster. Sometimes there was correspondence between the two branches, but never was any organic separation effected, much less any division of functions, such as consultation and administration for one group and judicature for the other.[1] This branching was certain to acquire endurance, though not rigidity, in the reign of a king resolved to keep all governments in his own hands, therefore needing a council with him wherever he went, and no less resolved to employ prerogative jurisdiction for abolishing disorder, therefore needing a permanent council in some one place. Such a king was Henry, and with him these necessities became unmistakable and continuous: they had been observable long before, as when in 1406 the house of commons petitioned the king to send all bills, by some of the councillors attendant, to the council remaining at Westminster.[2]

They were necessities which pressed on Henry's subjects no less than on himself, for there were things which they might properly want to get done and yet have no hope of procuring except from the council: so that it was with a note of querulousness that Sir T. Tyng wrote to Sir J. Paston (in 1494), "There hath been so gret counsell for the Kynge's maters, that my Lord chawnsler kept not the Ster Chawmber thys VIII days but on(e) day at London".[3]

It was not difficult for Henry VII to arrange for his council to be with him and at the same time to be at Westminster. It has been remarked that he was the first monarch since John who came to the throne without an influential party among the peers, but he was never without the attendance of as many as he needed: the king's favour and hospitality sufficed to attract those whose presence he thought desirable. Payment of councillors was by this time obsolescent: those, the most numerous and important section, who were not too grand for such considerations, were usually remunerated not as councillors but for the administrative offices which they exercised.[4] Appointment had

---

[1] The two sentences above are copied almost literally from I. S. Leadam and J. F. Baldwin, *Select Cases before the King's Council*, 1243–1482, p. xvi.
[2] *R.P.* III, p. 586, quoted by Leadam and Baldwin, p. xvi.
[3] *Paston Letters*, III, p. 385.
[4] Cf. p. 29 above.

come to mean appointment for life, unless the king should cut it short, and attendance continual or as continual as he wished. The traditional quorum was six, but it was not essential to validity. With the help of a dozen servants who could be trusted, the king may be said to have solved the problem of being in two places at once,[1] his council being, as the Venetian ambassador expressed it, his "ears, person, and voice itself",[2] and able to be active simultaneously at Windsor and at Westminster.

There is an instance early in 1494 of the way in which the bifurcation was managed. Henry was about to set out on progress, and a sort of roster was drawn up showing which councillors were to be in attendance for what periods.[3] But the distinction remained simply a question of fact: the council of the king *ubicunque fuerit* consisted of those who were with him, the council *in camera stellata* of those who were doing his business at Westminster. Any councillor could pass without notice or formality from one to the other, and either could do anything the other could do, at the king's desire. On 15 August 1494 Thomas Cresset appeared before the council attendant at Windsor on a recognisance entered into before the council in the Star Chamber. On 16 November 1501 the case of *Leech* v. *Galon, Moore and others* was remitted by the council attendant at Woodstock to the council in the Star Chamber.[4] In practice the attendants on the king had an advantage over their colleagues at Westminster, and might on occasion send them imperative instructions, because, the authority of both bodies flowing from the crown, that was superior which was nearer to the source. But both had full judicial powers, as is shown, for instance, by the statute 19 H. VII c. 14[5] providing informers with the choice of suing in Star Chamber, king's bench, or council attendant.

---

[1] As far back as the reign of Henry II the *Dialogus de Scaccario* showed two royal seals, *quod residet in thesauro* and *deambulatorium*: cf. Tout, I, p. 143: and p. 149, the exchequer seal being used as Henry III's "seal of absence" when he had taken the Great Seal abroad.
[2] *Ven. Cal.* 13 May 1557, quoted by Gladish, p. 44.
[3] Quoted from Caesar by Steele, p. lxxvi.
[4] Quoted from Caesar by C. L. Scofield, *The Court of Star Chamber*, p. 28.
[5] I.e. the fourteenth chapter of the statute made in the parliament which began in the nineteenth year (beginning on 21 Aug. 1503) of Henry VII's reign. Cf. p. 49 below.

It was largely to their position as residuary legatees and almost monopolists of feudality that the Tudors owed their ability to make the conciliar device effective not merely for central but also for local jurisdiction and administration, and even for reducing to a tolerable order and a manageable uniformity with the rest of the country those districts where frontier warfare, inaccessibility, and economic inferiority had kept alive feudalism, self-help,[1] faction and particularism. What they did in this way in the early sixteenth century, which was the decisive period, may be seen from the process by which the Councils in the Marches of Wales and in the North were made stable and strong.

The north country and Wales and its marches needed governance the more since, in spite, partly indeed because,[2] of their economic inferiority, they had played a quite disproportionate part in politics, and had provided the bulk of the forces for both sides in the Wars or the Roses.[3] Richard III had understood this, with respect to the north especially, as well as any one and with better reason, and this understanding was one of the many advantages which his vanquisher inherited from him. When Richard was the greatest lord in the north he had, like any other great lord, a council, which he kept when he was king. Bosworth transferred everything of Richard's to Henry, and his council in the north became the king's.[4]

Similarly, as far back as 1471 the council appointed to administer the Prince of Wales's possessions had been given judicial and military powers in Wales and the marches. It seems likely that in 1483 this council fell into abeyance, but it was revived and made into a permanent and satisfactory organ of government by the Tudors, who had special reasons for interesting themselves in Wales, and also special advantages, not least of which was that by Richard's defeat the earldom of March had been forfeited to the crown. Something was done towards turning the prince's council into the Council in the Marches, a professionalised

---

[1] In the sense of trusting to your force instead of your legal rights.
[2] Cf. R. R. Reid, *King's Council in the North*, p. 5.
[3] Cf. Reid, p. 41 and C. A. J. Skeel, *Council in the Marches of Wales*, p. 11.
[4] Cf. Reid, p. 46: and pp. 58–66, development of the council's authority and jurisdiction 1483–5: p. 75, no king's council in the north during the short time Northumberland ruled it (from Jan. 1486 for a little over three years).

and articulated part of the royal government, towards the end of Henry VII's time, but it was the first half of his son's reign which really settled the matter.[1]

In the north Richard, besides having been Edward's lieutenant and the greatest feudal magnate, had reigned in hearts, and had fallen only because of the desertion of the Percies, and there no doubt Richard's heir would have been proclaimed but for Henry's false announcement of his death. There there was danger not only of foray and riot but of invasion, and there in 1486, reluctantly, Henry made Percy Warden of the Marches and Lieutenant. Three years later Percy was murdered[2] (for trying to collect a subsidy voted by parliament), and Henry appointed the infant Arthur[3] as warden, with his best soldier, Surrey, as lieutenant.

Surrey had a council,[4] much like what Richard's had been: Henry took care that the preponderance of its membership was official, and this is the true beginning of the Council of the North. What commissions it had in the early years cannot now be exactly known, but they seem to have been expanding, under the incentive especially of need for meeting agrarian grievances and checking landlords, so that the council was steadily tending to become a court of requests and a star chamber for northern purposes.[5] This is marked by the fact that when in 1499 Surrey left the north, the government of Yorkshire passed not to his military successor, Sir Thomas Darcy, but first to the bishop of Carlisle and then (in 1502) to the archbishop of York, both chosen for their legal qualifications as well as for their clerical profession.

Another Yorkist attempt to adapt the conciliar method was taken up and exploited by the Tudors. The delegation of council sitting in

[1] Cf. Skeel, esp. pp. 28, 29, 31, 37.

[2] Leaving an heir eleven years old, and the Percy lands in the king's hands. Cf. p. 21, n. 4 above.

[3] He was succeeded in 1494 by his brother Henry, then four years old, who in the same year became also Duke of York and Lieutenant of Ireland: cf. Conway, pp. 34, 62.

[4] And so had the Warden of the West March (Dacre): in practice, the East and Middle Marches were left to the local officials, and Surrey governed Yorkshire: cf. Reid, p. 78. The royal officials in the north were paid by the assignment of manor revenues that had belonged to Richard, cf. Conway, p. 34.

[5] Cf. Reid, pp. 78–83: and below pp. 39 ff.

the White Hall, the Court of Requests, remained useful and popular
for generations. It was performing in the king's name his duty to see
that justice was done to the poor and friendless, a duty in performing
which he was entitled to the assistance of his councillors but which
could not be permitted to swamp king and counsel under a flood of
suits for small sums. As early as Richard III's reign, therefore, special
provision was made for such cases, and in December 1483, John
Harington "for his good service...especially in the custody, regi-
stration, and expedition of bills, requests, and supplications of poor
persons" was appointed "clerk of the council of the said requests and
supplications".[1] Such business was active, and the records of it have
survived, from the middle of Henry VII's reign.[2] At that time also
there began to be appointed special masters of requests, so that this
part of the council's business should neither interfere with the rest nor
languish for want of attention: the lord privy seal was their president.

The most solemn act of the council, and indeed of the realm short of
act of parliament, was proclamation. But though there can be little
doubt that proclamations came before the council and were issued
through it, they did not generally mention it, and indeed in this reign
the only one of which there is proof that it passed the council does not
refer to the fact.[3] The scope of proclamations can be indicated best
by examples. By proclamation in

1487 trade with the possessions of Maximilian was restrained, import and
export alike being forbidden without special licence under the Great
Seal. A staple of metals was incorporated at Southampton in 1492. The
duties payable by Venetian merchants were raised to equal those paid by
English merchants at Venice. The frequency of proclamations concerning the coinage show that it was a subject of preoccupation to the
king and his council. The undated proclamation against exchange and
export of the precious metals merely enforces the law if it is later in the
reign, or if it is early, continues an expired statute of Edward IV....
A number of proclamations for distraint of knighthood have been

---

[1] A. F. Pollard in *E.H.R.* xxxvii, p. 344, quoting J. F. Baldwin, p. 435, and *Pat.
Rolls* (1476–85), pp. 413, 538.
[2] For this and the following sentences, cf. I. S. Leadam, *Select Cases in the Court
of Requests*, pp. x ff.
[3] 16 July 1486, proclamation for aid to the fleet of Maximilian: Steele, p. lxxvii.

found.... The first results of the enclosure of arable land were now beginning to make themselves felt, and though we have found no proclamation against it, there can be no doubt that the proclamation against vagabonds of 1493, the first of a long series throughout the Tudor period, is a direct result.... The affairs of Calais are referred to several times.... It is significant that the first public proclamation of Henry's we have is an offer of pardon.[1]

There were proclamations also of peace, war, alliance, military discipline, national defence (even calling out all able-bodied men) for the expulsion of Scots, against the export of corn, for justices of the peace to execute their commissions and for persons aggrieved to resort to justices of assize or if necessary to the king or chancellor, against conveying any one overseas without licence, against retainers, and on many other matters.[1] There were cases before the council of breaches of proclamation, though they formed hardly more than an infinitesimal proportion of all its cases.

The council did other things besides issue general commands and occasionally punish neglect of them. It ordered Robin of Redesdale[2] to be arrested, concluded peace with the king of Scotland, settled that every lord or gentleman should be responsible for producing any riotous servant of his, commanded disturbers of the peace to lay down their arms and bound them over in large sums, ordered parties to drop suits which they had started, enquired into cases of perjury, piracy, murder, wounding, and even the title to land, levied fines,[3] arranged for the gentry of the south-eastern counties to reinforce Calais with armed men, received ambassadors, made official appointments and assigned their remuneration:[4] a committee of council was appointed by the king to make a list of mischiefs and corruptions so that remedy might be found in the next parliament, and, another time, commissioners to provide reformation of idleness and sumptuary excess as well by great lords as mean persons; it was decided in council that the king

---

[1] Steele, p.l xxvii, and pp. 1–6.
[2] A rather mysterious rebel: what follows, where not otherwise noted, is quoted from *Liber Intrationum* by Scofield, pp. 6, 7, 8, 18, 19, 20, 21, 23, 24.
[3] Campbell, II, p. 91.
[4] Campbell, I, p. 493.

himself should go to Ireland to suppress rebellion, and that he should take with him besides his household six thousand men well chosen, three great pieces, four hundred arquebuses, sixty fowkins,[1] and five hundred hand-guns. The council also exercised a general, sometimes a very active and exigent, superintendence over local administration.

Perhaps the most important work, certainly most of the work, of the council was judicial. It was Henry VII's most practical necessity as well as his highest vocation to be, in the words of an Elizabethan official, "a right reformer of a disordered Common Wealth":[2] his principal method was the punishment of offences which the ordinary course of fifteenth-century jurisdiction did not reach, and his principal tool the council. In Henry's time no new court was initiated, nor did the council receive any extension of competence; at most there was reinforcement of procedure.

Conciliar jurisdiction originated in the principle that it was the king's right, indeed his duty and almost his essence, to provide for the administration of justice to all his subjects. In this and his other tasks his sole assistance had once been the undifferentiated *curia*, the collection of his friends and servants who helped him to do his work. From it various branches had developed and had now been struck, so that they had each a life and a growth of their own, of which the fruit was the performance of this or that part of the royal obligation to provide justice: such were the court of common pleas, the king's bench, exchequer, parliament itself, and (latest shoot of all, hardly yet living its own life) chancery. But it was not to be supposed because the king had enabled other bodies to do for him some of the good for the sake of which he existed, that he had thereby precluded himself from making such further provision as might be necessary. There might still arise danger of injustice which none of these courts could prevent, and then the king should find in his bosom and might exercise in his council jurisdiction enough to fill the deficiency.

On the other hand, persons obnoxious to correction from this

---

[1] Presumably a sort of mortar.
[2] Steele, p. lxxv, quoting from B.M. Add. MSS. 4521, fol. 104. Cf. the coronation ceremonial, p. 11, n. 6 above.

residual jurisdiction and convinced that they would otherwise have escaped were likely to resent, and if possible to deny, its competence: its procedure, too, if it had not the restrictions of common law and statute, had not their certification either: and there was a perfectly real objection which could be quite honestly taken to conciliar judicature— that the first requisite of tolerable administration is the possibility of knowing the rules, that in general predictability, most of all about the grounds of legal decision, is a necessity, and a nice and detailed justice a luxury, even if it could be taken for certain that an unlimited and supereminent conciliar jurisdiction would always be used with a purpose of justice.

Rising then from this royal and supra-legal, at least extra-legal, source and hemmed in by these resistances of varying respectability, the stream of conciliar jurisdiction ran with inconstant volume in a winding and accidented channel from the remotest constitutional antiquity till it was canalised by Tudor practice and finally by Stuart statute stored in a parliamentary cistern, with parliamentary taps.

The modern terms of legislative, administrative, judicial, are in practice even now not exactly defined and mutually exclusive, and were at the end of the fifteenth century not yet familiar as categories of theoretical analysis. It has been said that "the jurisdiction of the King in Council was never *in its nature* directly judicial and original, nor even regularly appellate, but rather only protective, corrective, and restraining":[1] it is true that the council was not a court of judicature, but it could do what was necessary to correct the errors and supply the defects of such courts.

In Henry's time it sat regularly in the Star Chamber, during the legal terms at least as often as four times a week.[2] One of the principal reasons why the main business of supplementing the common law in civil cases fell to the chancellor, who would sit in vacation time, was the rule dating from 1426 that "out of terme tyme nothing be spedd in the counseil but suche thing as for the goods of the kyng and of his

---

[1] W. F. Finlason, *The Judicial Committee of the Privy Council*, p. 6.
[2] Gladish, p. 15, based on the *Liber Intrationum*.

land asketh necessarie and hasty speed":[1] that is, the council, though not incapacitated out of term time, was unwilling in vacation to transact any but urgent public business.

The king himself might be present: Edward IV at least once gave judgment and made the decree,[2] Henry VII often attended, and on one occasion (the same on which the arrest of Robin of Redesdale was ordered) "The L(ord) Lisle and Brightmere and others (were) dismist of the Riott, For that the Kinge himself would heare the same as his Atturney made Certificate".[3] The regular thing was for the king to instruct the council to make the decree, but stronger than any rule or custom was the word of the king. In any case he was always supposed to be present,[4] and the question, for instance, "whether the officials nominated by the Act 3 H. VII c. 1[5] were sitting or not, was, in the presence, real or constructive, of him from whom its jurisdiction flowed, a matter of no legal import".[6]

There were various ways in which cases might come before the council. It might be by way of petition from a private person with a grievance. The danger that the council in reply would override the forms and upset the certainty of law was one which parliament tried to guard against, by 5 E. III c. 9, for instance, and again in the twenty-fifth year of Edward III, when it was laid down that the council should not meddle with freehold.[7] Private persons might bring criminal as well as civil matters into the council, and were not checked here as in the process of *appeal* (i.e. private accusation at common law) either by the certainty of publicity or by the risk of having to venture their persons in trial by battle: so that the initiation of criminal charges by private *suggestion*, as it was called, was peculiarly odious, the more as it was officially, sometimes even pecuniarily, encouraged: it was therefore several times enacted that suitors should be required to give security

---

[1] Quoted by I. S. Leadam, *Select Cases in the Star Chamber* (Selden Soc. vol. XVI), I, p. lxviii.
[2] Quoted from *Cal. Pat. Rolls*, 20 E. IV, p. 218, by Baldwin, p. 433.
[3] Quoted from *Liber Intrationum*, by Scofield, p. 6.
[4] Cf. p. 39 above.
[5] Cf. p. 44 below.
[6] I. S. Leadam, *Select Cases in the Star Chamber*, I, p. lvii.
[7] Baldwin, p. 279.

for proving their suggestions, but these enactments do not appear to have much reduced the council's capacity for attracting information and delation, though they may have saved it from the pestering of private grievances.[1]

There were more general restrictions also, not always more effective, on the council's competence. In 1390 it was ordained by the council that business touching the common law be sent to be determined before the justices: in 1423 a proviso was added for the cases when the council might feel too great might on the one side and too great unmight on the other, and three years later a further proviso was appended—"or else other cause reasonable", and this was confirmed by parliament in 1429. In 1453 parliament went further, for 31 H. VI c. 2 was the first statutory reinforcement of the council's power to enforce attendance: this act specified also that matters determinable at common law should not thereby be withdrawn from the ordinary courts, and it was limited to seven years: but neither limitation seems to have been effective.[2] Nor was parliament's action always towards limitation, for sometimes it remitted to the council petitions which otherwise would have been left unanswered at parliament's dissolution. To sum up, the matters which by the end of the fifteenth century were settled to be unsuitable for conciliar jurisdiction were life and limb and freehold, and appeals in error from the common law courts, which should go to parliament (that is, as we should say, to the house of lords).[3] But this does not mean that in matters of common-law jurisdiction, even where life or land was at stake, the council was in practice impotent, though it was as a rule careful to observe its exclusion from matters of freehold: it enjoined, in 1488, for instance, the duke of Suffolk in his majesty's name not to proceed in an action of treason at the common law, and in 1506 it decreed that George Bardsey be "putt to silence, for ever, never to be heard in this Counsell, in anie Cause, And enjoyned to appeare on Fridaie next, and laie a Cause why he should not be Committed to Warde for his disobedience, in Counsellinge Kirkeby to make none aunsweare to

---

[1] Cf. Baldwin, pp. 286–8.
[2] I. S. Leadam, *Select Cases in the Star Chamber*, I, pp. xlix–lxii.
[3] Cf. Baldwin, pp. 334 ff., esp. refs. to the Year Books on p. 335.

the title of Land, Contrarie to the Comaundment and decree of this Councell".[1] It determined conflicts of jurisdiction, instructed judges about the conduct of cases, stopped, delayed and expedited actions, rebuked courts which it judged guilty of irregularity, and maintained control over the findings of juries.[2] The indication of the sort of cases with which the council dealt has led away from the consideration of ways in which cases came before it. Most came, naturally, by way of petition: but the most important, those with a political content, not less naturally were initiated by the crown or arose from a more than nominal exercise of its grace, the characteristic feature being in the first case a special kind of writ, in the second an enquiry into official conduct or royal rights.

The main motive of petitioning the council instead of proceeding at the ordinary law was that the council could do all that the ordinary courts could do (or make them do it) and more also: another was that a petition (unlike a writ) cost nothing: and a third that a petition might complain of "certain persons" or "parties unknown", and was not invalidated by technical defect, like a mistake in a name.[3] For the crown writs of privy seal[4] had charms much like those of petition for the subject. The privy seal had begun by being really privy, and when it had become the organ of the council and one of the regular tools of public business, the king being thrown back on the signet and then on the sign manual[5] for his private purposes, it retained some of the advantages of a position of greater freedom and less responsibility. Its writs[6] were issued on paper without sealed warrant, and were not registered or enrolled, so that they could not be delayed or published or investigated: they were no part of the common law, and therefore did not notice its limitations and were able, for instance, to penetrate districts protected by franchise. Similarly, when they expressed a

---

[1] Both instances quoted from the *Liber Intrationum* by Scofield, pp. 18, 20.
[2] Cf. W. S. Holdsworth, *History of English Law*, IV, p. 84: the instances there cited are not in reference to Henry VII, but there is no doubt that they might be applied to the council's habits in that reign.
[3] Cf. Leadam and Baldwin, p. xxvi.
[4] For their early development, beginning in the middle of the fourteenth century, cf. Baldwin, pp. 227, 255, 288.
[5] Cf. Tout, I, pp. 23, 29, 149, 151, 176; V, pp. 13, 59, 196, 207, 211, 212, 227.
[6] Baldwin, pp. 256, 288.

summons they did not need to convey its causes: *quibusdam certis de causis* and the later more usual *sub poena* ordered attendance without stating, as a common law writ must, what was the matter to be enquired into. Just the very reasons why these writs were dear to the crown made them hateful to their recipients, so that throughout the fifteenth century there were attempts to weaken them, and even to ignore them as invalid: but they were backed by fines for contempt, commissions of arrest, and proclamations of outlawry,[1] and the writs were irresistible when these reinforcements were real, which was the case under a strong monarch like Henry VII, as it had not been, for instance, under Henry VI. No doubt one of the motives of 3 H. VII c. 1[2] was to discourage any questioning of the privy seal writ's legality: the persons named in the statute had "authority to call before them by writ or *privy seal* the said misdoers".

The council's nature was to govern rather than to judge: and although its tradition did not emphasise that distinction, yet it had no love of judicature for its own sake: to exercise as much as might be necessary for the avoidance of injustice was its duty, and as much as might help the efficiency of government its interest, seeing that it was the supreme and central organ of the king's administration. These considerations affected the sort of cases which were held especially appropriate to the council, and the disposition which it made of those that came before it. By far the most of them it remitted to some other court, with any necessary directions as to their treatment: even those which received a partial hearing or preliminary examination from the council were usually sent for further deliberation to one of the courts, a board of arbitration, or a special commission.[3] Of cases fully treated in council in the two centuries before Henry VII's accession it would be difficult now to count a hundred, and it is not probable that the numbers have been much diminished by loss of records. A conciliar judgment was necessary only when the ordinary law was defeated by the excessive might of a party, or the undue influencing of judge or jury, or the novelty or

[1] Cf. Baldwin, pp. 290–4: and I. S. Leadam, *Select Cases in the Star Chamber*, I, pp. lix–lxv.
[2] Cf. p. 41 above, pp. 47, 64, 145 below.
[3] Leadam and Baldwin, p. xix.

enormity of the matter: most important of all were the cases that affected the king's interest, and indeed it may well be argued that in the council's relation to these lies the decisive characteristic of Tudor government.

In legal theory the king was the sole fountain of justice, and all courts were the king's courts: this formula does not altogether suffice for all the previous history of judicature, but in Henry VII's time it was and long had been orthodox. It was settled by judges and sanctified by antiquity that no one could sue or prosecute the king, that he could not receive a command or a summons.[1] In a legal sense the king could do no wrong, nor did his impeccability mean then, as it does now, that for everything which could be complained against the royal authority some of the royal servants must be responsible. On the contrary, the notion of the king and the crown as two entities was then hardly conceivable:[2] the king's servants were clearly part of the interests of the crown, and it was too well understood to be disputed that in such matters the judges should not proceed without consulting the king or his council: sometimes they would receive a writ to surcease, or not less often they would of their own accord decline to continue until they had received a writ to proceed. When, therefore, any matter affecting the prerogative or interests of the king or the conduct of his servants was submitted to his council and withdrawn from other tribunals, it was not a piece of tyrannical pretension or an arbitrary invasion of the liberty of the subject and equality before the law: it was a kingly concession to idealism and the rights of man.[3]

It was not only in the character of its writs and the use of petition and suggestion that conciliar procedure was different from that of the

---

[1] Pollock and Maitland, *History of English Law*, I, pp. 499–501.

[2] But cf. Tout for the first attempts at this notion: I, p. 5, discrimination in the fourteenth century between the king in his personal capacity and the crown as the mainspring of government (and, incidentally between legislative executive and judicial); II, p. 60, Edward I drawing the distinction between office and person of the king; p. 210, the distinction drawn by the younger Despenser; III, p. 27, John XXII's request in 1330 to the king for some sign to distinguish those letters which the king really meant from those which were merely official, and the answer—all requests under privy seal or signet with the words *pater sancte* in the king's own hand; on the other hand, IV, p. 468, the fourteenth century saw no difference between the king's public and private establishments.

[3] Cf. Baldwin, pp. 58, 271: Leadam and Baldwin, p. xxvii.

common law, or favourable to government. Pending or during trial, parties, accuser as well as defendant, might be kept in prison, even for years, though equally they might be restrained only by bonds to appear when called upon. They might be allowed to appear by proxy or attorney. In civil suits it was necessary that they should make their submission to the court. The record of any court which the pleadings made relevant might be procured by writ of *certiorari*. The council itself was not a court of record and therefore not bound by precedent, yet its endorsement on a bill (i.e. petition) was as valid a record as any other.[1] If on some point the verdict of a jury seemed necessary it might be had by writ of inquisition addressed to a sheriff. When such methods seemed unpromising, parties and witnesses might be sworn to tell the truth and then submitted to an inquisitorial examination. A defendant might be refused counsel, was not necessarily informed in advance of the charge, and might not be confronted by his accusers, when he swore to answer truly all questions put to him. Admissions of co-defendants were used against each other. Examinations were generally conducted by only a few of the council, or even by clerks or outsiders empowered for the occasion. Everything possible was in writing and was reduced to certainty outside the council room. Before a decree was made there might, and in equitable cases must, be a reference to the king. As to punishment, there was no limit, except that though the safeguarding of life and limb had failed to obtain statutory authority, yet the council was in practice careful to observe it. Nose-slitting and ear-cropping were not medieval penalties, and the cases collected by Doctors Leadam and Baldwin from the years 1243–1482 only once mention the pillory. Fines were generally much above the capacity to pay, and the crown collected as little as it would or as much as it could. Similarly, imprisonments were until further order. Defendants might be dismissed from office even though there had been no condemnation.[2]

---

[1] Baldwin, pp. 114, 376. Cf. I. S. Leadam, *Star Chamber* (Selden Soc. vol. XVI), pp. xlvi and xlvii (especially the notes), doubting whether the council were a court of record or not and suggesting that there was perhaps an attempt of the justices to have it so held in order to make their advice indispensable to the validity of its judgments.
[2] For all this paragraph, except where otherwise noted, cf. Leadam and Baldwin, pp. xxxv–xlv.

In this tribunal so acting the judges were in practice such of the king's councillors as he chose, assisted by his chief justices. There had been frequent statutory injunctions that it should not decide questions of law without the justices.[1] The Act 3 H. VII c. 1[2] attributed authority[3] to "the Chancellor and Treasurer of England for the time being and Keeper of the King's Privy Seal, or two of them, calling to them a Bishop and a temporal Lord of the King's Most Honourable Council, and the two Chief Justices of the King's Bench and Common Pleas, for the time being, or other two justices in their absence": but the council certainly did not admit that any such composition was essential to its judicial competence, nor is there any evidence of a bench so composed ever having sat. Similarly, it was recorded in the year-book of 1493[4] that all the judges had agreed in 1487 that under the statute 3 H. VII c. 1 only the chancellor, treasurer, privy seal were judges, though it was error if they did not call the others and act by their advice: but it is not clear that this dictum was unconditional or that either under Henry or at any other time the council was affected by it, and it was finally reversed in Proctor's case.[5] Indeed the effect of the statute, at least for Henry VII's reign and some time after, may be taken to have been no more than to stifle discussion of the privy seal writs, of procedure by inquisitorial examination, and of accusation without indictment.

It did not get its name *Star Chamber Act* or *Pro Camera Stellata* until much later, probably not till Elizabeth's time.[6] Perhaps it was

[1] Baldwin, p. 301.
[2] Cf. pp. 41 and 44 above: and 4 H. VIII c. 12, complaints against justices of the peace before the council, p. 64 below.
[3] To call before them by writ or privy seal upon bill or information, to examine persons so called, and to punish them if they were found defective as "if they were thereof convict after the due order of the law"; cf. J. R. Tanner, *Tudor Constitutional Documents*, p. 259.
[4] *Y.B.* (ed. Tottel), 8 H. VII fol. xiii: for a discussion of the whole question cf. I. S. Leadam, *Star Chamber*, I, pp. xxxv–xlv. A. F. Pollard, *Henry VII*, II, p. 57, prints the judges' opinion, and C. H. Williams (p. 166) gives a translation.
[5] Wm. Hudson, *A Treatise of the Court of Star Chamber*, pp. 30, 50: the date of the case is not there stated, but apparently it was when Lord Ellesmere was Lord Chancellor, i.e. between 1603 and 1617. Cf. p. 41 above.
[6] Cf. A. F. Pollard, *E.H.R.* XXXVII, pp. 521–5.

intended merely to help in clearing the royal household of retainder, maintenance, livery, and embracery, though probably the intention was wider than that, and if Henry had not known well enough what wanted doing, his judges very early informed him:[1]

And after dinner, all the Justices were at Blackfriars to discuss the king's business for the parliament. And several good statutes were mentioned, very advantageous for the kingdom if they could be carried out. These were the statutes compiled in the time of Edward IV and sent into each county to the justices of the peace, to be proclaimed and enforced, viz. Winchester and Westminster for robberies and felonies, the Statute of Labourers and Vagabonds, of tokens and liveries maintenance and embracery. And now they agreed that the Statute 23 H. VI concerning Sheriffs, &c. should be sent to them and then they would have enough, and if they were properly carried out, the law would run its course well. But the question was would they be carried out.

And the Chief Justice said the only hope was fear

of God or the King or both.... For he said that in the time of E. IV, when he was Attorney he saw all the lords sworn to keep and execute diligently the statutes which they with others had just drawn up by command of the King himself. And within an hour, while they were still in the Star Chamber, he saw the lords making retainers by oath, and swearing, and doing other things contrary to their above-mentioned oaths and promises.

At any rate, Henry fully intended that no one should doubt the availability of conciliar jurisdiction against that sort of offence by whomsoever committed, or should cavil at its writs or its oaths. In 1504 another statute[2] made it clear that the taking as well as the giving of liveries was punishable; it provided that quarter sessions should empanel a special jury of twenty-four to enquire into these offences by the evidence of bailiffs and constables, and that petty sessions should certify to king's bench all persons whom they found by examination to be retained; but what was most important was the provision that any individual might complain of these offences before

---

[1] *Y.B.* 1 H. VII Mich. pl. 3, trans. Williams, p. 169.
[2] 19 H. VII c. 14: cf. p. 34 above.

the Star Chamber or the king's bench or the council
he royal person.[1]
the tribunal whose structure and functions have been
dily adaptable to Henry's purpose. Its situation made
d assert its jurisdiction over any one: it could be set in
ne: its procedure was admirably adapted for extracting
: its special function was to do what good government
en the law as previously expounded had not authorised
ol a litigation without occupying itself with more of it
try: it could choose whether to act secretly (which
was the natural method of the councillors with the king) or publicly
(which was the method in the Star Chamber): its composition and
policy varied directly and automatically with the intentions of the
king. Never was there a judicial organ better suited to facilitate
administration: but in this connection it is necessary to note two facts
not familiar to twentieth-century thought—first that the England which
was emerging from the Middle Ages was accustomed to seeing its
administration done under the forms of judicature,[2] and indeed incapable of conceiving any other method; and secondly, that the council
in its judicial capacity behaved much more nearly like any other fifteenth-
century court than like any court in modern England.

Consider, for instance, the inquisitorial methods of the council:
they were peculiar as a habit, but as an expedient they were by no means
unprecedented. That a man should be tried without indictment (that
is, accusation by a jury of his neighbours) in a court of common law
was no doubt irregular and rare: but it had been done in king's bench,
before justices in eyre, in parliament itself. The statute 25 E. III
stat. 5 c. 4 tried to abolish or at least to limit very strictly trial without
indictment before the council: it enacted "that from henceforth none
shall be taken by Petition of Suggestion made to our Lord the King, or
to his Council, unless it be by Presentment or Indictment of good and

[1] For the relation between the first and the third, cf. p. 34 above, and *E.H.R.*
XXXVII, p. 530.
[2] Cf. p. 59 below: cf. Holdsworth, IV, pp. 134–50, especially p. 135, on the methods
of justices of the peace and their working of the more medieval officials into the
developed local government.

lawful People of the same Neighbourhood where such Deeds be done, in due Manner, or by Process made by Writ original at the Common Law; nor that none be out of his Franchises, nor of his freeholds, unless he duly be brought into answer and forejudged of the same by the Course of the Law".[1] If this act was meant to make trial without indictment impossible, it quite failed; and twelve years later it was enacted that "all they that make such Suggestions be sent with the same Suggestions before the Chancellor, Treasurer, and his Grand Council, and that they there find Surety to pursue their Suggestions, and incur the same Pain that the other should have had if he were attainted, in case that this Suggestion be found evil".[2] This provision and its frequent re-enactment show parliament's intention to regulate rather than abolish suggestion: on the face of it and in practice it limited the private accuser, not the crown, and apparently it did not do even that very effectively.

Nor was it only with regard to suggestion that the council had some precedent from common law courts and even some parliamentary authority. The same thing was true also of the sworn examination of a defendant, with its tendency to make a man convict himself. For this, too, there had been precedent in king's bench, common pleas, exchequer, parliament itself: this, too, was frequently the subject of parliamentary protests, but in individual cases of parliamentary encouragement, and even, in certain categories, of parliamentary authorisation. The most odious of all inquisitions, by torture, was less frequent in the council than in the common law courts.[3] And if its judges owed their appointment to the king and fixed their hopes upon the king, so did the other judges too.

---

[1] *Statutes of the Realm* (1810), I, p. 321.
[2] 37 E. III c. 18: on this and for the whole paragraph cf. Leadam and Baldwin, p. xxxvii, and Baldwin, p. 286.
[3] For this paragraph cf. Leadam and Baldwin, pp. xlii and xliii, Baldwin, p. 298, and *Henry VIII*, p. 361.

CHAPTER III

JUDGES, JUSTICES OF PEACE, FORCE, JURIES

Of these other judges, *the* judges, something must now be said, remembering how councillors were the king's instruments, tools and not partners of power, and how useful he made them, whether in the consultations in which, when he chose, he made up his mind, or in the proclamations and allocutions in which he announced it, or in the decrees in which he enforced it; whether he were present in person or only in construction; whether the persons concerned were the council because he had called them into the chamber where he happened to be or because he had left them in his Starred Chamber at Westminster; whether it was secret because he had something to hide or public because he had something he wished to be believed; whether what it was doing seems to us proper only to a parliament or only to a cabinet or only to a court or only to the Day of Judgment.

Not less than the royal councillors, the royal judges, whether in Westminster Hall or on circuit, owed their powers to the king's delegation of his unlimited capacity to provide justice for his people:[1] the jurisdiction they exercised was certainly of exclusively royal origin. To the king they owed their promotion, not only their nomination to the judicial bench but the necessary preliminary preferment to be serjeants, and all their hopes of future benefits: by him they might be dismissed, and mischiefs having arisen in Ireland from life appointments, it was enacted in 1494 that all judges there should hold office at the king's

---

[1] Edward IV sat in person for three days in King's Bench, *Three Fifteenth Century Chronicles* referred to by C. L. Scofield, *Edward IV*, I, p. 282. It had been settled by Henry VI's time that the king cannot order arrest outside his presence without a writ or warrant, *Y.B.* 37 H. VI Mich. pl. 20. The jurisdiction of the chancellor arose from the relation between the king's conscience and justice hindered by ordinary methods of judicature. "From the early years of the sixteenth century it is clear that it has become a separate court" (W. S. Holdsworth, *History of English Law*, I, p. 409): it protected trusts, contracts, and moral claims stopped by strict legality (pp. 453 ff. and v, pp. 215 ff.).

pleasure and that grants of a less slender tenure should be invalid.[1]
They got more from fees than from salaries and were therefore always
eager to widen their jurisdiction. They always sat, in the idea of the law,
in the king's presence. They existed not merely to hear disputes between
party and party but to do that and all the other things which the king
wanted done and which needed legal expertness. They might be
employed, for instance, to draft parliamentary bills, or to give the king
authoritative forecasts of the effect of such bills,[2] as when they decided
that it was unnecessary to include Henry's name in the reversal of
attainders.[3] They were consulted as to methods for giving increased
effectiveness to existing statutes, as when they met at Blackfriars for
the king's matters in the coming parliament[4] and there were discussed
several good statutes, very profitable to the realm if they could be
executed, statutes compiled in Edward IV's time and communicated to

[1] 10 H. VII c. 2 (Irel.), quoted in A. F. Pollard, *Reign of Henry VII*, III, p. 295.
[2] They were corporately consulted in another way also: "From the beginning of
the fifteenth century it became the practice to consult the judges [of king's bench
and common pleas and the chief baron, in the sixteenth century the other barons
also, of the exchequer] in the exchequer chamber in cases of...doubts on difficult
points of law, the inadequate knowledge of judicial authorities or a disinclination
to decide, unaided, points of law involving the interests of powerful litigants. This
practice was continued during the two following centuries, after which it was
gradually abandoned. The original purpose...was to deal with difficulties...whose
jurisdiction was outside the sphere of the common law...in the reign of Henry VI
...cases from the courts of common law quickly outnumbered all others, until
finally, at the close of the seventeenth century, common law and chancery cases
were the only ones argued before the assembly of judges...questions of disputed
jurisdiction were submitted to them, cases affecting the royal prerogative, problems
brought about by violent changes of dynasty, cases involving the rights and position
of foreigners...the chancellor was sometimes present at the hearing of a case, but
he rarely took part in any discussion, and his concurrence in the final decision is
not mentioned....In practice we find that a case was argued in court and then a
definite issue submitted to the...exchequer chamber. The adjournment thither
could only proceed on the motion of the court; the litigants had no right to demand
it...it is incorrect to describe the assembly of judges in the exchequer chamber
as a court: it was only an advisory body; yet so great were its prestige and authority
that its decisions were accepted and acted upon without question, although the
judges had no statutory authority for the function which they exercised in the
exchequer chamber" and sometimes at Serjeants Inn: quoted from the summary
of Mary Hemmant's thesis on the exchequer chamber, *Inst. Hist. Res. Bul.* VII,
pp. 116–18. Cf. Holdsworth, I, p. 242: and pp. 243 and 246 for Exchequer Chamber
amending error from King's Bench and Exchequer.
[3] Cf. p. 16 above.
[4] *Y.B.* I H. VII Mich. fol. 3, pl. 3.

the justices of the peace for them to proclaim and execute, statutes against disorder, especially riots and forcible entry, signs and livery, maintenance and embracery: and they agreed to send down to the justices of the peace the statutes 23 H. VI about sheriffs, but the chief justice said that the laws would never be well executed till the king on his part and the lords on theirs wanted them executed, and then every one would carry out the laws or if not they would be punished.

On at least one occasion,[1] it is true, the judges persuaded Henry not to insist on having their preliminary opinion on a legal point which was to be raised by the defence in a treason trial: but it is clear that Henry VII's judges were essentially different from George V's in that they were not safeguarded by security of tenure from interested complaisance with the crown, nor from unconsciously becoming the instruments of policy by exclusion from administrative and legislative cares. The right to administer the royal justice was so far from becoming in England, as it did in France, a freehold property hereditarily transmissible, that a judge lost it altogether when he died, lost it till he was reappointed when the king died, might lose it though both he and the king were still alive; and moreover, as the power of judging might be lost by a judge, so it might be granted to one who was not a judge nor in any way qualified except by the royal nomination. It is notable also that the one piece of professional freehold which was acquired by judges—certain patronage in their courts—was the one matter on which they were to stand up most firmly to a Tudor monarch.[2]

The law which the king's judges administered was applicable to the whole of the kingdom. In the palatinates (Durham, Lancaster, Chester, Wales and its marches) the rules of the common law and the statutes of parliament were enforced, and errors arising there could be corrected

---

[1] *Y.B.* 1 H. VII, fol. 25: this consultation about Stafford's defence raised two other interesting points: it was generally agreed that though the pope might "dedicate" a place and make it "sanctuary", only the king could make it a "tuition", a place of safety, for traitors: and Suliard "said that the king cannot grant this, but for the term of his life, for his heir will not be bound by this grant of his ancestor, And by this he means that these grants cannot be without Parliament".

[2] In Elizabeth's time, Cavendish's Case, Spedding and Heath's edn. of Bacon's *Works*, VII, p. 684: and cf. Skrogges *v.* Coleshill (1559): Holdsworth, I, pp. 257, 260–2.

by the King's Bench or the House of Lords. Men who were royal judges often sat in the palatine courts as well. By the end of the fifteenth century the relations between royal and palatine jurisdictions were so defined[1] and the relations between the monarch and the heads of the palatinates so intimate that the crown's control was in practice complete. The wearer of the crown was indeed, by inheritance and forfeiture, himself the palatine everywhere except in the bishopric of Durham. Of the lesser franchise courts it may safely be said that they were allowed to survive only because they were so effectively circumscribed as to be quite incapable of any political or constitutional importance:[2] and the old local courts—county court, hundred court, court leet, manorial court—besides being closely circumscribed were also in process of being superseded, for all but the pettiest purposes, by the justices of the peace, officers of royal appointment and having no authority but what came from the crown, though it was, indeed, the crown in parliament, since all their powers were statutory.

The judges sat, originally and theoretically, by commission from the king to do one part of his duty for him, and till the seventeenth century the king was not certainly excluded from still taking back to himself that part of his duty as occasion might seem good to him: but in fact no Tudor did offer to judge in person, and probably before the commencement of that dynasty it was if not decided at least understood that "as the king has entrusted his judicial power to his judges, he could not himself pronounce judgment".[3]

---

[1] Cf. G. T. Lapsley, *County Palatine of Durham*, pp. 168, 171, 210, 211, 212, 213, 215, 218, 220, 222, 228, 229.

[2] Cf. Holdsworth, I ,pp. 132 ff.

[3] Holdsworth, I, p. 207: cf. also Fortescue, *De Laudibus Legum Angliae*, ch. VIII (1464–70), in Lord Clermont's edition the Latin on p. 343 of vol. I, the English on p. 394: "you will better pronounce judgment in your courts by others than in person: it being not customary for the kings of England to sit in court, or pronounce judgment themselves: and yet they are called the king's judgments, though pronounced and given by others...". Cf. *Y.B.* 2 R. III, fols. x, xi, in the very year before Henry came to the throne, the king had summoned to the Star Chamber all the judges and put to them various important questions of law, which caused a series of consultations: one of the opinions that emerged, and that a unanimous one, was that where a man had been convicted his judges should ."take surety and pledges of the fine etc. and, after by their discretion let them assess the fine, and not the lord king by himself in his chamber nor elsewhere before him by his judges,

Such a restriction had obvious convenience, and was besides a natural corollary of the medieval idea of the supremacy of the law, an idea of which it is hardly too much to say that before the sixteenth century it was all there was in England in the way of a constitution, that during the seventeenth it was most of what there was, and during the eighteenth the best of what there was.

Yet "his judicial power" in the last paragraph but one is very far from meaning "all his judicial power". Henry IV[1] had not doubted that he could stop the flow of judicature if he judged that the political situation demanded it: "because of the war raised against us within our realm we might make all our courts cease in salvation of us and our realm". By Henry VII's time nothing had happened to impair this negative right, and positively also he still had a residue of judicature with which to supply the defects of the ordinary courts: a residue which might even be called infinite, since its nature was to provide remedy for every emergent injustice and since no bounds could be put to the universe's capacity for evil. How this residuary jurisdiction was exercised by the council and with what effect of reinforcement to the king has already been very slightly indicated: something must now be said of the jurisdiction entrusted to itinerant royal commissioners.

Already for something like two centuries commissions for this purpose had been issued at regular intervals and in definite forms. Of these commissions the one which was at first most important, the general eyre, authorising the hearing of all pleas whatsoever, fell into disuse in the first half of the fourteenth century: it had empowered the royal commissioners to seek and punish any dereliction of duty to the crown of which any one had been guilty since the last eyre: for this purpose they had before them all the officials and all the records of the county, and juries from each hundred were obliged to present to them all delinquents: so fines were collected and local government was kept up to the mark.

and *this is the will of the king viz. by his judges and his law . . .*". Cf. *Y.B.* 37 H. VI Mich. pl. 20, the king cannot order an arrest outside his presence without writ or warrant, p. 42 above.
[1] Cf. his letters to his council, 23. Oct. 1403, quoted by H. C. M. Lyte, *The Great Seal*, p. 130.

The general eyre deceased partly because, in Coke's words,[1] "as the power of the justices of assize by many acts of Parliament and other commissions increased, so these justices itinerant by little and little vanished away", partly because the king could now obtain the local information he needed from the developing organ, parliament: yet the successors of the justices in eyre did not at once become exclusively judicial officers but continued to be governmental personages as well, to enforce under judicial forms the will of government and the rights of the crown. The place of the general eyre was taken by various commissions: they were those of *trailbaston*,[2] *oyer and terminer*, *gaol delivery*, the peace, and assize.[3]

The first may be here omitted as of hardly more than antiquarian interest. The second directed certain of the king's justices and others to enquire into all crimes in a named district or into some special crime or class of crimes. The commission of gaol delivery gave power to deliver a certain gaol and to try all the prisoners found there. It might be in early times that not one of the commissioners was a royal judge. By the time of the Tudors there is no need to distinguish between gaol delivery and oyer and terminer, and indeed the two were generally issued at the same time to the same commissioners.

Both these commissions conferred a criminal jurisdiction (and so did that of the peace, which was attributed *ex officio* to the royal judges and therefore to the itinerant judges when they were selected mainly from among them, but which is not important for the present purpose). The commission of assize was civil,[4] authorising certain persons to try

---

[1] *First Instit.* 293 b, quoted by Holdsworth, I, p. 272: cf. also Holdsworth himself on that page *et seq.* for this and the following paragraphs.
[2] John Cowell's *Interpreter* says they were "a kind of Justices appointed by *King Edward* the firste upon occasion of great disorder grown in the Realme.... Their office was to make inquisition through the Realme by the verdict of substantiall Juries upon all officers, as Majors, Sheriffs, Bailiffes, Escheators and others, touching extortion, briberies, and other such grievances, as intrusions into other men's lands, and Barratours that used to take money for beating of men, and also of them whom they did beate: by means of which inquisitions many were punished by death, many by ransome, and so the rest flying the Realme, the land was quieted...".
[3] Holdsworth, I, pp. 273 ff.: and J. F. Stephen, *History of the Criminal Law*, I, pp. 105 ff.
[4] For all this paragraph, see Holdsworth, I, pp. 275 ff.

the possessory assizes of *novel disseisin, mort d'ancestor, darrein presentment,* and *utrum.*[1]

Such cases often involved difficult questions of law, and therefore
from the first at least one of the commissioners of assize was usually a
royal judge: with the elaboration of law the necessity for professional
equipment on the other commissions also became more urgent and
manifest: and no doubt the regular areas and dates of the circuits
(beginning in Edward I's time) tended the same way. In his reign and
the two reigns next following statutes repeatedly enacted that commissions of gaol delivery and of oyer and terminer must always include
the justices of assize or of either bench and must not be granted except
in the regular course: but there seems to have been some doubt about
the effect of these statutes, judging from a petition of the commons in
1383 for the limitation of the issue of the commissions, and from the
reply, "There are statutes made in this case, which the King wishes to
be held and kept, saving nevertheless to the King our Lord all his
regalie and prerogative entirely".[2]

Meanwhile the *nisi prius*[3] system had extended the civil competence
of the itinerant justices far beyond the possessory assizes:[4] so far indeed
that all sorts of civil actions could be heard on circuit.[5] And circuit
courts which had such a jurisdiction were clearly beyond the management of amateurs, so that though commissions continued to be issued
to laymen yet it was the judges from Westminster Hall who actually
executed them for all purposes, but still only in right of the specific
commission issued for the occasion, not at all in right of their status as
judges.

Such then were the king's instruments for what may be called the

[1] (a) Has A disseised B of his freehold? (b) Who is the next heir of a person deceased
last seised of a certain estate of inheritance? (c) Who was last seised of the right to
present to a certain vacant living? (d) Is certain land held by a lay or by a spiritual
tenure?
[2] *R.P.* 7 R. II no. 43 (III, 161). Referred to in Steele, p. xxv.
[3] Cf. Holdsworth, I, p. 278: custom, and particularly the Statute of Westminster II,
had given the justices of assize a general jurisdiction over civil cases begun in
common pleas or king's bench: these justices should be "two sworn justices", i.e.
judges of king's bench or common pleas.
[4] Cf. n. 1 above.
[5] Holdsworth, I, pp. 279 ff.

higher justice: men chosen by him, from a profession dependent on his favour, to sit in his hall at Westminster and administer his law to his subjects: dependent on him for remuneration and promotion and dismissible by him at will. In so far as the higher justice permitted or demanded local administration it was in practice entrusted to the same men,[1] though it would be excessive to assert that it could not be otherwise bestowed.[2] Not only were they accustomed to think of themselves as the king's paid deputies for purposes of judicature, but also they habitually acted as exponents of his policy and agents of his administration and were ready to draft or to interpret laws for him. Beside this very royal character of justice, the king's mere procedural advantages, even his power to stop a case in which his interests seemed concerned, nay even his immunity from suit, are comparatively insignificant. Nor as yet was the jury[3] anything like such a safeguard for the individual as we now are apt to assume.

But nothing could be more false than an impression that the judges were mere obsequious hirelings for enforcing the monarch's will. They were chosen for eminence in a profession whose pride was that its science had a rule for everything and whose oracle was precedent, they knew no sovereign but law and they knew that they alone knew the law, they knew each other and how to use each other, in their exchequer chamber assemblies they had a vast potentiality of co-operation.[4] And though to modern minds accustomed to the classification of Montesquieu and to the parliamentarism of Victoria the judicial may seem to

---

[1] "We have seen that the justices of assize were always on the commissions of Oyer and Terminer and Gaol Delivery; that the justices always included some of the judges of the two Benches and the Exchequer; and that, by virtue of the nisi prius system, they exercised a jurisdiction practically co-extensive with that exercised by the courts of common law", Holdsworth, I, 280.

[2] E.g. in Sept. 1498 a commission was issued to Thos. Harrys King's chaplain, Wm. Hatclyff clerk of the accounts of the household, and Roger Holland, to examine all persons in Devon and Cornwall who had adhered to Perkin Warbeck or Michael Joseph, and to impose fines and ransoms and exact recognisances: printed by Pollard, II, p. 111 from Rymer's *Foedera*, XII, p. 696 and summarised in English by Williams, p. 49 from *Cal. Pat. Rolls*, 1494–1509, p. 159. There is a similar commission dealing with the rebels of 1500 at Rymer, XII, p. 766. The 1498 commission collected nearly £9000 of fines, *L. and P.* II, pp. 335–7.

[3] Cf. p. 77–84 below.

[4] Cf. p. 52 above.

have been endangered by its association with the legislative and the administrative, it should be remembered that the two latter gained a great deal more than the first lost.

For it was not only, or even chiefly, the dispensers of what I have called the higher justice who did the work of judicature and of administration without any change of method[1] or any conscious change of function: this was especially the case of the men who did for the lower justice what Westminster Hall did for the higher, the functionaries whose development may without exaggeration be called the characteristic process in the essential Tudor exploit of substituting finally a national for a feudal administration—I mean the justices of the peace.

In the early days of the Anglo-Norman monarchy the sheriff was the king's representative in the county, the man whose business was to see that the king's will got down to the localities and that the king's dues came up from them. But the sheriff was a man with feudal interests and apt to fall into overmuch sympathy with his feudal neighbours: so the coroner was instituted to see that the crown's requirements were fulfilled. His office, however, went the same way as that of the sheriff, for, becoming elective, it became a weapon rather of the county families than against them. With the conservators, later justices, of the peace, one more attempt was made to get local authorities that should be amenable and trustworthy: it began towards the end of the twelfth century: by the middle of the fourteenth it was clearly successful and permanent, though most of the development was still in the future and though time was to show that even this institution could not be trusted to furnish quite every service which the crown might demand.[2]

What the functions of the justices of the peace were at the beginning of the Tudor period and how they were increased during it cannot be better indicated than in the words so often quoted from Wm. Lambard:[3]

if Hussey [the chief Justice 1 H. VII c. 3] did think it was enough to load all the Justices of the Peace of those days, with the execution, only of the

---

[1] Cf. p. 49 above and p. 61 below.
[2] Cf. p. 68 below, about the difficulty of enforcing, e.g., laws against enclosure.
[3] *Eirenarcha*, Bk. I, cap. 7 (edn. 1610, p. 34).

Statutes of *Winchester* and *Westminster* for Robberies, and Felonies: the Statute of Forcible entries: the Statute of Labourers, Vagabonds, Liveries, Maintenance, Embracery, and Sheriffs: Then, how many Justices, (think you) may now suffice (without breaking their backs) to bear so many, not Loads, but Stacks of Statutes, that have since that time been laid upon them?

Their main business was to preserve peace and order, and their main method the general sessions which they were bound to hold at least four times a year, when they could try every one indicted (that is, accused by a jury) of any crime but treason, unless the case were one of peculiar difficulty, and therefore referred to the justices of assize. By custom the competence of justices of peace was restricted to their own counties or other areas which by custom had special commissions. In petty sessions two or three justices of peace could enquire into misdemeanours (of ever-growing number) specified by parliament. As individuals they were specially bound to procure the apprehension of criminals and suspects, but that was an obligation which was shared generally by all citizens, and even at the end of the Tudor period it was not clear that the justices of the peace, although in this matter they had much more duty than Tom, Dick, or Harry, had much more power:[1] that is to say, any private person might arrest a man committing or having committed a felony or, provided a felony had actually been committed, a man whom he reasonably suspected of it. The superiority of the justice of the peace was not immense: he might issue warrants to bailiffs or constables to do these things for him, and by the end of the sixteenth century some justices were issuing such warrants not only on suspicion conceived by their own minds but also on suspicion communicated to them by others: though Lambard thought that they had no right to do so, unless the party had been indicted.[2] In Henry VII's time it was being settled that a constable could help in the arrest of some one reported for suspicion of felony, but only if the reporter were himself present at the arrest,[3] and that a justice of peace might

[1] Cf. Holdsworth, I, 294, and Lambard's *Eirenarcha*, Bk. II, cap. 6 (edn. 1610, p. 188) there referred to: and cf. p. 74 below.
[2] It was so held at *Y.B.* 14 H. VIII Hil. pl. 3 (Holdsworth, III, p. 601).
[3] M. Hale, *Pleas of the Crown*, II, p. 91. Holdsworth, III, p. 600.

order an arrest without written precept in case of riot under his own eye.[1]

Quarter sessions were much more than merely judicial in effect though all their methods were the methods of a law court: they were the chief governmental organs of the counties: they could investigate and punish the conduct of mayors, bailiffs, stewards, constables, gaolers,[2] and sheriffs.[3] The sheriff indeed was quite unable to stand up against the justice of the peace. He could not hold his office for more than one year at a time; in 1461 he was robbed of all his criminal jurisdiction, which went to swell the powers of the justice:[4] and by the beginning of our period his office, quite bereft of political and constitutional importance, survived only as a minor administrative convenience and as a tribunal for small debts.

Nor was it only the sheriff whom the justices were superseding. Towards the end of the Middle Ages the control of agriculture and industry was passing from feudal and communal to royal and national institutions and the justices of the peace were the local agents of this control. They fixed wages and prices,[5] supervised apprenticeship and conditions of service, enforced labour for the essential service of agriculture, adjusted the profits of victuallers, punished regraters of staple commodities, and enforced statutes regulating manufactures and exportation. They inspected the charters and censored the by-laws of gilds and companies.[6] They maintained the standards of coins, weights, and measures.[7] They were guardians of the coasts and conservators of rivers,[8] and they protected society against moral dangers to its unity and proportion by arresting Lollards and by combating the Englishman's fondness for costumes and pastimes above his station.[9]

[1] *Y.B.* 14 H. VII Mich. pl. 19, Holdsworth, III, p. 601.
[2] 12 R. II c. 10.
[3] 23 H. VI cc. 10, 11. Both statutes are referred to in C. A. Beard's *Justice of the Peace*, p. 57, where cc. 9, 10 are given inadvertently instead of cc. 10, 11.
[4] 1 E. IV c. 2: cf. Beard, p. 58.
[5] Cf. Beard, pp. 60 ff., and the statutes there quoted.
[6] Beard, p. 64: 15 H. VI c. 6.
[7] Beard, p. 65 and statutes there quoted: and 7 H. VII c. 3, 11 c. 4, for punishing local authorities who did not enforce the law about weights and measures.
[8] Beard, p. 69: 17 R. II c. 9 and 5 H. IV c. 3.
[9] Beard, pp. 69, 70, and statutes there quoted.

The office which bore all these responsibilities had run some danger of being made elective, but by the beginning of our period practically all the justices of the peace (except the dignitaries of some boroughs, who were on the commission *ex officio*) were appointed by the crown, by way of a nomination from the lord chancellor on the best advice he could get. The crown might dismiss them, but seldom found it necessary to do so. The service was obligatory and almost unpaid: that is, there were a few small fees, hardly considerable at any time and dwindling to insignificance. By a statute of Henry VI[1] justices of the peace must be worth £20 a year in land, but this was sometimes ignored in the case of persons learned in the law: in effect the chosen were those members of the prosperous classes whom the government considered most likely to sympathise and co-operate cordially with it.

Not only were they chosen as likely to be amenable, but there was a very complete and highly centralised machinery for keeping them so. The king's council[2] was constant and efficient in directing and investigating the conduct of justices of the peace and was not slow to punish it when necessary. Cases of maladministration could be heard in chancery also[3] or by the justices of oyer and terminer. The common law courts might be invoked against quarter sessions, by writ of *mandamus* ordering them to do what they had left undone or *certiorari* commanding them to explain what they had done. There was no danger, then, of quarter sessions developing independence for want of legal machinery to control them.

There might be danger, none the less, of their developing oppressive habits from the defencelessness of those who were the ordinary objects of their jurisdiction. Efforts were made to avoid this danger by the methods of appointing to the commission, the width of its representation, the exclusion of great men's dependents, the supervision of central authority: but no selection could ensure a bench beyond temptation, no supervision have its eye always on every bench in

---

[1] 18 H. VI c. 11.
[2] A councillor would be also a justice of peace, generally for several counties or for all of them; the number of justices of the peace per county tended to grow, t.r. R. II not less than six, 1533 thirty in Devon (e.g.), 1592 fifty-four.
[3] Beard, p. 152.

England. Henry VII provided another safeguard in the statute 4 H. VII c. 12: what the commission of the peace was and meant in his time may be indicated by a summary survey of his relevant legislation and may be begun with the act 4 H. VII c. 12, though it was not the first in point of time.

This statute[1] ensured, so far as such things can be ensured by law, that every one in the counties should be aware of the possibility and of the manner of complaining against maladministration by local magistrates. It enacted that every justice of the peace should be responsible for issuing at every quarter session a proclamation annexed to the statute: which proclamation recited how there were laws enough to secure peace and good government if only they were enforced and how the justices of the peace had authority enough to enforce them if only they would: if the magistrates found themselves hindered they were to inform the king of the hinderers, and any hindrance he might hear of from other sources would be counted against them: and the complaints of private persons poor or rich against justices of the peace might be taken before their colleagues or if that failed before the justices of assize or in the last resort before the king himself or his chancellor.[2]

This act begins not *Prayen the Commons* but the *King our sovereign lord...will that it be ordained and enacted by authority of the said parliament*: it need not be doubted that its assurance that to the king the poor and the rich were "all one in due ministration of justice" was absolutely sincere: or rather, if the sincerity was less than absolute, it was the rich and not the poor who suffered from the sophistication of the royal sentiments: if the poor on the whole were rather less punished than they deserved it would be no great matter, they were not to be feared anyhow: if the rich were rather excessively punished it would be just as well, or even all the better. Most of the king's work must be done by people who were neither poor nor rich but only well-to-do:[3] if this middling class was not to get above itself and if the lower orders were

---

[1] This and many other statutes of the reign touching justices of the peace are referred to in Beard, pp. 74, 77, 79, 80, 84, 98, 101, 103, 105, 106.

[2] That is, in later terminology, before the Privy Council or the Star Chamber. Cf. p. 44 above.

[3] Cf. p. 67 below.

to be kept available for the crown against the grandees, then the lower orders must be encouraged to provide the crown with information and to look to the crown for protection. All that was part of the same policy that was exemplified by the development of conciliar jurisdiction: there is no reason for supposing that it might not be reinforced by the unselfish impulses of the royal conscience.

In this connection reference may here be made to a statute of 1495,[1] though it has nothing to do specifically with justices of the peace. It provided that poor persons might at the discretion of the chancellor have writs without payment and might also be assigned counsel and attorneys without fee.

One of Henry's first statutes, 1 H. VII c. 7, was intended to prevent hunting[2] under cover of darkness or disguise, and it might seem to have an interest of curiosity rather than importance; but it contains provisions which may partly explain how the magistrates began to acquire their functions of issuing warrants for arrest, and of holding preliminary examinations of persons accused. For on information that any one was suspected of such unlawful hunting a justice of the peace might issue a warrant for his arrest and might then examine him: if under examination he confessed the charge and told all he knew about it, then it was a mere trespass to be purged by fine at the next quarter sessions: but if he were reticent, then the fact if proved was felony.

The next statute is that long famous as *Pro Camera Stellata*,[3] which ordained, among other regulations for the suppression of disorder and promotion of justice, that inquests might be held by justices of the peace to enquire into concealments by other inquests, whether held before them or not, and to punish the delinquent jurors.

3 H. VII c. 3 recited that there had been abuse of an act of Richard

[1] 11 H. VII c. 12: this statute begins *Prayen the commons*, but that by no means proves that it was not, as we should say, a government bill, and certainly the object aimed at was one with which Tudor kings sympathised more naturally than Tudor burgesses. It appears to have been in confirmation of the common law. Cf. Tindal C.J. in *Brunt* v. *Wardle* (1841) reported by Jas. Manning and T. C. Granger, *Cases in the Court of Common Pleas*, III, p. 542.
[2] Cf. 11 H. VII c. 17 (protecting partridges and the eggs of hawks and swans): 19, c. 11 (protecting deer and herons).
[3] 1487 (3 H. VII c. 1), cf. pp. 32–35, 39–42, 44–49 above, 145 below.

"late indeed, and not of right, King of England, the third" authorising every justice of the peace to bail "persons arrested for light suspicion of felony", and to remedy such abuse provided that in future at least two justices must be present to grant bail, of whom one must be a member of the quorum, and that they must certify what they had done to the quarter sessions or assize of gaol delivery. Here again, perhaps, is one of the germs of the later preliminary examination: here again is Henry's policy of strengthening the institution, but also of controlling it.

The parliament of Henry's eleventh year (1495) was the one which most concerned itself with the commission of the peace. They were to regulate beggars, vagabonds, and ale-house keepers.[1] They were empowered[2] to hear and determine without indictment (i.e. accusation by a jury) all statutory offences short of felony (but the first parliament of Henry VIII[3] took this power away again). Any two of them[4] (one being of the quorum)[5] might punish not only those who used false weights or measures but also mayors and bailiffs who failed in the duty of enforcing standards. They were to examine sheriffs,[6] bailiffs, etc. and if they found them guilty of extortion to punish them with fines of forty shillings and report their findings to the exchequer, and to audit and check the collection of fines and estreats, two of them being appointed for this purpose by the *custos rotulorum*. They could punish any labourer or artificer who refused to work at the wages they had fixed.[7] Jury panels returned by sheriffs to enquire for the king (not to decide between private parties) they could amend either by addition or by excision.[8]

And another attempt was made against riots and unlawful assemblies:[9] on complaint (by individuals) or indictment (by juries) of riot the justices of peace were to summon by proclamation the leaders to appear at the next sessions, to be tried according to the common law, punished, and bound over to keep the peace: non-appearance involved conviction: heinous cases were to be referred for punishment to the king and his

[1] 11 H. VII c. 2: cf. 19, c. 12.
[2] 11 H. VII c. 3: cf. pp. 69, 83, 84, below.
[3] 1 H. VIII c. 6.
[4] 11 H. VII c. 4.
[5] Cf. p. 67 below.
[6] 11 H. VII c. 15.
[7] 11 H. VII c. 22.
[8] 11 H. VII c. 24.
[9] 11 H. VII c. 7: cf. 19, c. 13.

council: costs and damages were to be paid to persons grieved by false complaints.

The parliament (1497) passed few statutes, and none relevant here except the Act for Fifteenths and Tenths,[1] which authorised justices of peace to hear complaints against collectors, and the Subsidy Act,[2] which directed them, with named assistants, to make assessments and appoint collectors.

Henry VII's last parliament (1504) did much to add to their powers and duties. They were to force mayors, sheriffs, bailiffs, and constables to accept legal coin of the realm at its face value.[3] They were to appoint searchers to see that pewter and brass were made of the prescribed fineness.[4] Their arm was again nerved against poachers,[5] by the provision that the penalties might be sued for as if they were debts before two justices of the peace by any one who suspected his neighbour. They were reinforced also against riot,[6] and in particular when a jury by reason of maintenance or embracery[7] failed to find a riot, rout, or unlawful assembly, the justices of the peace and the sheriff were to certify who were the maintainers and embracers, and the certificate was to be "of like force and effect in the law as if the matter contained in the same were duly found by the verdict of twelve men". And lastly,[8] the justices of peace were commanded under very severe penalties to cause the sheriff to empanel a jury of twenty persons of substantial landed property to present all cases within their knowledge, or reported by bailiffs and constables, of livery or retainders, and all persons so accused were to be examined and the results certified to the King in his Bench.

Of Henry's seven parliaments every one did more or less to increase the importance of the justices of the peace. In every activity of government as it was actually exercised in the localities and as it was made physically manifest to ordinary people, the justices of the peace were by far the most important organ, indeed on nineteen days out of twenty the only organ, other local officials being but instruments.

[1] 12 H. VII c. 12.
[2] 12 H. VII c. 13.
[3] 19 H. VII c. 5.
[4] 19 H. VII c. 6.
[5] 19 H. VII c. 11.
[6] 19 H. VII c. 13.
[7] I.e. undue influence.
[8] 19 H. VII c. 24.

The justices of the peace, collectively and individually, owed their creation to the crown, and the whole weight of the law placed them under the control of the king's judges and of his council. Complete legal subordination however does not of itself imply absolute ease of control. Something else was necessary: it was supplied partly by community of interest and sentiment, partly by the very number of justices of the peace, who were a check upon one another, partly by two institutions which have already been mentioned but which require some explanation: these are the *quorum* and the *custos rotulorum*.

It was customary for the chancellor in naming the commission of the peace for a county to add a shorter, select, list from among the same names. This shorter list consisted of the names of those justices whom the government considered particularly trustworthy because of their acquaintance with the law,[1] and they were men *of whom* some specified number must always be present whenever any of the more serious functions of the justices of the peace were in operation. This was some guarantee of the necessary minimum of legal knowledge when it was most needed, and also some assurance to the government that if it could not be certain of appointing only trustworthy men at least it should select a panel of those who were trustworthy and should know that some of them would be present on every important occasion. It happened however in course of time, partly from the unattractiveness of justice of the peace work to the legal members, partly from the employment of professional clerks with legal training, mostly from the crown's finding that its business did not require this safeguard, that first most and later all justices of the peace got put upon the quorum, which thus practically ceased to exist.

The office of *custos rotulorum* proved to have much more vitality. Its holder was responsible for the records, the rolls, of the county and appointed the clerk of the peace, so that he had at his disposition any information that might from time to time be required. He was by the fact of his appointment the principal personage on the commission, was chosen from among the leading men of the county, and was

---

[1] Often, no doubt, the acquaintance was not very deep, not much beyond having been a student at Clements Inn and having heard the chimes at midnight.

habitually named lord-lieutenant also when that office came into being.[1] The commission could not easily escape the royal control so long as he meant that it should not, and it was hard if the crown could not find in each county one serviceable agent.

At any rate, there is no doubt that Henry VII did find the justices of the peace thoroughly manageable, and the extent to which he developed their functions is proof enough. No doubt the reasons why his plans worked lay even more in the nature of the case than in any newness or ingenuity of method: that is to say, the essential factor was the existence of a class able and willing to do what the king wanted done: except, and this was to make much agrarian legislation ineffective, where their interest weighed too heavily the other way.[2]

Another factor so obvious that it is often neglected is the enormous difference made to governmental problems by variations in numbers. The population of England at the end of the fifteenth century was probably less than five million. There was hardly a county, and certainly not a town except perhaps London, where one man could not know of his own direct knowledge all that a government would care to ask about every inhabitant who was of any political or administrative importance. This was the more true since not only was the population sparser than we can easily conceive, but also the proportion of it capable of participation in politics or administration was much smaller and much more easily distinguishable than it is in modern conditions. Not that it is necessary to believe the level of intelligence then very much lower than it is now: but what was much rarer was to have time and energy left over from the primary occupation of making a living, or to have practised the intelligence in the primary political arts, reading, writing, discussion, association: life was short and working hours were

---

[1] Cf. G. S. Thomson, *Lords-Lieutenants in the Sixteenth Century*, p. 13, "Under Henry VIII these were military officers and little else besides, appointed only for a particular district during a time of crisis. By the end of the reign of Elizabeth they were playing a by no means unimportant part in the social and administrative history of the counties, though even so there was by no means a Lieutenant for every county in England".

[2] Cf. p. 69, n. 2 below.

long: communication was expensive: man, said Aristotle, is a political animal, but he did not count slaves as men, and in Tudor England it was only the well-to-do who could be political.

The well-to-do are the natural party of law and order, of which commodities recent reigns had provided woefully little: to supply the lack was no less a pleasure to Henry's temperament than a duty to his office, and because of the crown's enhanced resources it was a hopeful task. That was one reason why the class of which justices of the peace were made was ready to work with him. Another reason was that he had an economic policy beyond the mere prevention of disturbance and that this policy was agreeable to the opinions and ambitions then dominant. Governmental encouragement of the cloth manufacture and of shipping, restriction of the German Hansa's privileges, retaliation on Venice for her exclusive tariff, facilitation of intercourse with Spain and Burgundy, the enforcement of minimum hours of labour and of maximum rates of wages, care for the quantity and quality of coin, more effective steps towards making weights and measures uniform:[1] all these represented a policy to whose support the middle classes did not have to be constrained.[2] The royal intention was not always so unobstructed, but obstructions were seldom impassable: there was no individual who could stand up to the king, and hardly any English sovereign has had so little difficulty with corporations as Henry. Of the great corporation, the Church, something will be said later. The corporate towns were in decay,[3] no longer the monopolists of trade and industry but rather their deserted children, so that they had hardly the courage even to think of resistance to Henry's centralising measures.

---

[1] By a statute of 1495 the standards were to be distributed by members of parliament: cf. L. F. Salzmann, *English Trade in the Middle Ages*, p. 45.

[2] Cf. below, pp. 141, 148 (statutes on economic subjects), 174. But where the middle classes were not so complacent, the legislation was often ineffective: cf. I. S. Leadam, *Requests*, p. lv, "The policy of Henry VII had been to play off the official class against the hereditary nobles, and though he passed the act of 1489 with the object of restraining inclosure, a search of the Exchequer Rolls reveals that he allowed it to remain inoperative. The new policy of relying on the people against the aristocracy was the creation of Wolsey.... To the support of this policy the Court of Requests and the Star Chamber were alike invoked...".

[3] Cf. e.g. Salzmann, p. 87, for reports of this covering the period from 1447 to 1547.

He seems besides to have found no difficulty in remodelling their constitutions as he pleased.[1]

London was the only town that might have been formidable, and even London was well under control. In 1487, a city ordinance forbidding Londoners to take their goods to markets or fairs outside was annulled by statute.[2] In 1496, the richer London Merchant Adventurers having endeavoured to monopolise the Flanders trade by charging an entrance fee of £20, it was enacted that in future not more than ten marks should be charged.[3] In both these cases the hand that was raised to punish was careful to bless as well: in the first the blessing[4] was a confirmation of the city's ancient privilege of excluding strangers from retail trade within its bounds, in the second a grant of arms and of a charter.[5] It will be noticed how all this was part of the policy allegorised in the legend[6] that Henry had all mastiffs hanged because they dared to fight against their lord and master the lion, and an excellent falcon because he feared not to match with an eagle: a policy which the Spanish ambassador reported that the king himself had defined as an "intention to keep his subjects low, because riches would only make them haughty":[7] this was more fairly expressed by Polydore Vergil when he said that Henry "did his best to keep down his burghers, especially the richer among them, because he well knew that, as they grow richer,

---

[1] E.g. in 1486 York was let off the payment of nearly one third of its ferm and besides the mayor was taken into the king's pay, for he was henceforth to receive as chief serjeant at arms £18. 5s. od. a year out of what was left (Wm. Campbell, *Materials Illustrative of the Reign of Henry VII*, I, p. 462). Four years later at that city the mode of electing the mayor was altered by royal command so as to be less free (Campbell, II, p. 552). A similar alteration had already been made at Leicester, probably by way of a lesson for insubordination. Northampton had part of its ferm remitted on the ground that the burden was causing the town to be depopulated. Towns that were being treated in this sort of way could not form a serious opposition.

[2] 3 H. VII c. 10.

[3] 12 H. VII c. 6.

[4] Busch, p. 244: but it did not come till 1498, and then had to be paid for with £5000.

[5] Busch, p. 245: cf. also Busch, p. 299 for Henry's control of the election of Fitzwilliam to be Sheriff of London in spite of opposition.

[6] Harrison's Preface to Holinshed.

[7] Ayala to Ferdinand, 25 July 1498 in G. A. Bergenroth's *Calendar of the Simancas Papers*, I, p. 177.

men become overbearing, and allow their actions to be controlled by money interests alone":[1] the policy, in short, of encouraging the accumulation of wealth, but into many moderate heaps rather than into few great ones. It was a policy that had the economic tendencies of the time running with it.

In so far as Henry's favouring of the middle class was directed against either extreme it was against the rich, no doubt, in intention: but in effect it could not help being partly against the poor as well. Henry, as has been shown, depended on taxes less than any other English king: nevertheless taxes there were, and it was certain that there would be more taxes later. Who collected these taxes? who else but the same sort of men as sat in quarter sessions;[2] so that it is not surprising if there was some unfairness in assessment, if resistance to Tudor taxation usually came from the lower orders and got little help from the well-to-do. A benevolence was less an imposition than an equalisation of burdens: when parliament was actually brought to prefer benevolence (which would specially hit the classes which it specially represented) to taxation, it is a safe deduction that it must have been very conscious of having got off very lightly in the recent past, despite Bacon's encomium on its altruism.[3] Similarly, it was already the fact in Henry's reign, though it was not yet so apparent as it became later, that there were great obstacles in the way of royal attempts to guard the poor against hardships incident to the agrarian revolution, and its accompanying enclosures.[4] Well-meaning rules might be laid down by the crown in parliament though it was a landowners' parliament, but there was no one to enforce the rules except the justices of the peace: it was a little as if there were no one but cotton lords to enforce factory legislation.

Henry had, then, in the justices of the peace an instrument of local government at once more far reaching and more manageable than any of his predecessors or any of his contemporaries possessed, but

[1] As quoted by Busch, p. 297.
[2] Cf. 12 H. VII c. vii, M.P.s not to be collectors: complaints against the collectors, by constables or other officers in the names of the aggrieved, might be heard and determined by justices of the peace.
[3] Cf. Bacon's *Henry VII* (ed. Lumby), p. 92. Cf. p. 22 above.
[4] Cf. pp. 68, 69, n. 2 above.

it was not a mere instrument, and anyhow an instrument is a limitation as well as an extension of power: the hand that holds a poker is strengthened for poking but incapacitated for knitting. What the class from which justices of the peace were drawn wanted done, Henry VII could get done very easily: what they did not mind being done, easily enough; what would happen if the crown should want done something which that class was determined should not be done, was a question still to be settled, even still to be raised. It was a class very united in its wants—there was much less disagreement between town and country, especially, than anywhere else in Europe and perhaps less than at any other time in England—and where those wants differed from the king's it was not on essential matters: but also where their wills and his coincided, which was much the larger area, it was far from being simply because his was imposed.

There is another factor which must be reckoned in any estimate of the serviceability of the justices of the peace: not only was it limited by their character, by the fact that they remained private gentlemen more than government agents, with motives of their own; so that when any one motive was driving most of them the king could not get local action in the contrary sense; not only this, but also just as they themselves were private gentlemen unbound and unbought, occasionally doing public business, just in the same way they lacked almost entirely a professional and automatic ministerial service and were dependent on the good-will, or at the very least on the acquiescence, of the community. The modern apparatus of minor officials and clerks, of technicians and inspectors, of police and soldiers, was almost wholly non-existent: hardly anything which absolutely requires that apparatus could be done.

The justices of the peace partook equally of the nature of the feudal personages who had formerly directed local business and of the bureaucratic personages who were beginning to do so, in France, for instance. Like the first, they were pointed out by local considerations, their expertness came from local knowledge, their expectation of obedience (very largely, at least) from local respect, their respect (and their livings) from local property. Like the second, they owed all their legal authority to the central government, for whose purposes they were called into official existence, and might be expelled from it again. They resembled each in various features: they differed from both in one, and that one essential—they had not at their disposal the physical force either of feudal retainers or of royal mercenaries.

More than half their value to Henry lay in the first half of this double deficiency, but magistrates would have been twice as valuable still who had not been victims of the second: nor was the notion strange to Henry: he had lived in France, the kingdom then in the van of political progress, and had seen the advantages of a royal army, royal police, royal bureaucracy. At the very beginning of his reign he formed, probably in imitation of Louis XI, a royal bodyguard[1] of fifty men, which was afterwards increased, though never above two hundred: he took very special care for the safeguarding and arming and garrisoning[2] of his fortresses: he had even a few foreign mercenaries.[3] The Spanish ambassador[4] thought (and was not alone in thinking) that "he would like to govern England in the French fashion, but he cannot". There is strong evidence that Henry and his family were conscious imitators of the new French monarchy, for instance the naturalisation of such phrases as information, master of requests, privy council, secretary of state: but the Tudors did not (no doubt because they judged that they could not) imitate its essence—reliance upon salaried professionals for the actual enforcement of law and policy: the English government remained very feebly armed before a population which it had not disarmed.

The word *police* was hardly admitted as English by Dr Johnson, and only since 1856[5] have there been paid police for all England. The

---

[1] With a nucleus, no doubt, of those followers of Henry in exile who were below the rank of gentleman, cf. Campbell, I, p. 8, grant to Wm. Brown, yeoman of the king's guard, for service overseas "and at our victorieux journeye", 18 Sept. 1485.
[2] *Italian Relation* (Camden Society), pp. 45, 47.
[3] The English garrison in Ireland seems always to have been less than a thousand (cf. Conway, p. 78). And n.b. the acts of the Drogheda, Poynings, Parliament 1494–5, c. 20 for those with property above £10 to have bows, etc. and c. 23 no one to have guns, *ibid.* pp. 123, 124.
[4] Bergenroth, I, p. 178: referred to in Busch, p. 293.
[5] Cf. F. W. Maitland, *Justice and Police*, p. 105.

resources for police available to the Tudors were the constables—high constables, parish constables, special constables. Every hundred was bound to provide itself with a high constable, every parish with a petty constable. Appointment was generally in the hands of the justices of the peace, except where leet jurisdiction was still alive. Remuneration was by fee and was quite insufficient, so that compulsion was necessary to keep the office filled and every man was legally compellable to serve his turn.[1] As to duties and powers, there is a long history which has never been clarified. At any rate, the constable was the actual ministerial officer of government, which meant, for the great bulk of his activity, of the justices of the peace. In general it was his duty to repress felons and keep the peace, to which end he was entitled not only to arrest[2] a felon in the act or after the act but also to arrest for the purpose of preventing the probable commission of a felony, and to demand the assistance of third parties in so doing. He had no other special competence. Besides his general duty he was also obliged to execute the warrants, orders, and convictions of the justices of the peace, and to assist coroners and military officers on special occasions. He did not devote more than his spare time and energy to his constabulary duties and did not hold his office longer than he could help.

A force so constituted was not very formidable, nor was there behind it a military power which could be called in to strengthen it. A few mercenaries, a hundred or so of bodyguards, a dozen garrisons (of which the one at Calais, 800 men,[3] was the largest and was considered enormous)—this is not the makings of a military empire.

For other military purposes, Henry used parliament: statute imposed military service on two new classes, holders of offices, fees or annuities under the crown, and of honours or lands under the king's letters patent: they were to serve wherever called upon, at home or abroad, and were to be paid for their service.[4] Further, statute was used to

---

[1] For all this paragraph see H. R. Gneist, *Self-government in England*, 3rd ed. pp. 44 ff.
[2] Cf. p. 61 above.
[3] *Italian Relation*, p. 45.
[4] J. Fortescue, *History of the British Army*, I, p. 109. Cf. p. 16 above, parliamentary grants for military purposes.

strengthen the elementary rules of discipline: captains must always have been punishable for mustering fewer men or paying them lower wages than their contracts enjoined, and soldiers at sea or overseas for deserting, but now the penalties were fixed by parliament.[1] Parliament also gave various procedural advantages to persons in the king's service beyond sea,[2] and took care for archery,[3] and for the supply of chargers.[4] The trend of material development was in the king's favour: in 1483 ordnance had become sufficiently important to warrant the appointment of a Master-General, and it represented an element of force unprecedentedly apt for royal monopoly.[5]

The king might have spent his surplus on mercenaries: he did not: that left at his disposal the remnant of the feudal force, far gone in a not unwelcome decay,[6] and what could be made of the old common-law obligation on every subject to defend the kingdom[7] (reinforced by the practice of impressment[8]) and the chance of parliamentary grants for foreign expeditions. The actual practice was to issue, when an army was required, commissions of array,[9] each addressed to some dozen or score of the nobility and gentry in a county. The government's military

[1] 7 H. VII c. 1.
[2] E.g. 7 H. VII c. 2; 4 H. VII c. 4; 11 H. VII c. 1.
[3] E.g. 3 H. VII c. 12; 19 H. VII cc. 2, 4.
[4] 11 H. VII c. 13.
[5] Cf. p. 73, n. 3.
[6] Though it was used, e.g. Campbell, II, p. 384 (23 Dec. 1488), commissions to half a dozen of each county to examine how many archers each nobleman and knight is bound to find, and to muster them for the expedition to Brittany.
[7] Last defined by the Statute of Winchester 1285. The county levy should not be taken beyond the county, except to resist invasion.
[8] Cf. Campbell, II, p. 475, commission to the captain of the *Soveraigne* to impress soldiers and sailors, an armed force being about to put to sea, to resist the king's enemies, Aug. 1489. Impressment might be used for purposes hardly military (Campbell, II, p. 342, commission to Robt. Brikenden, familiar to Mr Kipling's readers, *Rewards and Fairies*, p. 82, to impress caulkers for repairing a ship, 4 Aug. 1488) or not military at all (p. 516, artificers, labourers and materials for the king's buildings to be taken on reasonable terms to be paid by the king, 17 Oct. 1490). Cf. Anson, II, pt. 2, pp. 168–70, especially for the fourteenth century statutes (and especially 4 H. IV c. 13) against constraining any one to find soldiers, unless he held his lands on such terms, or by assent of parliament; against service out of the county except against invasion; and that volunteers for overseas should be paid by the king. Cf. also G. S. Thomson, pp. 14–16.
[9] E.g. Campbell, II, p. 135, 7 Apr. 1487: the form authorised by parliament (*R.P.* III, p. 526, A.D. 1404) was not always strictly followed.

force was mainly and directly dependent on the good-will of the governed.

Similarly, the reinforcing of the constables with additional police was dependent upon popular sympathy: the justices of the peace it is true could compulsorily swear in as special constables for the preservation of the peace any and every citizen, or they could call out the whole neighbourhood in hue and cry for the pursuit of a criminal: but what was the use of that if they could not count upon good-will? Also, for the reporting of misdoers they could look to the juries as well as the constables: but what guarantee was there that the juries would perform their obligations? and anyway, was not the institution, however royal in origin, necessarily popular in effect? To answer, even to understand, these questions it is necessary first to enquire into the character of the jury system at the beginning of the Tudor period: and before doing that it is convenient first to emphasise the ways in which English government at the end of the fifteenth century was characterised by the development of the commission of the peace.

That commission gave the king, at no expense, in every district, urban or rural, a representative of his power: collectively these representatives wielded a preponderance of the property and energy of the country: their characters and interests inclined, even constrained, them to protect the crown of England against foreign invasion and oligarchic faction and popular sedition; they owed to the crown their appointment, which they felt a considerable obligation, and their authority, which they enjoyed very much: the law kept them completely subordinate, and their numbers were not yet so great nor their business so bulky that this legal subordination could not be made the basis of a real control. All this made an organ of local government (and all government is in one sense local) unprecedently efficient and amenable. On the other hand, the efficiency rested mainly on the fact that the justices of the peace were the natural leaders of their neighbourhoods, so that it was apt to dissolve if applied to driving instead of leading: and the amenability came mostly from gratitude and sympathy, political forces which more than any others require continual renewal and preclude arbitrary command. The whole effect may be fairly put in one sentence thus:

Henry VII was stronger than any of his predecessors to enforce his will throughout his dominions on condition that his will was actively shared by the prosperous and passively shared, or at least not actively resented, by the masses: conditions which on the whole he fulfilled without difficulty.

Closely connected with the justice of the peace and with his usefulness for enforcing the will of government was the jury: it was the older institution of the two: it resembled the other in several respects—its origin was due to royal initiative: it was a device for improving the performance of a governmental function: its effectiveness depended on the general good-will of the governed, especially one great class, the smaller landowners. It was an essential part of the ordinary judicial machinery, and also part of the characteristic process by which the business of administration was managed under judicial forms, part of the general method of establishing facts that were in dispute: finally, the juror, even more than the justice, was a changing, developing personage, and his development was a matter much less of statute, much more of practice, so that there is greater difficulty in giving a full and fair description of it at a stated time.

The jury might be used in various forms and for various purposes: the varieties of which some knowledge is requisite on the threshold of a study of Tudor government are the grand jury, the petty and civil juries, and the jury of attaint.

"The earliest recorded juries were employed to discover and present facts in answer to enquiries addressed to them by the king";[1] as, for instance, the sworn representatives of each neighbourhood who enabled William I to compile Domesday Book or Henry II to collect the Saladin Tithe. The grand jury presented rather suggestions of probability than answers of fact, and though special topics might be propounded to them, their duty was to answer the most general question —Has anything happened in your neighbourhood, whether by fault of commission or of omission, which ought to be legally punished, and who seem most likely to be the responsible persons? They might answer of their own knowledge or with reference to

[1] Holdsworth, I, p. 321.

accusations made by others, finding a *true bill*, that is, "This accusation seems likely and ought to be investigated", or *ignoramus*, that is the contrary. Their presentment was by a simple majority of the twenty-four jurors and was made after considering in private the grounds for accusation, without any safeguard of publicity, of direction by a judge, or of hearing what was to be said on the other side, and thereupon the person presented was indicted at the king's suit: the twenty-four jurors were substantial freeholders, preferably knights, chosen by the king's officers in earlier days from the several hundreds, as being thus more likely to have full information, but by our period from the county in general. By this time, also, this method of accusation had in all but very exceptional cases superseded the ancient procedure of *appeal* by a private person against the accused, because the modes of proof on an appeal—compurgation, ordeal, battle—were out of date.

For prosecutions, then, the crown relied mainly on the good-will of a large and preponderant class of its subjects: for convictions it needed the assent of a class not quite identical but, so to speak, continuous with it: for the petty jury also, which did the trying of persons indicted, like the grand jury which did the presenting, was made up of freeholders: rather smaller freeholders they might be, but still their holdings must be of at least forty shillings a year and the larger the better: and they also, like the grand jurors, were chosen by the sheriffs.

The action of the grand jury in Henry VII's time was like enough to modern practice to be sufficiently understood without much explanation: this is not so with the trial jury, whether in civil or in criminal cases: the whole idea of its object and method was very different from what it has now become: exactly how different cannot be shortly and plainly stated for it was as yet neither fixed nor explicit.

Anciently the separation[1] between the indicting jury and the trial jury was far from absolute: they might be identical or the second might be the first afforced as seemed convenient to the court, and for long therefore it remained necessary that some members of the grand jury should be upon the petty jury. This was altered owing to a qualification

[1] For the early history of juries cf. J. B. Thayer, *Preliminary Treatise on Evidence at the Common Law*, chs. II, III: here specially pp. 82 ff.

of what was said above about the empanelling of jurors: it is true that they were nominated by the sheriff, but they were subject to challenge by the accused, and it came to be settled by the middle of the fourteenth century that on his challenge every indictor was excluded as a matter of course from the petty jury, which thus became a self-subsistent entity. Not much later it was settled that its number should be twelve and that its decision must be unanimous.

This was very far, however, from marking arrival at the modern notion by which the virtue of the trial jury is that its composition, size, and single-mindedness preserve it from all fore-knowledge or pre-conception about the case, and thus render it a perfect umpire for disentangling facts from a conflicting mass of evidence and argument whose relevance is controlled by the court. At the end of the fifteenth century the jurymen were still some way from becoming judges of fact, and had not ceased to partake of the character of witnesses. Juries in criminal cases should come from the neighbourhood where the alleged facts happened.[1] As late as the middle of the sixteenth century a pro-portion of half the jury from the hundred where the matter had arisen was still to be required in civil cases.[2] It was still in Henry VII's time assumed that they had some knowledge of their own, but they could take what ways they found for getting more, and the court was only beginning incidentally and very slowly to see that they disposed of all the procurable and available information and that they were not influenced by anything which seemed more likely to be misinformation. Criminal procedure retained a similarity to the old method of appeal: "the new procedure becomes as accusatory as the old",[3] and the notion persisted of the accused as a defendant against whom a plaintiff (in this case the crown) must prove a case.

How did the jurors make up their minds? The system of special

---

[1] Cf. Hale, II, pp. 262, 272: and cf. 4 H. VIII c. 2 (continued by 22, c. 2 and 32, c. 3), to avoid the inconvenience of "foreign Pleas, triable in foreign Counties". 33 H. VIII c. 23 (see also 28, c. 15; 35, c. 2, 1 and 2 P. and M. c. 10), no "Challenge for the Shire or hundred" where there has been confession to or vehement suspicion by three of the king's council.
[2] 35 H. VIII c. 6, para. 1.
[3] Appeal was accusation by an individual who undertook to prove it: the quotation is from Pollock and Maitland, *History of English Law*, II, p. 655.

pleading meant that there appeared on the pleas a good deal which nowadays would be put in evidence, and this process was developing in the fifteenth century.[1] Documents were submitted to the jury: and the judge would explain how far they were relevant and conclusive, and this was the beginning of the law of evidence: but the jury might act on documents not known to the court or the parties. People engaged in any transaction whose authentication in a court of law was likely to be desirable some day were careful to perform it with every circumstance of publicity. Parties and their counsel plied jurors with both assertion and argument. It was lawful for parties to endeavour to convince the jurors before they met, and only since 1361 was it unlawful to do so after they had retired. The judge's charge isolated for them the points which they were to decide.

It is intelligible that with all this assistance—and with a small, homogeneous, and sedentary population—juries could arrive at verdicts not scandalously often conflicting with the facts, even though they had not what seems to the modern mind the first essential of trial by jury, witnesses giving in open court testimony controlled by cross-examination and by rules of evidence. Nevertheless, witnesses in something the modern sense, and developing more and more towards it, were appearing before the time of the Tudors.

But as yet they were not the essence of jury trial, only a novel and by no means indispensable adjunct to it. The truth of this and the effects of it on the constitutional import of the jury are comprehensible only in the light of the conditions which were evolving the witness.

It was, probably, for a quite incidental purpose that witnesses in the modern sense were first used, for the purpose of trying the challenge of a juror.[2] Already the jury might accept information from the parties or others out of court, and it heard statements from the parties and their counsel in court, and even heard witnesses examined by the court, "pre-constituted" witnesses who had been appointed to be the living registers of some transaction. It was an easy step, with all these habits well established, from the use of witnesses for confirming the challenge

---

[1] Thayer, p. 114.
[2] Thayer, p. 123.

of a juror to their use for confirming the statements of a party, and it was a step which was quite often taken in the fifteenth century.

Yet it was not in every trial matter of course, still less matter of necessity. The characteristic crime of the age was maintenance,[1] interested support of one party in a suit in order to abuse legal process for private ends, and the development of the use of witnesses was much hindered by the extreme anxiety of courts to discourage this abuse and of private persons to avoid being accused of it. There was no process for summoning any witnesses but the pre-constituted sort,[2] and when other witnesses did begin to be found useful it was for long very much easier for the crown to use them than for any one else, nor was it till the seventeenth century that a man accused of treason or felony could enforce the attendance of his witnesses, nor till the eighteenth that he could have them examined on oath.

At the beginning of our period, then, witnesses were still a very minor part of a trial, except in the sense that jurors were still regarded as being to a very large extent witnesses, certainly as partaking of the nature more of witnesses than of judges. In Fortescue's account[3] there is a place indeed but a very small place for witnesses in the modern sense, but he says of the jurors: "These witnesses are neighbours, able to live out of their own property, of good name and unsullied reputation, not brought into court by a party, but chosen by an official who is a gentleman and indifferent, and required to come before the judge. These men know everything which witnesses can tell them: these are

---

[1] For embracery, improper influencing of juries, and its close connection with maintenance, cf. P. H. Winfield, *History of Conspiracy and Abuse of Legal Procedure*, ch. VII: and cf. 3 H. VII c. 1; 11 H. VII c. 3; 32 H. VIII c. 9. "In the Star Chamber, it was affirmed that a party to the suit, his son, servant or near kinsman might exert himself to procure the jury to appear, if there were no other ill-qualified circumstance in it; but no man might write to another to get him to appear in a case in which the persuader was not interested" (Winfield, p. 172, with references to t.r. El. and J. I). "The Solicitor-General to Queen Elizabeth was standing behind Robert, Earl of Leicester, among other lords when a cause was being heard concerning the writing of a letter to a juror to appear, and the great Earl asked if that were a fault, and swore that he had committed it a hundred times" (Winfield, p. 166, referring to Hudson, p. 92).
[2] Thayer, pp. 126–9.
[3] *De Laudibus Legum Anglia*, written probably shortly before 1470: here I refer to c. 26, quoted by Thayer, p. 131.

aware of the trustworthiness or untrustworthiness, and the reputation of the witnesses who are produced". In 1499 another judge was no less explicit, and this time not in writing a commentary but in deciding a case:[1] "Suppose no evidence given on either side", said Vavasour J., "and the parties do not wish to give any, yet the jury shall give their verdict for one side or the other. And so the evidence is not material to help or harm the matter".

Enough has been said to show the comparative unimportance of witnesses at the beginning of our period, and to make clear how it affected trial by jury as a safeguard of the subject. It gave the party accused or impleaded no assurance that the jurors would give due weight to everything which could be said on his side, nor that they would not give weight to things on the other side that never ought to have been said—hearsay, prejudice, irrelevancies—nor even that he should know what were the considerations which influenced them. Beyond all this, it left them still so far from having become unprejudiced judges of fact and nothing else, that it was still possible without obvious impropriety to subject them to measures of control which would have been intolerable if jurors had been simply twelve honest ordinary ignorant men, and their duty simply to hear all that could be said in accordance with the rules of evidence on both sides, and then to come down unanimously on one side, as a guarantee that there must be a great preponderance of probability on that side to have convinced so much honesty and mediocrity and ignorance. That is what the jury became by the time of Charles James Fox and Henry Erskine, but really not so very long before: at the beginning of the Tudor period at any rate it was very far from having become so. It was necessarily, therefore, still subject to some measure of control.

The classic check upon the jury was the attaint, when it was tried for false verdict at the suit of the injured party before another jury, of larger number and more respectable property qualification.

If the suit were successful the offending jurymen were punished, and the verdict was reversed.[2] It seems that the crown might proceed by

---

[1] *Y.B.* 14 H. VII, fol. 29. 4, quoted by Thayer, p. 132.
[2] Except in the Grand Assize: cf. Thayer, p. 141.

attaint against an acquitting jury, though it had preferable methods of ensuring convictions:[1] there was never any question of attainting a jury which had convicted[2] (but, of course, the court might recommend the victim of a wrongful verdict to the royal pardon). The penalty on an attainted jury was enormous—imprisonment, forfeiture, and loss of civil rights. It was no defence for the attainted jury that it had decided in good faith: if its decision was wrong it was punishable.[3] On the other hand, it was settled in 1467 that the attaint jury could not regard evidence which had not been at the disposal of the original jury.[4] But even so, and even after the attempted modification of the penalty in 1495, the attaint, besides being plainly a clumsy and difficult procedure, was generally disliked[5] as being peculiarly odious and severe, so that resort to it was rare, and in the sixteenth century obsolescent. Other checks remained, if less violent no less efficient.

Something was done by the court itself: not only did medieval judges assume the right to punish juries for such transgressions as separating, or eating or drinking, before giving their verdict, but also they went very far in the way of persuading them what their verdict should be,[6] might grant new trial where a verdict seemed objectionable, and sometimes arbitrarily punished them when it was not what was wanted. Nor did this practice cease altogether with the Middle Ages, for Chief Justice Hale[7] speaks of it, with disapproval indeed but still as a matter of present practical interest.

[1] Cf. later paragraphs.
[2] Holdsworth, I, p. 340; Thayer, p. 156; Winfield, p. 195. The crown's right to attaint an acquitting jury was denied as to felony and murder by Hudson in his *Treatise on the Star Chamber*, p. 72, and by Vaughan C.J. in *Bushell's Case* (1670). Vaughan was denying an opinion of Thirning C.J. in 1409, and in Vaughan's own day Sir M. Hale was against him. Thayer explains that the criminal had in theory chosen trial by jury, and therefore for him to claim attaint would be *facere probationem suam nullam*.
[3] Holdsworth, I, p. 341.
[4] Holdsworth, I, p. 341; Thayer, p. 138; *Y.B.* 7 E. IV Hil. pl. 14. This may perhaps be taken as the decisive moment in the process by which the jury was to become a corporate referee on what was put in evidence, and on nothing else.
[5] Thayer, p. 138.
[6] Thayer, pp. 155, 157: the accused had no right to counsel or witnesses, but as early as 1302 it had been good doctrine (recently confirmed by Fortescue) that it was better to leave a guilty man unpunished than to punish an innocent.
[7] (1609–76): in his *Pleas of the Crown*, II, p. 160: cf. also pp. 309, 313, and Winfield, p. 198.

Another check upon juries was the control of conciliar jurisdiction: how indefinite this jurisdiction was has already been shown, and how its function was to supply the defects of ordinary judicature. Nothing could be more strictly in the line of this function than to supervise the working of juries, peculiarly susceptible to perversion by corruption, faction or coercion, and not to be trusted to supervise each other's working.[1] So it happened that, in Hudson's words,[2] "when a corrupt jury had given an injurious verdict, if there had been no remedy but to attaint them by another jury, the wronged party would have had small remedy, as it is manifested by common experience,[3] no jury having for many years attainted a former": and "in the reigns of Henry VII, Henry VIII, Queen Mary, and the beginning of Elizabeth's reign, there was scarce one Term pretermitted but some grand inquest or jury, was fined for acquitting felons or murderers".[4] Conciliar action, says Holdsworth,[5] "with respect to the jury had the same effect as it had in many other spheres of government—it restored its proper working": it certainly made it work much better.

It is clear enough that besides all its other advantages for getting favourable verdicts, the crown had this also, that it could punish jurors who found verdicts that were not favourable: and even though, in the light of differences between the juries and witnesses of those days and of these, such royal control was defensible, indeed necessary, yet we should not forget that it did withhold from the English method of trial what we assume as its essence and glory, the safeguarding of judicature from being exploited for the convenience of administration.

So much for the stage of evolution reached by the jury when Henry VII came to the throne, and for the manner in which it affected

---

[1] For a petition to the king and council against an alleged false verdict (about 1490) in a civil case, cf. Williams, p. 174, quoting from P.R.O. Star Chamber Proc. H. VII, no. 132. It is to be noted that the petitioners were servants of Thomas Garth, who was an important member of the royal bureaucracy: cf. Conway, index, and especially pp. 50–1.

[2] In his *Treatise on the Star Chamber*, written early in the seventeenth century.

[3] Quoted by Thayer, p. 139, as from Part I, S. 4, p. 11: in *Collectanea Juridica* it should be p. 14.

[4] Hudson, p. 72, quoted by Thayer, p. 162.

[5] I, p. 343.

the method and character of English government: some of the statutory regulations of the jury passed in Henry's time will next be reviewed by way of indicating from this point of view the policy of the first Tudor towards the governmental arrangements which he had inherited.

It was a policy directed above all towards efficiency, especially towards the rigorous infliction of penalties upon such as by force or fraud interfered with the due course and proper effect of law. Some of the ways in which this policy affected the jury system have already been mentioned incidentally.[1] 3 H. VII c. 14 recited that recent troubles had been principally occasioned "by envy and malice of the King's own household Servants", and that by the common law there was no remedy for conspiracies against the king's councillors and ministers unless they had emerged in actual deeds: and accordingly the statute empowered the steward, treasurer, and controller, or one of them, to enquire into such conspiracies by a jury of twelve of the household, and the same officers or two of them to try any one indicted by that enquiry with a similar jury. 7 H. VII c. 4 removed the difficulties put in the way of forming juries in London by want of qualification or contempt of the summons. Thus the jury system was adapted to meet the characteristic evils of the time: and for the same purpose a little later it was partially suspended, when 11 H. VII c. 3 made a great exception to the general rule that for putting the law in motion the government relied upon the community, by dispensing with indictment in cases of riot and retainder, and other crimes not endangering the life or limb of the accused.[2]

---

[1] Above, pp. 65, 66.

[2] Cf. pp. 65, 77 above and p. 148 below. The purpose of this act may be believed to be set out fairly enough in the preamble (*Statutes of the Realm* (1816), II, p. 370), where the king notes regretfully that though there are statutes in plenty against the prevalent evils yet in consequence of the defects of presenting juries there is too little punishment: the evils specified are "riots, unlawful assemblies, retainders, and giving and receiving of liveries, signs and tokens unlawfully, extortions, maintenance, embracery", offences all tending to the abuse or overriding of the law by the strong, but other offences also were aimed at, "excessive taking of wages...unlawful games, inordinate apparel": and the act proceeded to empower justices of assize or of the peace to hear and determine on information for the king (that is, on information supplied by any inhabitant of the shire as the ground for a criminal charge) all statutory offences: the limitations were the exclusion of treason, murder,

This same parliament, besides thus rendering the jury of indictment unnecessary in a large class of cases and proportionately strengthening the hands of administration, also endeavoured[1] to make juries in civil cases and juries of inquisition more trustworthy. To prevent perjury in London jurors they were in future to be property holders to the value of forty marks, or a hundred marks where there was matter in dispute worth more than forty: moreover, attaint, hitherto unknown in the city, was henceforth to be suable there, the jury for the purpose being of the highest respectability, all men of the substance of £100 or more, and being authorised to find the previous jury corrupt[2] even though its verdict should be found true. Similarly, it was attempted to make attaint in other parts of the country more effective by strengthening the juries and by making the penalty more reasonable.[3] Most important of all, justices were empowered to amend jury panels returned by sheriffs in criminal cases.

11 H. VII c. 25[4] gave them the power in inquests, in which cases also every private person was given the right to complain of perjury, and to have his complaint heard by the "Chancellor and Treasurer of

and felony and of any accusation endangering life or limb from this procedure, and the provision that if the party were acquitted he should be entitled to costs and damages from the informer, and that the information should not extend to any person dwelling in another shire than that where the information was given. The statute was repealed in the first year of Henry VIII. There had been an act of 1468 opening the king's courts of record and of quarter sessions to the common informer, but it had been ineffective (cf. I. S. Leadam, *Select Cases in the Star Chamber*, I, p. xcix).

[1] 11 H. VII c. 21, 24, 25 justices of the peace to revise panels for inquests of office, 26: 11 H. VII c. 24 was continued by 12 H. VII c. 2 and 19 H. VII c. 3 and 1 H. VIII c. 11, and 11 H. VII c. 25 by 12 H. VII c. 2. Where the trial had been "by half tongue" (i.e. between an Englishman and a foreigner, by a half-and-half jury, cf. *Italian Relation*, p. 32) the attainting jury was to be half and half.

[2] And fine them £20 or more and imprison them for six months or less: their corruptors were to be fined ten times the amount of the bribes.

[3] On a verdict for £40 the party aggrieved might sue attaint before a jury with qualifications of twenty marks per annum freehold, in cases of less than £40 five marks per annum: attaints were to be brought only in king's bench or common pleas. The jury attainted might be fined at the discretion of the court, but this provision did not prove very effective since parties might still proceed at common law, where the penalties were much greater.

[4] Chapter 26 increased the penalties on jurors who did not appear when summoned, and provided that where there was an insufficiency of qualified jurors others might be sworn.

England, the chief Justices of either Bench and the Clerk of the Rolls".

19 H. VII c. 13 was again concerned chiefly with "riot, assembly, or rout of people against the Law". For enquiring into such offences jurors were to be 20*s*. freeholders or 26*s*. 8*d*. copyholders, and if the offence were not found "by reason of any maintenance or embracery of the said Jurors", then the justices were to certify the said maintenance or embracery and their certificate should be of the same effect as an indictment.

The first Tudor's statutory dealings with juries were clearly intended to make them more effective, but no less clearly[1] to maintain and even to increase their sympathy with government and their docility. Their composition from the classes least inclined to recalcitrance, the control of that composition by royal judges, the increased applicability of attaint and of conciliar correction—such were the tendencies of Henry's statutes. In cases where experience had shown that efficiency was not to be expected from the jury, where offences which cramped the heart of government and drained the vitality of the community could not be punished except on the initiative of juries and where their initiative was certainly inadequate, in such cases Henry substituted other machinery. This might have been the beginning of a great change in the character of the enforcement of English law,[2] a change which nowadays would amount to a constitutional revolution, and which then would have been the greatest possible constitutional revolution, if *constitutional* is a word that may be used of those times. It did not happen: to know all the reasons why it did not happen would be to know everything about sixteenth-century England. Two reasons, neither of them far-fetched, are enough: it need not be believed that the increased freedom of accusation was used for nothing else but extorting fines, and for that unconscionably and enormously, yet it may well be supposed that "many Sinister and craftily feigned informations have been pursued against the King's subjects",[3] and that even when informations were not feigned they were

---

[1] No less clearly to us: it is not suggested that Henry or his advisers made the distinction.
[2] Cf. p. 148 below.   [3] 1 H. VIII c. 6.

not liked. On the other hand, it would be excessively optimistic to assume the disappearance by 1509 of all the real evils which the extension of information had been legitimately designed to check, and yet it may well be believed (and was indeed the fact) that Henry VIII, quite unlike his father, inherited a kingdom in which it was tolerably easy to hope that riot and maintenance would not exceed manageable proportions. Nor should it be forgotten that though 11 H. VII c. 3 was repealed it has been succeeded by many statutes giving power to punish without indictment.

CHAPTER IV

PARLIAMENT

Fortescue, in the last considerable account of English government[1] written before the sixteenth century, devotes but three hundred words or so to the making of statutes, after the recital of other kinds of law, and devotes practically all the rest of his book to the ways in which justice is done. Similarly, although the Tudors did much to fix that characteristic feature of modern politics, the distinguishing of legislation as the specific function of government, yet the first and the most considerable account of English government written in the Tudor period (Sir Thomas Smith's *De Republica Anglorum*,[2] dating from the fifteen-sixties) devotes almost all its space, except what is taken up with general and theoretical considerations, to courts, their procedure, and its effect.

So it may be hoped that the length at which modes of judicature in the first Tudor reign have been here treated is less disproportionate to the material facts of those days than to the ordinary assumptions of ours. The government was the king's government: to know what the king's government was like it is necessary to enquire what force had he? what money? what advice? what courts? To these questions some sort of answer has now been given: showing especially how highly centralised the courts were, how much royal organs, how careful of royal interests, how flexible to royal purposes: but yet also how open to popular approach, how dependent on popular and especially landowning good-will, how profoundly and inexorably correspondent to national character and history. Of the greatest court of all, the grand inquest of the nation, the high court of parliament, nothing has yet been said except incidentally: this is the next branch of the subject to be discussed.

By 1485 the king's high court of parliament had already for long been the supreme organ of English government: that is to say, for the

[1] *De Laudibus Legum Angliae.*
[2] Best in the edition of L. Alston, whose introduction also is valuable.

business of this kingdom there was no higher authority. It was the highest court of English Law, the embodiment of English unity, the great cistern of English resources, in idea it was the method by which all the information in England could be gathered together to define a question and the whole will of England could be uttered to decide it. Even in idea parliament did not claim competence to decide all questions, still less to create in advance general rules for all contingencies: in practice the will which it expressed was almost always a great deal less than general and was often extremely particular.

The names *house of lords*,[1] *house of commons*[2] were brought into use

---

[1] This name appears first in 1544 according to A. F. Pollard, *Henry VII from Contemporary Sources*, p. xxxiii, referring to C. H. Parry, *Parliaments and Councils of England*, p. xlii.

[2] (*a*) *R.P.* III, p. 523, 5 H. IV, 1403/4, part of the speaker-elect's petition was "that the Chancellor would command, in presence of the King and of the Lords in Parliament, to all the Knights of the Counties, Citizens, and Burgesses come to the same Parliament for the Commonalty of the Realm, that they and each of them should be, every day during that Parliament, at Westminster *a lour Maison a eux assignez pur le temps* at eight o'clock at latest...".

(*b*) *R.P.* IV, p. 422, 11 and 12 H. VI, 1433, "Concordatum fuit etiam, eodem Tertio die Novembris, et ordinatum, quod prefati Communes in eorum Domo communi Promissionem et Juramentum hujusmodi facerent...". See also p. 432*b*, the same year.

(*c*) *R.P.* V, p. 177, 28 H. VI, 1450, "Item, the XXVIII day of Januar next folowyng, the Speker of the Parlement opened and declared in the Commen House, before the Chaunceller of England and other Lordes with hym accompanied...".

(*d*) P. 337, 33 H. VI, 1455, from Thos. Yong's petition, "...alle suche persones as for the tyme been assembled in eny Parlement for the same Comyns, ought to have theire fredom to speke and sey in the Hous of their assemble...".

(*e*) P. 374, 39 H. VI, 1460, from the petition of the commons about Walter Clerk "which com by your high commaundement to this youre present Parlement, and attendyng to the same in the house for the Commens accustumed...".

(*f*) *Paston Letters* (ed. J. Gairdner, 1896), I, p. 273, 1454, "a full straunge acte is passed agayn me in the Higher House. I hope to God it shal not passe in the Comon House".

(*g*) Same date, "whan thai undirstood the disposicion of the Comons House agayn their billes".

(*h*) *Hardyng's Chron.* (ed. Hy. Ellis, 1812: the first version was presented to Henry VI in 1457, *E.H.R.* XXVII, p. 740), pp. 353–4n., "Also I herde the seide erle of Northumberlande saie divers tymes, that he herde duke John of Lancastre, amonge the lordes in counsels and in parlementes, and in the common house, amonge the knyghtes choseyn for the comons, aske be bille forto beene admytte heire apparaunte to kyng Richarde...".

(*i*) *Y.B.* I H. VII Hil. pl. 25, "A great question was asked by the Chancellor of

in the sixteenth century, but the things were already there in the fifteenth. Yet in one sense it would be premature to say that there were two houses of parliament when the Tudors began to reign. There was the king in his parliament, surrounded by his barons and councillors, with his commons not present, or present only as spectators, when they made by the mouth of one of them, their speaker, a report upon which they had previously agreed in private consultation.

The parliament chamber was a room in the royal palace of Westminster. Its salient feature was a royal throne. As lately as in the reign of Henry VI it had not been clear without anxious discussion that parliament could transact any business without the physical presence of the king.[1] He was of course ideally present in all his courts, but in his highest court and the one that was most especially his it was arguable that something more was required. Nor even when its presence had ceased to be absolutely necessary did the person of the king become incapable of attendance or inactive when absent or merely ceremonial when present. It has been shown[2] how in his first parliament Henry VII with his own mouth eloquently expounded to the commons the justice of his title. On 19 November 1485 there was an extraordinary instance how much the parliament chamber was at the king's disposal and how paramount a distinction was the king's service: it was thought that the characteristic vice of recent reigns, disturbance of due process of law, might be mitigated by the administration of an oath to those most liable to temptation: an oath was therefore framed against misprison of felony, retainder, livery, maintenance, riot, hindering of writs: to take this oath[3] there were summoned before the king and his lords in the

England of all the Justices, *de ceo* que lou bill fuit mise en le commen house a les Seigniours en l'Parliament, eux priant d'assentir etc.".

(k) Thos. Marowe's reading, 18 H. VII, on keeping the peace, printed by Dr B. H. Putnam in *Early Treatises on the Practice of the Justices of the Peace*, p. 303, "Item le comen howse del parliement poient graunter surete de peas...".

Note that (g) (Paston, 1454) is the first unequivocal use of *house* to mean an institution or body of men not a place or edifice, and that (k) (Marowe, 1502/3) is the only other such use among these quotations.

Some of these references I owe to Dr S. B. Chrimes, and one to Mr G. T. Lapsley.

[1] A. F. Pollard, *Evolution of Parliament* (2nd edn.), p. 92.
[2] Above, p. 12: and *R.P.* VI, p. 268, 8 Nov. 1485.
[3] *R.P.* VI, p. 288.

parliament chamber first several notable knights and gentlemen of the Household and of the house of commons, and then after their departure, whether encouraged or shamed by their example, still in the presence of the king, the lords spiritual with their hands on their hearts and the lords temporal grasping the Gospel, all took the same oath. On 10 December 1485 Henry received graciously the request made by the speaker and backed by the lords that he should marry Elizabeth of York, a request which the speaker would certainly not have proffered without the best reasons for knowing that it would be agreeable to the recipient. Again, eleven years later, the king with his own hand delivered in a bill of trade then read.[1] Moreover, when the king was absent it was his principal and most trusted servant, the chancellor, who presided over the parliament chamber and very actively directed its business.

The chancellor need not himself be a lord and if he were not received no summons: he was there simply because he was chancellor, and all the rest were there because he had summoned them. Nor was he the only one whose attendance had in it nothing of peerage or barony. Many of those he summoned came like him by reason of profession, not status—judges, attorney- and solicitor-general, masters in chancery, serjeants-at-law, royal secretaries. These experts were not full members[2] and had no right to vote, but they were constant attendants and, as will be seen, were the most effective element in Henry VII's parliaments.

Of members not "under the degree of a Baron of the Parliament" the majority were ecclesiastics, with habits of mind not dissimilar to those of the official attendants, and not much less apt to serve the king. The two classes indeed overlapped a good deal, Henry choosing his officials and confidants largely from among churchmen: his chancellors, for instance, were all bishops. From some churchmen he got his

---

[1] A. F. Pollard, *Evolution of Parliament*, p. 264, quoting from R. B. Cotton's *Posthuma* (1672), p. 54.
[2] As early as t.r. Edward III: cf. A. F. Pollard, *Evolution of Parliament*, p. 105. In 1539 Henry VIII's Act for the placing of the lords in the Parliament (31 H. VIII c. 10) provided only for the chancellor, treasurer, president, privy seal, chief secretary if under the degree of baron.

most valuable and enlightened co-operation, and opposition from none.[1]

To Henry's first parliament came thirteen archbishops and bishops and seventeen abbots and priors: about twenty-nine abbots and priors had been summoned [2] and the same number of laymen, of whom eighteen actually came. The spiritual lords were there because, holding baronies, they were liable to summons and because the crown was desirous of their counsel and assistance: there had been more who were liable to summons, but in the days when the liability was a burden many had shaken it off:[3] not so many, however, but that now, even when lay attendances increased, prelates entitled to summons were still numerous enough to make a majority.

The primary question of parliamentary procedure is this—shall a mere majority bind the whole assembly? It had not always been clear in the English parliament that it should, but by the fifteenth century it was well established, taken for granted, that where either house was not unanimous the greater number should prevail.[4] Such grumbles as those of Betanson [5] are not evidence to the contrary: "Howbeit [he says, speaking of the bill of attainder passed in December 1485] ther was many gentlemen agaynst it, but it would not be, for yt was the Kings pleasure". The king's pleasure went far to make a majority, but majority was the criterion.

The average number of lay lords in recent reigns had been something above forty. Why were there now so few? The simple explanation is

---

[1] When he came to the throne most of them were of Yorkist appointment: but of his first dozen councillors three were bishops (Morton, Courtenay, Fox). By June 1486 he was able to issue as a proclamation the papal bull of recognition which required obedience on pain of excommunication: in Dec. 1498 after Innocent VIII's death, he got Alexander VI's confirmation of this and plenary indulgence to all killed by rebels: the threat of excommunication was used also in 1502 and 1503.

[2] Cf. J. R. Tanner, *Tudor Constitutional Documents*, p. 514: there were summoned to Henry VII's parliaments two archbishops, nineteen bishops, twenty-eight abbots. Henry VIII added three more abbots.

[3] L. O. Pike, *Constitutional History of the House of Lords*, p. 349.

[4] But cf. p. 124 below: an act about Lancashire repealed (1492) on the ground that the Lancashire members were absent when it passed: and p. 163 below, an abbot estopped by the acts of convocation because he had not protested against them, cf. p. 159 below.

[5] To Sir R. Plumpton, *Plumpton Correspondence*, p. 48.

that the Wars of the Roses had been extremely destructive of the baronial class, and this explanation is true, but not in its simplest sense. It was not simply because families entitled to seats in the upper house had been extirpated that Henry's first parliament had so small an attendance of temporal lords.[1] In some cases there was an heir, but he was disqualified by attaint, or by infancy. And then, *entitled to seats* is an expression rather too strong for the period under discussion. The rule that a baron once summoned must be summoned henceforth, himself as long as he lived and his heirs as long as he had any, was in the tendencies and intentions of the fifteenth century, but it was not yet fixed and obligatory.[2] The connection of baronage with landowning had hardly ceased to be essential. As late as 1477 Edward IV by act of parliament[3] deprived George Neville of his dukedom and all his titles because he was neither owner nor heir of a sufficiency of land.

More striking still, as late as the reign of Henry VIII a certain Wimbish[4] claimed to sit in right of Elizabeth, daughter and heiress of Gilbert baron Talboys of Kime, who was his wife but by whom he had no children. There was sound precedent for the claim: nevertheless the king, by his own mere authority, pronounced that "neither Mr Wimbish nor none other from henceforth should use the title of his wife's dignity but such as by courtesy of England has also right to her possessions for term of his life", that is, in right of being not merely husband to the holder but also father to the heir. In this case the interest is not less in the manner of the decision than in the connection between peerage and land. The lords were still far[5] from the claim to be final judges of the composition of their own house. When the lords did come to be judges in peerage cases, it was only on express reference from the crown that they were able to act, and at the end of the fifteenth century a long

---

[1] Cf. Wm. Stubbs, *Seventeen Lectures on Medieval and Modern History*, pp. 407 ff.
[2] Cf. Pike, pp. 88 ff., 238: and Tanner, p. 513.
[3] *R.P.* VI, p. 173, quoted by Pike, p. 82: cf. T. Smith, *De Republica Anglorum* (ed. Alston), p. 32, on decayed lords not admitted to the upper house although they keep the name.
[4] Pike, p. 107.
[5] The commons even further: cf. below, pp. 110, 111, 112.

development was still necessary before the crown should be bound to resort to this mode of decision.[1]

It had always been the royal writ that entitled a lord to come (or a borough to send) to parliament, and though use and custom had done much to fix the destination of writs their issue had not yet become quite independent of royal choice. To some lords Henry VII did not address his summons:[2] his descendants achieved the same result by accompanying the writ of summons under the great seal with an intimation under the privy seal or signet that it was not meant to be obeyed.[3] The king was able also to compel attendance by fine, as well as to dispense with it, and if he gave license for absence could veto the favoured peer's choice of proxy.[4]

It was to the dynastic wars very largely that the Tudors owed the tractability of the peerage: not only that some peers were dead without heirs, some with infant heirs, some were attainted, some were the apprehensive survivors of a defeated party, but still more that from the alternate rise and fall of the great feudal families the crown had emerged the almost universal legatee. Where now were the Veres? "Where is Bohun? where's Mowbray? where's Mortimer?"[5] Henry VII inherited not only from the kings of Lancaster and York but from the kingmakers too. The upper house had been formidable because the great accumulations represented by these names were personified in it: now they

---

[1] As appears from the FitzWalter Case (1669), which though first referred to the house of lords was during a prorogation transferred by the king to the arbitrament of the privy council, Pike, pp. 130, 285.

[2] Cf. Stubbs, *Seventeen Lectures*, p. 406; Pollard, *Evolution of Parliament*, p. 273; Hy. Elsynge, *Manner of Holding Parliaments*, pp. 32, 59. And of course the king could license absence, as he did on 22 Dec. 1505, for Lord Stourton, with exemption from attending any parliament or council that might be summoned even though writ, letters or mandate should be sent him, Williams, *England under the Early Tudors*, p. 134 from *Cal. Pat. Rolls*, 1494–1509, p. 491. Similarly, the earl of Desmond was exempted, at the end of 1495 or beginning of 1496, from attending Parliament or Grand Council in Ireland, Conway, p. 91.

[3] Cf. Pollard, *Evolution of Parliament*, p. 306 n.

[4] *Ibid.* p. 273: cf. E. Lodge, *Illustrations of British History*, I, p. 255, for a case in 1555, where Mary licensed the absence of the earl of Shrewsbury, and at the same time suggested Lord Montague and the bishop of Ely to be his proxies.

[5] Chief Justice Crewe, giving judgment in the Oxford (Vere) Peerage Case, 1625, quoted by C. H. Firth, *The House of Lords during the Civil War*, p. 7.

were concentrated in the crown. There were the Stanleys, but Henry proved quite strong enough to deal with them:[1] the Howards returned to favour in 1489[2] and to the house of lords, and to a century of very chequered eminence: Ferrers[2] was restored in 1487, Zouch[2] in 1495: Henry created five new peerages, and his later parliaments contained about forty lay lords, which was very near the usual figure: but the house of lords never presented any difficulty either to him or to his descendants.

The house of commons was already in 1485 a house in a fuller sense than the other, but it was as yet hardly a house of parliament, while the other in a very important sense was parliament. The commons first achieved a corporate identity and a name just because they were not parliament. They had to be called something: and were called *domus communitatis* because they represented the communities—counties, cities, and boroughs: they had to meet somewhere, and did in point of fact meet habitually in the chapter house[3] of Westminster Abbey. The lords being assembled to parley with the king and his council, conducted their deliberations under royal guidance, and their chairman was the chancellor. The commons had nothing to do in parliament but to listen when they were desired to hear and to report the results of their own debates, and they chose[4] one of their own number to preside over their debates and to report them to the chancellor.[5]

The house of commons numbered something under three hundred. For every shire (but not yet including Wales, or the counties palatine of Chester and Durham) two knights[6] were elected by the freeholders

---

[1] Cf. p. 29 above.

[2] Stubbs, *Seventeen Lectures*, p. 406.

[3] Since Richard II's reign at least. T. F. Tout, *Chapters in Medieval Administrative History*, III, p. 293, says that by 1376 parliament had been meeting at Westminster for forty years, and the house of commons had its accustomed meeting-place in the chapter house.

[4] Regularly and continuously since Richard II's reign: in Tudor times they always chose some one who was making a career in the service of the crown. Cf. p. 108 below.

[5] On a very exceptional occasion some other commoner might speak in the parliament chamber: Burley, who on 15 Nov. 1455 led a deputation of the commons to explain to the lords the desirability of appointing a protector, was not speaker: cf. H. L. Gray, *Influence of the Commons on Early Legislation*, p. 75.

[6] That is, a total of seventy-four.

of lands to the annual value of forty shillings at least.[1] The knights had a certain precedence over their colleagues: no burgess was speaker till 1544: knights were complimented by the assumption that they were richer than burgesses, and were privileged to be booted and spurred in the house;[2] they took the lead in ceremonial[3] and although they were in a minority they had something of preponderance too as well as pre-eminence, for they were men of higher social position and bolder habit of mind, accustomed to taking the lead and apt to look down upon townsmen.

The constituency that returned citizens and burgesses cannot be defined with anything like the brevity and clarity with which that of the knights can be treated. What towns were represented? and what was the qualification to vote in each town? Neither question can be more than partially and vaguely answered.

Henry VII was to claim the infrequency of his parliaments as a merit.[4] In earlier days representation had often seemed nothing but a burden, the aspect of it of which townsmen were most keenly aware being the obligation to pay wages and travelling expenses. On the other hand, what the crown wanted was communication with every town that was at all considerable, and so there was no general question—which boroughs had the right to be represented in parliament?—but only a series of special questions which may be divided into two classes—from what towns did the royal authorities on each occasion think it worth while to summon burgesses? from what towns did burgesses actually come when they were summoned? It was by a long succession of answers to questions of this sort, from Edward I's time onwards, that urban representation reached the relative fixity which it possessed at the end of the fifteenth century.

Every town that was of any importance received the parliamentary writ and sent, as a rule, two representatives; and in those days five thousand inhabitants meant a town of very considerable importance. Thus the urban representatives amounted to some three quarters of the

[1] So settled by statute 8 H. VI c. 7 (1430).
[2] E. and A. G. Porritt, *The Unreformed House of Commons*, pp. 502, 503.
[3] *Red Paper Book of Colchester* (ed. W. G. Benham), p. 62.
[4] *R.P.* VI, p. 526: Elizabeth was to make the same claim.

commons. But though all the towns of size and wealth were represented, it was not simply for those qualifications that they had been selected to receive the summons, and so it was not only from such towns that burgesses came. Of the great variety of boroughs from which in the course of parliamentary history sheriffs had summoned burgesses,[1] many had by the end of the fifteenth century dropped out of representation, and of the fallen no doubt the great majority were from among the smaller towns, but still there were certainly not more than a hundred considerable towns in England at that time, and so while all the towns represented (except London) were very small by modern standards, some were very small by any standard.

As far back as 1382 statute had forbidden the sheriff, under penalty, to withhold his precept from any city or borough accustomed to receive it: this was not immediately or absolutely effective, nor did every town always think it worth while to answer the summons: as late as 1614 the borough of Minehead[2] made no answer.

Meanwhile, another method of promoting a town to representative rank had been added to the mere selection by fourteenth-century sheriffs. In 1445 the crown begun the practice of creating, or more often reviving, parliamentary boroughs by royal charter:[3] eight boroughs were thus called into existence by Henry VI and four by Edward IV. It was a method which the Tudors were to employ freely: so long as that was possible, it was clearly difficult to think of the house of commons as an independent entity over against the crown.

If first the king's officer, and later the king himself, assigned representation to this town and that, what authority settled the method by which each town should choose its representative? The answer is that the towns were left to arrange it for themselves, with occasional interference from the king.[4] There was, until 1832, no general rule

---

[1] G. L. Riess, *Geschichte des Wahlrechts zum englischen Parlament*, pp. 31–5.
[2] Porritt, I, p. 6.
[3] Cf. Homersham Cox, *Antient Parliamentary Elections*, p. 158.
[4] Cf. Campbell, *Materials Illustrative of the Reign of Henry VII*, II, p. 456, writ to Leicester reciting the practice there of assembling as well as the rich the poor, "persons as be of little substance or reason", to the subversion of good policy and discouragement of the governors, and directing that in future the mayor should summon the king's bailiff and forty-eight of the most wise and sad commons.

laying down who should be borough electors, like the forty-shilling freehold rule for counties, though no doubt the statute which made that rule[1] marked the establishment for boroughs as for counties of the principle that elections should be by majority, a principle which seems now self-evident but which had not previously been matter of course, and though for boroughs as for counties electors and elected must alike be inhabitants: neither even of these principles proved in practice very restrictive. As for the second, it could be got over easily enough, as soon as there were any temptation to get over it, by making the favoured outsider an honorary burgess. And as for the first, it was impossible that majority votes, so long as they were calculated in public, should be the mere counting of individual inclinations: so long as the process is so public, votes will be largely a matter of weighing, the leading men will lead, and in a fifteenth-century town (or county, for that matter) leading had a great deal more to do with lucre than with light. An election of that period may be imagined as resembling less the modern counting of bits of paper than what would happen at an open poll of the forty or fifty inhabitants of a public school "house", or members of a university faculty: only, for physical force and athletic prowess (or for the commensurable academic qualities) substitute landed property and governmental influence.

In an election meeting of those days, in town or county, the decision was a matter much more of weight than of numbers. But who were present at the meeting? In the county, as has been seen, forty-shilling freeholders, and forty shillings then meant perhaps sixty or seventy pounds now. In the boroughs it is not so simple.

Roughly speaking, the town voters were the persons summoned for the purpose by the administrative authorities of the town. In some towns they summoned no one but themselves, in some a few other important personages, in some the holders of certain traditional pro- perties, in some all burgesses (but then who were reckoned burgesses was a matter of borough custom:[2] at any rate they must be house-

---

[1] 1430: 8 H. VI c. 7.
[2] Cf. Riess, p. 62; *Red Paper Book of Colchester* (ed. W. G. Benham), p. 26; Porritt, I, p. 42.

holders paying scot and lot, not living by wages or by innkeeping, brewing, baking, butchering). In the fifteenth century, and in the sixteenth, there was a general movement towards oligarchy, though not towards an absolutely closed oligarchy. Economic influence was in the same direction: "the government of the English towns in the sixteenth century had everywhere passed into the hands of oligarchies of traders, and if these bodies established and maintained their rule without much opposition, it was because they kept an open door for the successful craftsmen".[1] There may have been a few instances of parliamentary representation moving in the opposite direction,[2] but on the whole, town electorates were small and tended to get smaller, and this tendency obtained a new force and rigidity from the grant to towns of royal charters of incorporation, which began in Henry VI's reign and which very often directly or indirectly handed over to the municipal governments the election of parliamentary representatives.

In little more than a century it was possible to assume election by an oligarchy as a general rule, and an honest and well-informed writer, displaying English parliamentary institutions for imitation in Ireland, wrote in 1569 without misgiving or qualification:

the sheriff of every county, having received his writs, ought forthwith to send his precepts and summons to the mayors, bailiffs, and head officers of every city, town, corporate borough, and such places as have been accustomed to send burgesses within his county, that they do choose and elect among themselves two citizens from every city, and two burgesses for every borough, according to their ancient custom and usage... and the head officers ought then to assemble themselves and the aldermen and common council of every city and town, and to make choice among themselves of two able and sufficient of every city or town to serve for and in the said parliament.[3]

The constituency of the house of commons, then, was a class constituency: lords of parliament could participate in elections, and did so,

---

[1] G. Unwin, *Industrial Organisation in the Sixteenth and Seventeenth Centuries*, p. 74.
[2] Cf. Porritt, I, p. 41–6 for all this paragraph, and esp. the case of Ipswich in 1474, deciding that "all burgesses resident, and no others shall have their free votes": but "burgesses" was far from synonymous with "inhabitants".
[3] Quoted by Porritt, I, p. 43, from Hooker, *Statement of English Procedure*, reprinted in *History of the Irish Parliament*, by Lord Mountmorres.

sometimes with great effect. Members were elected in the counties by substantial landowners; in the towns mostly by the thriving managing part of the population where there was population enough for such an aristocracy, in which case it was very closely related to the surrounding landowners: and where there was not enough urban population to produce such a class, there it was not difficult for surrounding land-owners to manage what population there was as often as they thought it worth while. It was an electorate large enough to be able to identify the nation with itself, homogeneous enough to be not incapable of thinking and feeling as a unit without organised communication and discussion, not so small nor so resourceless as to be easily regimented, yet not too big to be manageable nor too haughty to sympathise and co-operate with government: of a character, indeed, very apt to be exploited by Tudor government.

Such was the character of the electorate: even more notable here than its character is its mode of definition, or its lack of definition: another occasion to remark how far the fifteenth century was from anything which can very usefully be called a constitution. There was no doubt, indeed, how many counties were to send knights to parliament, who might send, or who might be sent: but even here there was a great deal that was very vague and very slack. County members ought to be knights since 1445 [1] or if not knights at least gentlemen of good repute. Even the slighter qualification does not seem to have been in practice restrictive: not since 1450 has there been objection to a candidate for want of gentility.[2] And even then that objection was incidental to another much more serious: the really serious grievance was that the ungentlemanly candidate's supporters had forcibly prevented those on the other side, who were the majority, from taking their oaths that they were forty-shilling freeholders and thus entitled to vote and to carry the election. All this was irregular enough: it seems still more irregular that the protest was in effect unnecessary since the sheriff had ignored all difficulties of form and done what he thought substantially just by returning the candidates whose party was really the greater.

[1] 23 H. VI c. 14.
[2] Cf. Homersham Cox, p. 117; Prynne, *Brevia Parliamentaria Rediviva*, pp. 156 ff; and below, pp. 105 and 111.

When such things could be, the method of making a knight of the shire was neither exact nor unmistakable: but it was by no means absolutely fluid: parliament in the fifteenth century had fixed the franchise, enforced residence for electors and elected,[1] and done what it could against falsification of returns by commanding that they should be made by indenture certified by the seals of electors: but still the actual machinery of election was left to local habit and discretion; not so much as the simple device of counting heads, the majority's most elementary guarantee, was matter of course nor even matter of right on demand.

Even for knights of the shire, then, and even after the fifteenth-century statutes about election, the machinery was still rudimentary and such as would have been intolerable on the assumption that every detail of the composition of the house of commons was matter of first-rate national interest: much more unregulated still, as has been seen, was the election of burgesses, where central authority had not troubled to decide how many of them there should be or from what towns, or how elected—had decided nothing, except that they should be residents elected by residents (and this it made no effort to enforce), and that they should be entitled to standard wages and expenses from their constituencies (and that not if the towns could find representatives willing to contract out).

In short, when Henry VII came to the throne the house of commons had not yet got so far towards the likelihood of having a will of its own apt for rivalry with that of the crown as to convince the crown of any urgent need for active and general control of its constituency. In Henry's time seats in the lower house were still far from being the objects of an organised competition between government and opposition: but it is an undue simplification to suppose that they had not yet become objects of desire: some political significance of that sort they had already acquired, and some remarks on the manner of it (though it was a manner that with the establishment of the Tudors became demoded)

---

[1] This requirement was not new, the form of the writ had always intended it: nor did it prove very effective. Even the fixing of the franchise was not absolute: "freehold" was to add much to its meaning for electoral purposes.

may help to show what the house of commons signified, what was its place among political forces, at the beginning of the Tudor period.

It is easy enough to show both that there was competition for seats in the fifteenth century and that there was not enough of it to make demand everywhere overtake supply. For the first proposition there is the evidence of the legislation already noted: there would have been no object in beginning to regulate elections and returns if no one minded who was elected.[1] Constituencies often found men who were willing to serve for less than the fixed rate of remuneration or for none at all.[2] As early as 1441 some candidates thought it worth while to pay money for the possession of the writs, so as to forestall their rivals, and by 1467 they were adding to their expenses by entertaining the electors.[3] The men of Kent who followed Jack Cade in 1451 complained of letters sent to "the great rulers of all the countrie the which imbraceth their tenants and other people by force to choose other persons than the commons' will is".[4] The complaint was not unfounded. The duchess of Norfolk wrote to John Paston in 1455: "forasmuch as it is thought right necessary for diverse causes, that my lord have at this time in the parliament such persons as belong unto him, and be of his menial servants:[5] we heartily desire and pray you, that at the contemplation of these our letters...ye will give an apply your voice unto our right well beloved cousin and servants John Howard and Sur Roger Chamberlayne, to be the knights of the shire...". Another letter of about the same date explains how the dukes of York and Norfolk and the earl of Oxford had arranged for the election of knights of the shire. In 1472 Sir John Paston was prevented from sitting for Norfolk because "my Lord of Norfolk and my Lord of Suffolk were agreed...to have Sir

---

[1] Cf. Riess, p. 49.
[2] Porritt, I, p. 155.
[3] Porritt, I, pp. 21, 22.
[4] Quoted by Homersham Cox, *Antient Parliamentary Elections*, from Holinshed, III (edn. 1586), p. 633. Cf. C. H. Parry, *Parliaments and Councils of England*, p. 186.
[5] *Paston Letters* (edn. 1904, III, p. 34). But *menial* had not yet its modern meaning, and Norfolk was not the last leader to desire the election of his followers: cf. p. 107 below. And cf. *Paston Letters*, IV, p. 26, letters from the king to all gentlemen of reputation to attend the duke of Suffolk at Norwich next Monday for the election of knights of the shire.

Robert Wingfield and Sir Richard Harcourt"; but his brother wrote that he was trying to get him in for Maldon, and "if ye miss to be burgess for Maldon and my Lord Chancellor will, ye may be in another place. There be a dozen towns in England that choose no burgesses which ought to do it, and ye may be set in for one of those towns and [i.e., if] ye be friended".[1] Moreover, membership had such possibilities of usefulness that it was worth not only wholesale purchase by way of procuring election but also occasional hiring by way of bargains for a member's support: in 1472 Nicholas Statham made provision in his will[2] for restitution of money accepted in respect of parliamentary services: "Item, I received ten shillings of...Bemont a worshippful Squire of the West Country by the hands of Page in the last Parlement. I did nothing there...and if I did, it is against my conscience for so moche as I was one of the Parlement and should be indifferent in every matter of the Parlement, I will he have it ageyne".

The returns for Henry VII's parliaments are not available. The nearest pairs of parliaments whose compositions can be compared are those of 1472 and 1477/8, and of 1529 and 1541/2.[3] It seems that in the 1477 parliament out of just under three hundred names nearly sixty are identical with names which appeared in 1472, thirty-three for the same, twenty-six for different, constituencies. For the parliament of 1541 many of the names are missing, and in the long interval since 1529 there had been two other parliaments for which returns are not available: so that sixteen cases of nominal identity with the 1529 parliament may be held to show that the habit of seeking re-election had at least not much diminished. In all four parliaments, also, surnames often recur with different Christian names, and in all four names suggestive of the royal service are not infrequent.

Here is evidence enough that before the Tudor period began the time was already past (if it had ever existed) when a seat in the lower house was necessarily a mere nuisance alike to the man who had to

---

[1] *Paston Letters*, V, p. 149.
[2] Quoted by B. G. Skottowe, *Short History of Parliament*, p. iv: Statham sat in the parliament of 1467 for Old Sarum (*Return of Members of Parliament*, I, p. 359).
[3] *Return of Members of Parliament* (1878), pt. 1.

waste his time in it and to the community which had to waste its money on his remuneration. There is a little more evidence[1] (very little, but not quite negligible) that kings themselves had taken trouble to obtain such members as would serve their turn: and the use of royal charters to create parliamentary boroughs and to influence their methods of election may have had this as one of its motives. The petitioners against the ungentlemanly Gimber[2] were anxious that the king should know that *their* candidates were "men of your Honourable Household, named in your Checker-Roll...most like the expedition, and to execute and assent to the said aydes": and the manner of taking the oath against hindering due process of law in the 1485 parliament,[3] first by several notable knights and gentlemen as well of the Household as of the house of commons, looks as if the advantages of royal representation in the lower house had not been forgotten. So that to explain the absolute ease of Henry VII's, and the great ease of his family's, dealings with the house of commons, it will not do simply to assume that no constituency had ever yet learnt to be interested in its representation and that no ambitions had yet begun to exploit parliamentary elections, that any monarch could do as he liked with the house of commons because no one cared whether he were represented in it or how, and because no one wanted to be a member of it.

It is not quite so simple as that: and yet it is clear enough that Henry VII did do as he liked with the house of commons. For this there are many reasons;[4] one is that the very evidence that parliamentary representation in the fifteenth century was not mere matter of indifference, that that very evidence itself largely explains the ease of Tudor control.

If there were many constituencies willing to elect any one who would serve for nothing, was not the crown in a peculiarly favourable position for profiting by their complacency, whenever it should seem worth

---

[1] Cf. Porritt, I, p. 369, esp. the reference to Whitelocke, *Notes on the King's Writ*, I, p. 384.
[2] Prynne, *Brevia Parliamentaria Rediviva* (1602), p. 158, and cf. pp. 101 above, 111 below.
[3] *R.P.* VI, p. 288, 9 Nov. 1485: cf. p. 91 above.
[4] Below, p. 126.

while?[1] If the house of commons was tempting to ambition, lawyers and courtiers were the most easily tempted, the one class almost, the other quite, necessarily royalist. If members were worth influencing, the crown had resources, material and immaterial, such as were at the disposal of no one else. Besides the advantages already enumerated the king could grant exemptions from being elected, and exemptions from attendance after election:[2] which meant, again, that seats in parliament were not yet always objects of desire, and that in so far as they were political resources the king had special opportunities to dispose of them.[3] And then, consider how feudal were the fifteenth-century instances of election management, how much in the hands of "the great rulers of all the countrie", of dukes and earls and large landowners, how it is in times of factious and dynastic strife that it becomes most active; now, it was the characteristic of Henry to have swallowed the feudalisms and united the dynasties which had busied and rent the preceding generations. Faction he still had to face, but faction with foreign roots and to be met in the field rather than in the council chamber. Great men were again to make members: in Henry VIII's time, for instance, there are Thomas Cromwell and Stephen Gardiner in rivalry for the electoral management of Surrey and Hampshire, and the Elizabethan duke of Norfolk returned ten members in Sussex alone. But in the first case both competitors owed their influence to the king; and as for the second, when Elizabeth's duke of Norfolk began to act as if he were back in the fifteenth century, he lost his head for it. At any rate, Henry VII had no need to regard any possible borough-monger or master as a threat to his freedom of action: procuring elections had been part of the struggle for power between feudal families, and was to be between political parties: but for a time it was very nearly true that the crown was itself all the feudal families and all the political

---

[1] E.g., Garth, who served Henry in a military capacity especially in Ireland and on the Scottish border, sat in the English parliament of 1491, for Blechingley, probably as the nominee of Buckingham, in whose Lancastrian rebellion he had probably taken part (Conway, pp. 50–1), and similar identifications of king's servants and M.P.s could be made.

[2] Holdsworth, IV, p. 93, for such an exemption in 1514.

[3] Cf. A. F. Pollard, *Evolution of Parliament*, pp. 161, 332.

parties too, and it was quite true that of that special weapon at least it was the unrivalled master.

It is necessary to use the phrase *house of commons* as the name of part of the governmental organisation which the Tudors found in being: but the phrase is more misleading than helpful unless the reader remembers how immensely less of organisation it connotes for the early Tudor than for the early Windsor period. Not only was its composition so little organised, and in so far as it was organised, with royal machinery and open to royal influence, but also its conduct and procedure after assembly were still rudimentary and hardly yet capable of independence.

How the commons conducted themselves when they were in their own house cannot be very copiously expounded since it is a subject of which no official records were kept and very few unofficial reports have survived. Since the fourteenth century they had utilised to some extent the large assembly's natural device of the committee and had provided themselves with the large assembly's primary necessity of a chairman. Being, if not a court, at least a body attending upon and helping to give capacity to a court, and being individually all more or less familiar with common law methods, they naturally took as a matter of course some of the lawyers' rules about debate and evidence, and especially the lawyers' method of discussion by a series of speeches for and against some specific motion.[1] They formed the community of communities, the corporation of corporations, but as long as they were acting alone their proceedings were private and preliminary, they could hardly be regarded as a public constitutional organ, could not indeed be literally regarded at all.

When the house of commons did come to the parliament chamber it had no means of utterance save the mouth of its elected speaker, and his election by the house was really a formality which disguised appointment by the king. A parliamentary session lasted only for a few weeks, and if Richard II's and Edward IV's device of calling back the same parliament for a second session was utilised, as it was three times by Henry VII, the second session was also very short, and was the last:

[1] Cf. J. Redlich, *Procedure of the House of Commons*, III, p. 60; I, p. 11 (receivers and triers of petitions); II, p. 203 (early committees); and below, p. 128.

it was only his son's repeated prorogations of the 1529 assembly which began the modern parliament, something which has a life instead of being an occasion. As early as Richard II's reign the same individuals had frequently been returned,[1] but when the Tudors began to reign (and for long after) it was still true that this was much the most likely to happen with royal servants, and lawyers ambitious of royal favour, and that they were the only men in the commons with much notion what was the business before the house and how it should be done. There is an account of the 1485 parliament written by the Colchester burgesses for the information of their constituents,[2] which shows how the house of commons in action impressed two at least of its members: they report that they were directed by the chancellor to choose a speaker, and that they elected Thomas Lovel (how, or on whose proposition they do not say, but Lovel, like all the speakers of the reign and indeed of the dynasty, was engaged in making a career in the royal service):[3] they go on to say that they were then instructed by the Recorder of London (who was presumably himself a member) that the usual next step was to appoint a committee of twenty-four to ask the chancellor to report their choice to the king: which was accordingly done.

Moreover, the speaker was paid, and might be very handsomely paid, by the king. In view of these considerations it is not strange, and at any rate it is quite certain, that he was in practice a royal nominee, at least as much the king's servant for managing the commons as the commons' representative for communicating with the king in parliament.[4]

It is through the speaker that the house of commons has established those privileges which have now for centuries been its main distinction and have enabled it to become the principal constitutional organ: it is often assumed that those privileges are in essence so inseparable from

---

[1] M. McKisack, *Borough Representation in R. II's Reign*, printed in the *E.H.R.* XXXIX, p. 518.

[2] *Red Paper Book of Colchester* (ed. W. G. Benham), pp. 60 ff.

[3] Cf. p. 96, n. 4 above: and cf. Porritt, I, p. 433, "the Commons were never in a position to elect whom they pleased" till towards the end of Charles II's reign.

[4] To understand how all this was changed, cf. the cases of Speakers Onslow (1566), Lenthall (1640), Seymour (1679), Foley (1695).

the very idea of the house of commons that they must always have been in force. Some indication of the point at which the history of privilege had arrived when the Tudors began to reign may help towards an understanding how different the house of commons was then from what the words suggest now, how much the idea of it was something hardly to be conceived by a mind in which the words chime resonant with the history of another four and a half centuries.

The only privilege which the speaker in 1485 [1] asked was

that everything to be proffered and declared in the aforesaid Parliament in the name of the said Commons, he might proffer and declare under such Protestation, that if he should have declared anything enjoined on him by his Fellows, otherwise than they had agreed, or with any addition or omission, that then what he had so declared might be corrected and emended by his fellows; and that his protestation to this effect might be entered on the roll of the aforesaid parliament.

Almost exactly the same formula was used throughout the reign: but it does not represent all the legal advantage which the house of commons had over a mere collection of private citizens.

The true justification of that advantage can hardly be better put than at the beginning of John Hatsell's *Cases of Privilege of Parliament*: [2]

As it is an essential part [he says] of the constitution of every court of judicature, and absolutely necessary for the due execution of its powers, that persons resorting to such courts, whether as judges or as parties, should be entitled to certain Privileges to secure them from molestation during their attendance; it is more peculiarly essential to the Court of Parliament, the first and highest court in this kingdom, that the members who compose it, should not be prevented by trifling interruptions from their attendance on this important duty, but should, for a certain time, be excused from obeying any other call, not so immediately necessary for the great services of the nation.. . .

So it was that members [3] of the house of commons, being by the very fact of their membership assistants in the most important of all legal processes, were exempted from other legal processes and placed under

[1] *R.P.* VI, p. 268.
[2] But cf. p. 110 below.
[3] A fifteenth-century usage, cf. p. 110, n. 6 below.

the king's special protection, lest the smaller should defeat the greater. The exemption had its inconveniences, but less serious then than when parliamentary sessions became longer: nor was it absolute; when the commons in 1404 petitioned[1] that since by ancient custom they (and the lords) and their servants ought not to be arrested for any debt, account, trespass, or contract, that therefore it might be established that in future any one attempting anything against this custom should make fine and ransom to the king and treble damages to the party grieved, they got no more satisfactory answer than "There is already sufficient remedy in such cases". Here may be seen both the limitation of their privilege, since they did not claim that it extended to criminal charges,[2] and its dependence on the king's assistance for realisation. Against mere acts of violence they did get the protection of special penalties[3] by general statute, but for their immunity from arrest they continued dependent upon occasional good-will.

It was of the greatest importance that this immunity was not automatic nor enforceable by the house of commons itself. Every court of the king was of course armed with as much of his authority as was necessary to protect its functions, but the house of commons was not a court,[4] hardly a part of a court, rather was it in the relation of a jury to the court, a court which we should call the House of Lords, or better, the King in the House of Lords.

It is easy to exaggerate the extent to which the house of commons failed to participate in parliament:[5] remember,[6] for instance, that the

---

[1] *R.P.* III, p. 541.
[2] In Lark's Case (1429) (*R.P.* IV, p. 357) it was assumed that Lark being a member's servant was "by the privilege of your court of parliament...safeguarded from all arrest during your said court, save for treason, felony, or surety of the peace". The petition for Lark's request was granted (with the consent of the counsel of Marjerie Janyns, at whose suit he had been arrested, and promising her execution of the judgment), but not the added general request that all lords, commons and their servants coming to or being in parliament be not arrested except for treason, felony or breach of the peace: cf. Gray, p. 327.
[3] Hatsell, pp. 15 ff., 24 ff., esp. the act 11 H. VI c. 11.
[4] Cf. p. 111 below, but cf. also p. 125 below.
[5] Cf. p. 107 above.
[6] *R.P.* v, p. 240 and pp. 374, 375 (Thorp's Case and Clerk's Case): note also on p. 374 the form of the speaker's request and of the grant of commons liberties in 1460.

justices in 1454 thought of the speaker (and apparently any one in the commons) as "a member of this high court of Parliament", and that in 1460 the house of commons assumed that a member was attending parliament "in the house for the Commons accustomed". Yet it remains true that it was a membership constrained to be silent except by the mouth of the speaker in (as we should say) the house of lords, and that it was attendance upon a court rather than judicature within it. At the beginning of Henry IV's reign the commons had themselves protested[1]

that the judgments of parliament belong solely to the king and the lords and not at all to the commons except in cases where it pleases the king of his especial grace to show them the said judgements for their ease, and that no record be made in parliament against the said Commons that they are or will be parties to any judgements given or to be given in parliament. To which they had answer from the Archbishop of Canterbury by the command of the king, how the same Commons are petitioners and requesters, and that the king and the lords of all time have had, and of right will have, the judgements in parliament, in manner as the Commons have shewn. Save that in statutes to be made, or in grants and subsidies, or such things to be made for common profit of the realm, the king wishes to have especially their advice and assent. And that such order he held and kept in all time to come.

Similarly, disputed returns, even after the statute of 1410 authorising judges of assize to enquire into them, were matters for the king, with the help of the lords or the judges.[2] And the house of commons itself could not on its own authority deliver a member who had been arrested, but required the co-operation of the rest of parliament, or at least of the lord chancellor. How far these resources were from guaranteeing the persons of the commons may be seen from Thorp's case[3] in 1453/4. Thorp, not merely a member but actually speaker, was imprisoned on a civil suit instituted by the duke of York, and the commons "by certain of their members made request to the king and to the lords spiritual and temporal in the said parliament, that they might have and enjoy

[1] *R.P.* III, p. 427 (3 Nov. 1399), referred to by Pike, p. 290. Cf. p. 116 below.
[2] Stubbs, *Constitutional History*, III, p. 423: and p. 105 above, for the petition to the king against Henry Gimber.
[3] Hatsell, pp. 28 ff.; *R.P.* V, pp. 239, 240: cf. p. 139 below.

all such liberties and privileges, as have been accustomed, and of ancient time used for coming to parliament; and according to the same liberties, and privileges that Thomas Thorp their common speaker" might be set at liberty.

Exactly what were the facts and all the significance of this case cannot be confidently explained. For the point here in question—that the commons could not unassisted define and vindicate their privileges— what has been quoted is already evidence enough. But there is more: for though the chief justice (in the name of all the justices, whose expert advice the lords had asked), after denying "That the justices should in any wise determine the privileges of this high court of parliament", proceeded to declare the custom that "a member of this high court of parliament...be released of such arrests", yet in spite of this de- claration, the lords agreed that Thorp should remain in prison, and when in the king's name they reported this decision to the commons, the election of another speaker was undertaken without further re- monstrance.[1]

To return to freedom of speech: there was more of it than was asked in the speaker's petition, but it was no more self-subsistent than freedom from arrest, no less dependent for vindication upon external authority. It had one root in the essentially private character[2] of the commons' debates, and one authority[3] goes so far as to deny that it can "appear by any ancient record that the king did ever take notice of any of the commons speeches or consultations, until they were reported unto His Majesty in open parliament". The commons themselves were not always so confident. In January 1400/1 they petitioned[4] Henry IV

---

[1] Two years later a commons bill to punish Thorp for alienating the king from the duke of York was rejected: cf. Gray, p. 123.

[2] Cf. pp. 96, 107, 111 above.

[3] Hy. Elsynge, *Manner of Holding Parliaments* (edn. 1768), p. 180. Elsynge was Clerk of the Parliaments from 1632 to 1648.

[4] *R.P.* III, p. 456: cf. Carl Wittke, *English Parliamentary Privilege*, p. 24: the commons cannot yet have forgotten Haxey's Case (1397), where it had just been ruled by the king on the petition of the commons that all the proceedings against him were null and void: Haxey was not a member of parliament and was a royal official: he had initiated a bill to limit the expenses of the king's household, especially on ladies and bishops. The king told Lancaster to get the name of the bill's sponsor, and the commons delivered the bill to the lords and said it had been handed to them

that he refuse to give credence to any one bearing reports of matters under discussion in their house: Henry replied "that he would hear no such person, nor give him credence, before such matters were shown to the king by advice and assent of all the Commons according to the purport of their prayer". Half a century later the position was still not satisfactorily settled: in 1455 Thomas Young complained to the house that for words of his in the house of 1451 reported to the king he had been imprisoned in the Tower. His petition was sent to the lords and the king ordered that "the Lordes of his Counsell do and provide in this partie for the said suppliant, as by their discretions shall be thought convenyent and reasonable". 1455 was the year when the Wars of the Roses began, and Young's proposition in 1451 had been for the duke of York to be declared heir to the throne:[1] moreover in this case freedom from arrest was involved as well as freedom of speech: much most important of all, the expectation of favourable treatment, however legitimate, was not crystallised into a definite and unmistakable privilege and could not be enforced without the co-operation of the king, who remitted the case to the discretion of the lords: nor was redress asked for any injury to the house of commons, nothing more than a personal and private indemnity.

These fifteenth-century cases are all from troublous, even revolutionary, occasions, they are none of them perfectly comprehensible, and none of them drawn from Tudor times: indeed, the Tudor history of privilege begins in the middle of Henry VIII's reign, and till then what has been said above may be sufficiently convincing that when Henry VII reigned the commons could not assert their privileges without royal help, and consequently not against the royal will unless the

by T. Haxey. Then they were summoned before the king in full parliament, and begged pardon for their presumption in meddling with things which appertained to the king: the king renounced his demand for extraordinary supplies. The lords resolved that it was treason for any one to excite the commons in parliament to reform anything touching the king's person, government, or regality. Two days later Haxey was condemned to the penalties of treason for having offended in this way. He had already been successfully claimed by Canterbury as a clerk, and three months later he was pardoned. Cf. T. F. Tout, *Chapters in Medieval Administrative History*, IV, p. 17.
[1] Cf. Stubbs, *Constitutional History*, III, p. 493.

king had reason to be afraid of them: but also that it was a part of the good order and known custom of England that parliament business should not be impeded by the process of other courts nor by royal proscriptions of obnoxious debaters.[1]

There is a natural connection between the privileges of the commons and the officers at their disposal. Among these mention has so far been made only of the speaker, and it has been shown that he was by no means completely at their disposal. The house had also, from as far back at least as 1388,[2] a clerk and a serjeant-at-arms. The clerk has always been appointed by the crown: as lately as Elizabeth's time his chief emolument came from gratuities given by members, until the eighteenth century part of it by fees on bills, until the nineteenth part from the patronage of the under-clerks: the salary paid from the king's exchequer, which was a comparatively small part of his payment, is now the whole of it. The serjeant-at-arms has remained what he always was, an officer of the crown lent to the commons. Clearly the house could have no servants upon whose obedience it could rely until it could be sure that its orders to them would not be countermanded or diverted by the crown. What Dr Stubbs said of them, speaking of the "parliamentary antiquities" of the fifteenth century, may be repeated of Henry VII's reign—"The development of their functions, and all matters of constitutional importance connected with them, are of later growth".[3]

From what parliament at the beginning of the Tudor period was, it is time to turn to what it did. To contemporaries it was, in thought and speech (as it still is in the prayer book),[4] the high court of parliament. It would be rash to deduce that all, or even most, of its function was by

[1] Harpsfield, p. 15, writing in Mary's time, attributes the alleged underhand action of Henry VII against More (supposed to have resisted his financial proposals in the parliament of 1504) partly to royal reluctance "lest he might seem thereby to infringe and break the ancient liberty of the Parliament house for free speaking touching the public affairs (which would have been taken odiously)".
[2] Stubbs, *Constitutional History*, III, p. 452; cf. also Porritt, I, ch. XXIV for all this paragraph.
[3] Stubbs, *Constitutional History*, III, p. 452.
[4] The prayer is a little later than Tudor times: it first appeared in an "Order of Fasting" in 1625, and was probably composed by Laud: *History of the Book of Common Prayer*, by F. Proctor and W. H. Frere.

way of jurisdiction: nor is it possible to reckon the proportions of its activities—judicial, legislative, and whatever else—by any convenient rule of thumb, marking off this day's business or that mode of procedure as purely judicial or absolutely legislative, though a leading authority asserts that "as late as the reign of Henry VII, half the time of parliament was occupied with purely judicial functions".[1]

The practical purpose and effect of Henry VII's parliaments were mainly legislative, in the sense of affirming general rules and allotting general taxation;[2] at the same time, and even later, it remained true that the normal processes and conceptions of parliament, alike those of which it was the subject and those of which it was the object, were mainly judicial by origin, judicial in the sense of applying punishments and remedies to particular failures of the rules: this truth had immense constitutional importance, and it is convenient to indicate what were the resources of judicature at parliament's disposal in Henry's time before enquiring into the methods and amounts of parliamentary legislation and into the sense in which it was "legislation".

The criminal side of parliamentary jurisdiction may for the present be very roughly sketched. The part of it which was to affect constitutional development most was impeachment. The word had originally signified any kind of accusation in any court. The process to which it was later appropriated—accusation made by the house of commons to the house of lords—was first employed in 1376.[3] In the ensuing period the process was well organised and repeatedly used, and the term became technical. At the same time the crown's power of accusing offenders in

---

[1] A. F. Pollard, *Evolution of Parliament*, p. 61.
[2] Its aspect as a taxing authority was the most familiar, along with or next after its aspect as a court. Cf. Harpsfield (writing in Mary's reign, *Life of More*, E.E.T.S., p. 15, and see above, p. 24), on the 1504 parliament, called for levying two aids: "Now considering the continual custom almost of all times and of all Princes, at least from Henry I...and as well the great and present as the long durable commodity as it was then likely that should ensue to this Realm by the marriage, it was thought there would be small reluctation or repining against this Parliament" (my spelling). Cf. above, p. 97, n. 4.
[3] L. O. Pike, *Constitutional History of the House of Lords*, p. 205: and generally for the early history of impeachment, cf. that and the following pages, and the book *passim*.

parliament was questioned and dropped,[1] and the right of an individual subject to accuse (technically *appeal*) another before parliament was annulled by the fourteenth chapter of Henry IV's first statute.

The trial in an impeachment was before the whole house of lords, the judgment given by vote of the majority of the lords on the demand of the commons made through the speaker.[2] The great period of impeachment was the seventeenth century,[3] and there are no examples of it between 1459 and 1620: so that its importance for immediate purposes lies precisely in its intermission: it was the classic method whereby discontented parliaments struck at royal servants,[4] and throughout the Tudor period it was wholly neglected.

A lord of parliament indicted of treason or felony[5] was entitled to be tried by his peers,[6] all of them if parliament was sitting, and if not a jury of them, the court in either case presided over by a lord high steward appointed for the occasion, and advised on legal points by the justices as assessors.[7] The steward was the only judge,[8] the peers present being no more than jurors—jurors, however, not like others obliged to unanimity, but permitted to arrive at a verdict[9] by a mere majority: this rule, and the royal appointment for each occasion of a steward and of a jury of about twenty lords,[10] gave the court a pronounced inclination towards subservience, which accounts for the practical supersession by it, during the Tudor period, of the upper house's jurisdiction on indictments of peers.

For the upper house's jurisdiction in cases of parliamentary privilege,

---

[1] 1377, the case of Alice Ferrers, *R.P.* III, p. 12, referred to in Holdsworth, I, p. 378. Remember Charles I's attempt to revive this power.
[2] Holdsworth, I, p. 380.
[3] Cf. Tout, III, pp. 293–7, on the stiff behaviour of the commons in the "Good Parliament" of 1376, and how they went to the "house of parliament" and co-operated with a committee of lords, and their parts in devising the method of impeachment. The next parliament (1377) is the first of which packing (by Gaunt) is recorded, and it included only eight knights who had sat in the Good Parliament.
[4] Though on the last occasion (1459) on which impeachment was attempted before Mompesson's Case in 1621, it was vetoed like a bill by the formula "le roi s'avisera".
[5] Cf. Holdsworth, I, pp. 385 ff.
[6] To understand how little this privilege might mean in the fifteenth century, cf. L. W. V. Harcourt, *His Grace the Steward and Trial of Peers*, esp. p. 398.
[7] Harcourt, p. 438.   [8] *Ibid.* p. 302.
[9] *Ibid.* p. 434.   [10] *Ibid.* p. 436.

it is not here necessary to say more than that at the end of the fifteenth century it was accustomed to exercise that jurisdiction for the protection of the other house as well as of itself. How this defence of privilege worked has already been indicated;[1] how in the middle of the Tudor period it began to be altered, and with what great effects will be shown in a later chapter.[2] Till later also may be left the other original jurisdiction against whose exercise there had been in the fourteenth and fifteenth centuries a growing tendency although, "If the king's interest was specially concerned he would commission the Lords to hear the case. Thus petitions of right and monstrans de droit, cases of lunacy, cases where, owing to the turbulence and strength of one of the parties, justice could not be got in the ordinary courts, were heard by the Lords in this way".[3] This sort of jurisdiction was quite discontinued during the sixteenth century.[4]

Most important of all, for the notions and methods of English government, most important in the past and for the future though in Tudor times its animation was suspended,[5] was the jurisdiction of parliament in correcting the errors of the common-law courts and especially of king's bench. Appeal in the modern sense, from court to court, did not exist, but it was well established that a supreme remedial jurisdiction was inherent in parliament, which could try any complaint that there was error on the record of a case heard elsewhere, and could also provide for the rectification of any error which it found.[6]

[1] Cf. p. 111 above.
[2] Cf. *Henry VIII*, pp. 465 ff. Ferrer's Case, 1543.
[3] Holdsworth, I, p. 365. *Petition of right* is "that remedy, which the subject hath to help a wrong done, or pretended to be done, by the King. For the King hath it by prerogative that he may not be sued upon writ" (Cowell's *Interpreter*). *Monstrans de droit* is "a suit at Chancery to be restored to lands or tenements, that indeed be mine in right, though they were by some office found to be in possession of another lately dead" (*ibid.*). *Office* here is "an Inquisition made to the King's use of anything by virtue of his office who inquirith" (*ibid.*), e.g. the finding of a coroner's court.
[4] When the house of lords had exercised it, it had done so as the council in parliament: when a similar jurisdiction was needed in Tudor times it was exercised by the council elsewhere, especially in the star chamber.
[5] Cf. McIlwain, pp. 118, 133, and his references to Palgrave, *Report on Public Petitions*, Parl. Papers, 1833, XII, p. 19, and to Hargrave's Preface to Hale's *Jurisdiction of the Lords House*, p. viii.
[6] Holdsworth, I, p. 214.

But *parliament* as the corrector of error means *king in parliament*. A writ of error was a royal mandate issued at the royal discretion, directing the court complained against to send the record "to us in our Parliament... that we may further cause to be done thereupon, with the assent of the Lords Spiritual and Temporal in the same Parliament, for correcting that error, what of right and according to the law and custom of England ought to be done".[1] The lords were accustomed to exercise this jurisdiction also, and in 1485 it was decided by all the judges to be vested exclusively in them:[2] it was little used under the Tudors, but began to be revived at the end of their time.[3]

Such were the specifically judicial functions of parliament (which meant the lords of parliament) at the end of the fifteenth century. The comparative judicial somnolence of parliament at that time was due to such reasons as the weakness of the nobility, the irregularity of sessions, the increased activity of chancery and conciliar jurisdiction, the preoccupation of parliament with purposes which to us look legislative, and its use for purposes that were or should have been judicial of forms apter (by modern notions) for legislation.[4] I mean acts of attainder and of reversal. Unlike the other judicative capacities of parliament, important for the Tudor period merely because they existed and were not used but might be, on the contrary attainder and its appendants were then at their most active: they were unlike most parliamentary jurisdiction for another reason too, because with regard to them it was natural to assume the participation of the commons.

The proper and full effect of attainder was to inflict a more than capital punishment:[5] the victim might lose not only his natural life but also his legal life and all the consequences of ever having had a legal life, so that for legal purposes no descent could be traced from him, his children were disinherited, and all his property forfeited to the king. The method was by bill originating from king or either house, passed by both houses and completed by the royal assent, alleging the mis-

---

[1] Pike, 294.
[2] *Y.B.* 1 H. VII Pasch. pl. 5 (p. 20), quoted by Holdsworth, I, p. 362.
[3] Holdsworth, I, p. 370.
[4] Cf. McIlwain, p. 132.
[5] But the extreme penalty was not necessarily awarded.

deeds of the accused and affixing the penalties with all the legal force of the kingdom.

This process became usual during the factious struggles of the fifteenth century, when the alternations of conflict installed in power now one government and now another which was tempted by the desire of revenge and driven by the need of security to destroy the leaders of the vanquished as speedily, as utterly, and with as much appearance of legality as possible: it had the special advantages that not merely the attainted but his family also was destroyed, and that there was no escape, even by death, from its jurisdiction.

Attainder was thus habitually the act of a parliament which was itself the result of a battle or a revolution. It is not surprising if the accused had no guarantee of judicial treatment and if the procedure was summary and undefined; no more, indeed, was indispensable than the reading of a bill in the parliament chamber and its acceptance by the king.[1] Even the necessity of consulting the commons had not yet become matter of course, for in 1489 "in the parliament the king wished that so-and-so be attainted and lose his lands: and the Lords assented and nothing was said of the Commons. Wherefore all the Judges hold clearly that it was not an Act. Wherefore he was restored, &c."[2] Moreover, it is to be remembered that the occasion when "ther was many gentlemen agaynst it, but it wold not be, for it was the Kings pleasure",[3] was the wholesale attainting of 1485, and that there is no evidence of the assent of the commons being as yet necessarily anything more than the merest and most passive acquiescence.

Henry VII submitted without protest to the judges' opinion that the consent of both branches of parliament was requisite to an attainder.[4]

[1] Pollard, *Evolution of Parliament*, p. 263.
[2] Pollard, *Reign of Henry VII*, ii, p. 19, prints the quotation in the French of the Year Books, 4 H. VII, p. 18.
[3] Cf. p. 93 above.
[4] Henry VIII in 1538 (Countess of Salisbury's Case, cf. Coke, *Institutes*, iv, pp. 37, 38) thought necessary to get a judicial opinion (which proved to be grudging) that parliament could attaint without trial or citation to appear. Attainder had habitually been used "to confirm a sentence already passed in some court of law, or to ensure the destruction of such as might possibly escape by the openness of a common law trial": e.g. Empson and Dudley, Exeter, Montacute, Darcy, Hussey, were all formally tried. Cf. J. Reeves, *History of the English Law* (2nd edn. 1787),

In a matter closely related, the reversing of attainders, he was again respectful of parliament and may be thought to have begun that characteristically Tudor process by which monarchs, confident of their ability to manage their parliaments, made parliamentary sanction of their whole conduct habitual and thus tended to make it for their successors indispensable. The reversal of attainder has always been a matter for royal initiative, it might have been argued that it was altogether within the prerogative of pardon, and there was precedent for acting on that view, at least to the extent of relieving from attainder by advice of the council only.[1] Henry preferred another method: the twenty-eighth chapter of the acts of the parliament of his nineteenth year[2] accordingly recites how "the King Our Sovereign Lord considering that divers and many persons were and be attainted of High Treason,...and have made instant and diligent pursuit in the most humble wise to his Highness, of his mercy and pity, to have the said Attainders reversed", and how he is "inclined to hear and speed reasonably the said petitioners, so if there were convenient time and space in this present Parliament, as it is not, for the great and weighty matters concerning the common weal,...and that the said Parliament draweth so near to an end, and that after the same his Highness is not minded, for the ease of his subjects, without great necessary and urgent causes, of long time to summon a new Parliament, by which long tract of time, the said suitors and petitioners, were and should be discomforted...": in consideration of which premises "the King's Highness is agreed and contented that it be enacted by assent of the Lords Spiritual and Temporal, and the Commons..." that he shall have

---

IV, p. 408: he mentions also "the attainders of Sir Thomas More and bishop Fisher for misprision of treason; which, perhaps because a case that did not extend to life, they ventured on without the examination of witnesses, or hearing them in their defence. On the other hand, in a capital case, the Maid of Kent and her accomplices were all examined in the star-chamber, though not in parliament, before the bill of attainder passed upon them...we do not find that the result of such examination was always laid before parliament to enable them to form a judgement.... The privy counsellors had taken their resolution; and if they were satisfied, the houses seldom concerned themselves as to any further enquiry".

[1] *Cal. Pat. Rolls*, 4 E. IV, p. 321, quoted by J. F. Baldwin, *The King's Council*, p. 427.
[2] Feb. 1504: my quotation is (spelling apart) from Pollard, *Reign of Henry VII*, p. 17, referring to *R.P.* VI, p. 526 and *S.R.* II, p. 669.

power during his life by letters patent in the cases of the persons named and their heirs, and of any other persons and their heirs attainted by act of parliament or the common law since August 22 of his first year or during the reign of Richard III, "to reverse, annul, repeal, and avoid all the attainders" and "to restore the same persons so attainted and their heirs..., as if the said attainders or any of them had never been made...".[1]

Attainder and reversal were judicative in effect, though essentially unjudicial by modern standards, the attainted not being entitled to opportunity of presenting argument or evidence.[2] The procedure was procedure by bill: this was the parliament's common procedure for all sorts of work,[3] whether a modern analysis would label it legislative, judicative, executive, or taxative. Such analysis was not practised, but there were different sorts of bills, and the names and something of the stories of them are necessary to an understanding of what parliament meant at the end of the fifteenth century and what were its relation and its potentiality to Henry VII.

The clearest distinction was that "if it is a common bill it will be enrolled and enacted, but if it is a private bill it will not be enrolled but will be filed on the files and that is good enough, but if the party wishes to sue for the entry to be more sure it could be enrolled".[4] There had been another distinction, that private bills, just because they were less matters of general interest to be fortified by general consent, had been much less parliamentary in a modern sense, much less connected with anything legislative or representative, than commons bills, and had not required commons approval. As has been seen,[5] the commons in 1399

---

[1] In 1523 similar power was given to Henry VIII for life.
[2] Cf. p. 119 above.
[3] Cf. p. 142 below.
[4] Kirkeby clerk of the rolls in *Y.B.* 33 H. VI Pasch. pl. 8, fol. xvii: cf. H. L. Gray, *Influence of the Commons on Early Legislation*, p. 7, for the same rule in the seventeenth century. The difference of intention was roughly what it is now: "Parliament now understands by private Bills all those projects of law which affect the interests of particular localities, persons or corporations, and are not of a public general character", Wm. F. Craies, *Treatise on Statute Law* (edn. 1923), p. 465 (edn. 1911, p. 480), p. 482 (edn. 1911). Cf. Riess, *Geschichte des Wahlrechts zum englischen Parlament*, p. 106, and his reference to *R.P.* II, pp. 201, 316; III, p. 45.
[5] Above, p. 111.

had disclaimed participation in the judgments of parliament and had been excused from advising or assenting save "in statutes to be made, or in grants and subsidies, or such things to be made for common profit of the realm". The corresponding procedural distinction[1] had been that private bills were handed not to the clerk of parliament but to receivers[2] of petitions, who passed them on to auditors or triers, a committee of anything up to a dozen lords, bishops, and judges, the co-operation of the judges not being indispensable.[3]

The primary purpose of this committee of grandees and ministers was to find remedy for what could not without parliamentary help be remedied: the help would generally be by way of deciding which court the petition should be remitted to:[4] and though the help was thus parliamentary, its basis seems to a modern mind very "unparliamentary", the receivers and triers being chosen before parliament met, their names announced at the very beginning even before the speaker was elected.

But as the weight of the commons increased, it was drawn in to push bills that were not public: already by the end of Richard II's reign there were premonitions, it was no longer quite true that private bills addressed to king and lords were never referred to commons, and at the very end some were even addressed to the commons.[5] Under Henry IV "they were coming within the survey and competence of the commons",[6] and it was becoming usual to enter them on the parliament roll. An increasing number of private petitions was being addressed to the commons, and even to the commons alone,[7] and the commons were forwarding to the lords private bills endorsed with their assent,[8] and

[1] Gray, pp. 338, 339, quotes only the case of 1346 as drawing the distinction with absolute clearness, but alleges "every reason to think that the procedure was maintained throughout the fourteenth and fifteenth centuries".
[2] Chancery clerks.   [3] McIlwain, p. 198
[4] Cf. Stubbs, *Constitutional History*, III, p. 469; McIlwain, p. 200; Maitland, *Memoranda de Parliamento*, pp. lvi, lxviii–lxxii; and J. F. Baldwin, p. 325, in the time of Edward III at the request of the commons the auditors deprived of power to answer petitions when the determination of any point of law was involved.
[5] Gray, p. 336.   [6] Gray, p. 342.
[7] Gray, pp. 352, 356.
[8] Instead of adopting such a bill and forwarding it as their own, cf. Gray, pp. 367, 242, 243.

were beginning to express assent to private bills sent down to them from the lords[1]; and the first case[2] appears of their assent being asked to a bill not addressed to them, when the archbishop of Canterbury brought to them his petition against a papal bull exempting the Cistercians from tithe, with the king's declaration, backed by the lords, that the bull should not be put into execution and that he would ask the pope to annul it, and when the commons agreed. By 1509 commons were actually among the auditors, four of their members being included.[3] But by then for a long generation private bills had been established in the modern sense, to be introduced in either house and then passed in the other:[4] and by then, on the other hand, the private petitioner seems to have been once again trusting to king much more than commons, for once again most of the private bills enrolled were addressed to the king.[5] And the old function of private bills and auditors, the supply of extraordinary jurisdiction for unusual needs, was being performed by the Tudor adaptations of council and chancery.

If private bills had thus been getting more like public bills, and both kinds becoming round the turn of the century in some sense "less parliamentary", more royal, it had been just as much because the public bill was copying the private as the other way about.

Besides private bills there were two other sorts distinguishable from the ordinary public bill: subsidy bills were in the fifteenth century called *indentures* or *indentured schedules*,[6] and were actually in two halves indented, serrated, like many other contracts. And bills of general pardon were called *pardons* or *cedules*:[6] they were entirely of royal grace and naturally required no form of advice or assent, only acceptance.

[1] Gray, p. 370.
[2] 1401, Gray, p. 364.
[3] Gray, pp. 29, 338.
[4] Gray, p. 376: he suggests that the reference to the auditors may now have been at the stage of forwarding from one house to the other.
[5] Gray, p. 377.
[6] Gray, pp. 45, 41: where did the commons put their copies? Gray suggests that they formed the germ of commons records: he reports also, p. 41, a case from 1453 where a grant appears to have been amended to the advantage of the government, with "no clue as to how the assent of the commons to the change was got, if, indeed, it was got".

Public bills may be divided into two kinds, commons bills and those which originated with the lords or the government: not that commons bills might not be government bills,[1] only that lords bills always were. Commons bills in the fourteenth century were comprehensive documents each containing all the commons requests of a session,[2] and the result was a statute of several articles which between them re-phrased and enacted such of the requests as were granted. In the fourteen-twenties the comprehensive petition was rapidly and completely replaced by separate specific petitions, some of which now began to be in English.[3] They were forwarded to the lords with an inscription denoting commons approval,[4] and very likely the formulation into specific bills and the treatment of them were imitated by the commons from their practice in forwarding private bills.[5]

The single specific bill was much apter to be developed into something that might give the commons a real control of legislation than had been the comprehensive petition: and there was a beginning of a subsidiary development, an interior hardening of bill procedure which might make it less manageable from above except by way of a disciplined majority in the commons. From the middle of the fifteenth century[6] there are notes of bills having been "read" in either house, and a likelihood of the process having been much like that of 1509; in Henry VII's time the reading might be *sepius, persepe, plerique*,[7] and the bill would be debated, *plenius intellecta*: the readings were beginning to settle down to a ritual number: in 1495, 1497, and 1504 there were triple readings,[8] and that became so much the regular thing that in the next reign a bill could be noted as receiving a third reading twice over.[9]

---

[1] E.g. in 1351 the Statutes of Labourers and Provisors were both initiated by commons requests, Gray, p. 250.

[2] Gray, pp. 210, 223, 229.

[3] Gray, pp. 231, 303.

[4] Soit baille as seigneurs.

[5] Gray, pp. 373, 374: cf. also pp. 54, 336.

[6] Early t.r. Henry V in the lords: cf. Gray, pp. 164, 165.

[7] Cf. the quotations from *R.P.* VI in Pollard, *Reign of Henry VII*, II, p. 20, and references by Gray, p. 166.

[8] Cf. Stubbs, *Constitutional History*, III, p. 459.

[9] E.g. *L.J.* I, pp. 239, 240, A.D. 1543: it looks as if *third reading* had become a special *sort* of reading so that *third* ceased to have a merely numerical significance

If the time was yet far off when a fixed procedure might serve the commons against the crown, on the other hand the commons had long been more than suppliants, had had a legislative history, for which the classical starting-point[1] is 1322. Then, Edward II's parliament rolls spoke of the law made in parliament by king and lords "et tout la Communalte du Roialme". Enactments were not to be made in parliament on petition of the clergy, who had ceased, except the bishops, to attend parliament.[2] In the second year of Henry V the commons petitioned "consideringe that the comune of youre lond, the whiche that is and ever hathe be, a membre of youre Parlemente,[3] ben as well Assenters as Peticioners", that therefore "fro this tyme foreward, by compleynte of the Comune of any myschief axkinge remedie by mouthe of their Speker for the Comune, other ellys by Petition writen, that ther never be no Lawe made theruppon, and engrosed as Statut and Lawe, nother by addicions, nother by diminucions, by no maner of terme ne termes, the whiche that sholde chaunge the sentence, and the entente axked by the Speker mouthe, or the Petitions biforesaid..., without assent of the forsaid Comune". The commons had begun their preamble with the debatable claim that it had ever been "thair liberte and fredom, that thar sholde no Statut no Lawe made of lasse that they yaf therto their assent": the king's reply ignored this, and granted a good deal less than was asked—"that fro hens forth no thyng be enacted to the Peticions of his Comune, that be contrarie of hir askyng, wharby they shuld be bounde withoute their assent".[4] There might still be bills without them,[5] and in 1420 they petitioned

and meant a reading in certain conditions, after certain processes conferring finality. Cf. also *Henry VIII*, p. 458 for bill of attainder receiving second reading on each of two successive days.

[1] Cf. e.g. Holdsworth, I, p. 360 and Pollard, *Evolution of Parliament*, p. 241 for their treatment of the 1322 statute and its requirement of the "commonalty's" participation in "the matters which are to be established for the Estate of our Lord the King and of his Heirs, and for the Estate of the Realm and of the People" (*S.R.* I, p. 189). [2] Cf. Stubbs, *Constitutional History*, II, pp. 596, 597.
[3] But cf. p. 109 above.
[4] *R.P.* IV, p. 22, quoted in Holdsworth, II, p. 439: cf. Pike, p. 325. In the next few parliaments "amendments to commons bills were enrolled with the statement that they had the commons' assent; but after a little the statement no longer appears", Gray, p. 174: cf. also pp. 262, 282, 285, 314, 320, 321, 415.
[5] Cf. p. 122 above.

unsuccessfully against the validity of bills endorsed *per auctoritatem parliamenti* without their assent or request.[1]

Amendments, in the fifteenth century, were often included in the answers endorsed on commons bills,[2] or in later years appended to them on separate parchments,[3] and Henry VII certainly added such provisos without consulting lords or commons—generally, indeed, to make some mere personal exception,[4] but on occasion also to make some real general legal change.[5] Of the few amendments to commons bills which survive from 1444 to 1503 none is inscribed with the commons assent.[6] But in order to understand the extent to which commons bills could at the end of the fifteenth century be amended without their consent, it is necessary to consider a little what "commons bill" had by then come to mean.

Money bills were still far from being purely a matter for the commons. Henry IV in 1407 stated that "grants were granted by the commons and assented to by the lords",[7] but in 1455 Kirkeby,[8] clerk of the rolls, assumed that the lords might reduce, though not increase, the grant of the commons as they pleased without consulting them, and in 1489 the lords by themselves granted a tenth of their income from land, and the commons with the advice and consent of the lords a tenth on their lands and twenty pence on every ten marks of goods.[9]

Throughout the first half of the fifteenth century almost all statutes

[1] Cf. Pollard, *Evolution of Parliament*, p. 327, referring to *R.P.* IV, p. 127: the point seems to have been that bills should not be so endorsed for committal to council or chancellor, so that without the assent of the commons a man might be put to answer "encountre les Leyes de le Roialme d'Engleterre".

[2] Gray, p. 169.

[3] Gray, p. 170.

[4] E.g. the provisos for Anthony Fetiplace and David Philip, *R.P.* VI, pp. 462, 496, quoted by Pollard, *Reign of Henry VII*, II, p. 16: cf. Gray, pp. 177, 192.

[5] Cf. *Y.B.* 1 H. VII Hil. pl. 11 fol. 10 about sanctuary-men making over their property and defrauding their creditors, and the statutes against this which "the king had enlarged so that execution would be made as well of the lands and tenements put in feoffment to their use *bona fide* as of those that were put in feoffment by collusion": cf. p. 178 below. That Henry had recent precedent (1483) is shown by Gray, p. 173.

[6] Gray, p. 177.

[7] *R.P.* III, p. 611.

[8] *Y.B.* 33 H. VI Pasch. pl. 8: cf. p. 133, n. 1 below.

[9] Stubbs, *Seventeen Lectures*, p. 409.

had arisen from commons bills:[1] but in Henry VII's reign although all public statutes were still marked *communes petitions*, yet this no longer meant that there had been even formally commons initiative. The change happened in this way.

From about 1350 to 1450 nearly all statutes were based on commons bills:[2] towards 1430 official bills began, but for another twenty years infrequently, to be enrolled[3] under the caption *communes petitions*:[4] in the 'fifties and 'sixties bills of attainder were drafted so as to be formally commons bills though really official in origin:[5] in the 'sixties bills of resumption ceased to be commons bills and became official:[6] Edward IV's government sometimes, "in order to put its measures in the mouth of the commons, had bills which were properly official bills presented as commons bills":[7] and, generally, in the third quarter of the century there began to be a considerable, and in the last quarter a large, proportion of statutes which were not of commons origin,[8] even though marked *communes petitions*: at the same time, commons bills were very apt to be rejected, and the more important apter than the less:[9] of the later fifteenth century as a whole it may be said that "the share of the commons in legislation was not great",[10] by the time of Richard III "nearly all significant statutory legislation"[11] was based, in Professor Gray's opinion, on official bills.

Accordingly, that government amendments of commons bills do not

---

[1] Gray, pp. 258, 334: cf. Stubbs, *Constitutional History*, II, p. 589: and for the different indorsements on bills of lords and commons origin, cf. *Y.B.* 33 H. VI Pasch. fol. xvii and 7 H. VII Trin. pl. 1, fol. xiv, Vavisor J., "the order is to begin at the commons, and then to the lords by request to the king and then the king says that the king wishes it, and so at the request of the commons and lords, and sometimes the bill is first shown to the lords and then to the commons. . . .". See also in this second case what the other judges said about the nature and effect of statute, and Fineux J.'s remark, "an act of parliament is only judicium and an act like a judgement, And the king, lords and commonalty require to make that judgement, and none of them can be left out".
[2] Cf. the last note, and Gray, p. 168.
[3] Gray, pp. 304, 307, 310.
[4] Gray, p. 90, *communes petitions* "not necessarily commons petitions or bills at all", cf. also pp. 91, 98, 100. Note that the obvious translation of *communes petitions* is "*common* petitions".
[5] Gray, pp. 89, 115.
[6] p. 128.
[7] pp. 67, 107.
[8] p. 310.
[9] pp. 122, 125, 136, 333.
[10] p. 160.
[11] p. 138.

seem to have increased during the century, and that any such amendments under Henry VII can hardly be traced,[1] is much less indicative
of the proportional weight of government and commons in making
acts than is the absence in the later fifteenth century of any evidence
that the commons amended official bills at all.[2]

Henry VII was Lancastrian enough to make use of parliament, but
he was monarchist enough and sufficiently of his time to see and
develop the advantages of what Edward IV and Richard III had begun.
"To the parliaments of Henry VII there was to be presented a greater
number of official bills than of commons bills and the content of the
former was to be more significant than the content of the latter. The
government was largely to replace the commons as the initiator of
statutory legislation."[3]

This was true enough for it to matter less to Henry's royal authority if
it did come at the end of a century of stiffening procedure, of hardening
in the commons share in the process of bill; even if Stubbs[4] were right,
that "the weak point in the position of the commons was their attitude
of petition. The remedy for this was the adoption of a new form of
initiation; the form of bill was substituted for that of petition; the
statute was brought forward in the shape which it was intended ulti-
mately to take, and every modification in the original draught passed
under the eyes of the promoters. The change took place about the end
of the reign of Henry VI".

The words *petition* and *bill* certainly formed no such contrast at the
time: they were "used interchangeably in the chancery down to the
Tudor times, and the same is true in Parliament as well as in the ordinary
speech of the people".[5] Bill was the ordinary means for petitioning
chancery or council for relief. Connected with this is the fact that all
parliamentary deliberation is in the form of a debate, speeches and
replies upon some specific motion.[6]

---

[1] Gray, pp. 188–9.   [2] Gray, p. 199, and the five previous pages.
[3] Gray, p. 141.   [4] *Constitutional History*, II, p. 577.
[5] McIlwain, *High Court of Parliament*, p. 211: cf. his reference to D. M. Kerly,
Hist. Sketch of the Equitable Jurisdiction of Chancery.
[6] For these two sentences, cf. Holdsworth, II, p. 432 and his reference to Redlich,
Procedure of the House of Commons, II, p. 203: cf. p. 107 above.

As has been seen,[1] *communes petitions* were by Henry VII's time not necessarily of commons origin at all, the phrase having become merely a name for bills that were intended for public general statutes. In the first parliament of Henry VIII probably more than a third of the fifteen *communes petitions* originated with the lords.[2]

But, all the same, there was in some sense a tendency from petition to bill, a tendency sufficiently important in Henry VII's reign and later to justify some enquiry what its sense was.

The bill *formam actus in se continens*, formally drafted so that its acceptance meant the enactment of more or less detailed regulations instead of a mere promise to remedy more or less specific grievances, the bill in this sense seems to be almost as old as the fifteenth century, to be so designated since 1461, to have been employed at first for the most important official enactments and then for private bills, but not for commons petitions till the time of Henry VIII.[3]

Along with this development went another, that of "a closer correspondence between many bills and the statutes which arose from them", due to "the increasing tendency to draft a condition attached to the acceptance of a bill as a proviso" inscribed and enrolled, instead of "as an undifferentiated part of the answer":[4] in other words, there is no proper contrast between bill and petition, but there is a greater formality about amendment and a closer identity between bill or petition and the resulting act, and by Henry VII's time all private bills were submitted to the commons,[5] official and private bills were described as drafted to contain in themselves the act form, bills really governmental in origin and intent were labelled *communes petitions*: in Henry's first parliament the only two commons bills[6] of any importance (affirming Henry's title and facilitating the repression of night wanderers) were certainly governmental in origin: generally, official bills throughout the reign preponderated over commons bills.[7] The few

---

[1] Above, pp. 127, 128.
[2] Gray, pp. 30–3.
[3] Gray, pp. 178–82, 412.
[4] Gray, p. 183.
[5] Gray, p. 378.
[6] Cf. Gray, p. 142: and cf. p. 64 above, where I think the act 1 H. VII c. 7 against nocturnal hunting a good deal more important than Gray does.
[7] Cf. Gray, pp. 143–60.

later commons bills that were of any importance seem clearly to have been essentially governmental, as in 1495 enforcing a benevolence and strengthening council and justices of peace against rioters,[1] or as in 1503 dealing with uses.[2]

In the formal ready-drafted bill, in the formal debates and readings and the fixed number of them, in the submission of all bills to the commons[3] and in the ruling against uncovenanted amendments, in all these things there might be the means for the commons some day to rival with the king in the making of statutes, but all these things together did not amount to anything which Henry VII felt as a limitation. Henry never once found it necessary to veto a bill:[4] it is pretty safe to conclude that no bill ever got so far if he disapproved of it. The king might deliver in a bill with his own hand, or a bill might begin "Prayen the commons" or it might begin "The king remembering", or in other ways: but every one of Henry's acts, whatever its nominal origin, must have begun with the royal tolerance at the very least, and some of the proposals made by the commons were certainly made because it was known that they would be welcome to the king. The will of the crown was, at least in matters of what we should call public legislation, the principal factor in the action of the commons.

Bill might, as its use got wider and its method stiffer, develop into an engine by which the commons should share and even control the highest activities of parliament: but it was as yet far from the end of that development, and was indeed even for the first of these purposes, for mere participation, as yet hardly emancipated from the preliminary necessity of royal authorisation: not only that then as now it was convenient, if not indispensable, for government to be represented in the commons sufficiently to preclude the passing of bills likely to embarrass policy or administration, but also that the crown had a large

---

[1] On the lines of 1 H. VII c. 7: and cf. Gray, p. 152.
[2] Cf. p. 166 below, and n.b. that one of Henry VII's first acts, an official one, assisted plaintiffs baffled by feoffments to use, cf. Gray, p. 143.
[3] In 1492 they obtained the repeal of an act on the ground that it had been passed at the suit of a private person in the absence of the "Knyghtes of Shyres and other Noble persounes of" Lancashire, to which it referred, *R.P.* VI, p. 456.
[4] J. Gairdner, *Henry VII*, p. 212.

right to veto bills at their beginning as well as at their end. To exactly the extent to which bill was restrictive, contained in itself the form of an act, to that same extent was its use against the crown improper. To promote a bill for the restriction of the king's rights, the curtailment of his prerogative, or the control of his will, would have seemed hardly less than revolutionary, and as late as the end of Elizabeth's reign arguments of this sort were used against bill procedure in the matter of royal grants of monopolies, though perhaps the arguments might not then have survived destruction if the queen's timely concessions to the practical grievance had not rendered argumentation about principle unnecessary. Certainly the queen thought she was entitled to instruct the speaker to stop the introduction of obnoxious bills, and certainly such instructions from her were effective. At any rate, Henry VII had no need to fear that his commons would pass bills of an unacceptable kind, and throughout the period of his dynasty bill was not a device for use by the commons against the crown.

CHAPTER V

LAW AND STATUTE, KING AND CROWN

Although the judges had long lost their right to consent to acts of parliament, yet they continued to play a great part in the making of them.[1] They were the king's legal experts, summoned to parliament as such, and it was natural therefore that statutes should owe much to them. Examples have been given above of their deciding how parliament should act—that the king's attainder did not need reversal, for instance, or that the participation of the commons was necessary to an attainder. They were the natural draughtsmen, also, of statutes (though the development of bill was tending to reduce their opportunities in this connection), and the natural experts on the legal and, as we should say, constitutional effects of a proposed bill. In Henry VIII's reign it was the custom for the lords to receive copies of bills under discussion in the commons so that they might hear the judges' opinions of them before they were sent up,[2] and if it were not the custom in his father's time the reason was, no doubt, that the judges had discussed the bills before the commons. The judges were always among the triers of petitions. If the lords thought it necessary to send a bill to committee the judges were members of the committee, long after they had ceased to be members of parliament, as late as Henry VIII, as late as Elizabeth.[3] Moreover, not only were the judges the interpreters of statute but also they decided whether something which was asserted and denied to be a statute was effectively a statute or not, and before deciding they could

[1] McIlwain, p. 35.
[2] Pollard, *Evolution of Parliament*, p. 34, referring to *L. and P.* H. VIII, vol. xii, pt. i, no. 901 (39, 40): Aske's report in 1537 of what he had heard from Darcy, that the lords received upon request a copy of the bill to be scanned by their learned counsel, and that lately it had not been so easy.
[3] T. E. May, *Parliamentary Practice* (13th edn. 1924), p. 195, and his references to *L.J.* I, pp. 586, 606, and S. D'Ewes, *Journals*, pp. 99, 143. (D'Ewes evidently thought the committal to the judges odd.)

discuss parliamentary procedure and question the officials of the rolls and the clerk of parliament.[1]

It was well-established law[2] (as it still is, but with great reservation and a different connotation[3]) that the crown is not bound by statute unless there are express words to that effect. The king's right to limit the operation of a statute by suspending it for a period or dispensing with it for a person was as yet very far from definition. His right to legislate without statute, by proclamation, was large, was not by any means precisely limited, and was highly effective so long as he could rely upon his prerogative courts to punish breaches of proclamation. The judges in applying statutes had wide rights of interpretation and construction.

But there was no doubt that statute was the highest legal act there could be in the kingdom of England. And it might seem at first sight equally clear that there was no limit to its competence: in 1453[4] the judges excused themselves from participation in a case of parliamentary privilege on the ground that the "high Court of Parliament...is so high and so mighty in his nature, that it may make law, and that that is law it may make no law....". Even two generations earlier than this there had been a declaration of similar appearance, for in the "appeal and process" (1387–8) against Nevill, Vere, and the other king's friends, the basis of the fifteenth accusation was that "the law of the Land is made in Parliament by the King, and the Lords Spiritual and Temporal, and all the Commonalty of the Realm".[5] Yet both these assertions were made at moments of revolutionary crisis: the lords appellant were not really claiming for the organ they controlled a legislative omnicom-

---

[1] *Y.B.* 33 H. VI Pasch. fol. xvii: in the discussion one judge pointed out that "the court of parliament is the highest court the king has", and another, after stating that the disputed matter was an act of parliament, added "we wish to be well advised before we annul any act made in the parliament". And it was incidentally argued, and apparently accepted, that the lords could alter a bill coming from the commons without consulting them so long as the bill so altered did not grant more than the commons had granted, "as if the commons grant tonnage and poundage for four years, etc. And the lords grant, but for two years, it will not be re-delivered to the commons": cf. p. 126 above.
[2] Cf. P. Vinogradoff, on p. 281, vol. XXIX, *Law Quarterly Review*.
[3] Wm. F. Craies, *Treatise on Statute Law* (2nd edn. 1911), p. 376.
[4] Cf. p. 111 above, Thorp's Case.   [5] *R.P.* III, p. 243.

petence but rather an unbounded jurisdiction, an illimitable right to try and condemn: and the king granted that great matters moved or to be moved in parliament touching peers of the land should be decided not by civil law nor by common law but by the course of parliament.[1] If the appellants had been desirous of acting as a revolutionary tribunal, a committee of safety, that was precisely what in the later case the judges did not wish to become: it would be easy to hang too much deduction on the expression of their timidity or on a short passage[2] of Fortescue: "the statutes of England are...not enacted by the sole will of the prince, but with the concurrent consent of the whole kingdom, so that it is morally impossible but that they are and must be calculated for the good of the people: and...full of wisdom and prudence". Every judge of the later fifteenth century knew that acts of parliament were not all the law in England and that he himself had very wide powers of interpreting statutes and, however reluctant to "annul any act made in parliament",[3] would have agreed with a legal writer[4] a generation later that "against this law (of Reason) prescription, statute, nor custom may not prevail: and if any be brought in against it, they be not prescriptions, statutes nor customs, but things void and against justice....If any general custom were against the law of God, or if any statute were made directly against it..., the custom and statute were void". Or, to show from a different angle the way in which the very mind of those times limited the competence of statute, for them the year-book[5] was but perpetuating a truism when it said, "the

---

[1] *R.P.* III, p. 244: when the sages of the common law and the civil law had said that the appeal was not according to the one law or the other, the lords had declared, by assent of the king, that with so high a crime, touching the person of the king and the state of his whole realm, perpetrated by peers of the realm, the case must be tried by law and course of parliament, and it is the liberty of the lords by ancient custom of parliament to be judges, and to adjudge the case by assent of the king; England was never governed by the civil law nor ever should be (p. 336).

[2] *On the Laws of England*, ch. XVIII (I, p. 402 in Lord Clermont's edition), written about 1470. Cf. p. 163, n. 4 below.

[3] Fortescue in *Y.B.* 33 H. VI Pasch. pl. 8, fol. xvii: cf. p. 133, n. 1 above.

[4] Christopher Saint-German, whose *Doctor and Student* (in which see dialogue I, chs. 2 and 6) was published from 1523 to 1531 (*D.N.B.*). Cf. McIlwain, p. 300.

[5] 19 H. VI Pasch. pl. 1, fol. lxiii. The speaker was Chief Baron Fray: the deductions to be made were not axiomatic, indeed the deductions Fray proceeded to were at once disputed. Cf. Plucknett in *Tudor Studies*, p. 164.

Parliament is the King's Court and the highest court he has, and the Law is the highest inheritance that the King has, for by the Law he himself and all his subjects are ruled, and if there were no Law there would be no King and no inheritance". Law was what princes (if they were not mere tyrants) and their courts (however high) and all political institutions hung upon, and they could not unfix it.

"Law", writes a learned medievalist,[1] "is here sovereign, and not the State, i.e. the Community, the Authority, the Prince.... The State cannot alter Law. That would be to commit something like matricide.... A Law which is identical with the Good-in-Itself is of course before and above the State...it is not to be deduced that in practice also the Law was respected with especial sanctity". That was still the natural way of thinking and feeling in Henry VII's time: Law, the Law which all temporary and local arrangements must subserve, was still in theory a matter of knowledge, however much in danger of being disputed about or sinned against, and not a matter of will, however widespread or solemnly asserted: but for long already there had been in practice ways of modifying, even of abolishing or new modelling, the rules on which the courts could be expected to act, that is, the law with a little l: and there had been expressions from high authorities which might seem, to those who half saw a new theory or had half forgotten the old, to admit the possibility of altering Law. The possibility drew nearer with the habituation to statute: statute was in idea "a modification of the law of the land, which henceforth the courts would apply[2]...something which extended the common law and had the same validity as the common law":[3] it might be held void for conflict with the law of the land[4] (including the law of God, reason, and the king's prerogative): but in so far as it partook of the nature of Law and

---

[1] Fritz Kern, "Recht und Verfassung im Mittelalter", published in the *Historische Zeitschrift*, CXX, p. 11 (1919). The whole article is very clear and instructive.
[2] H. L. Gray, *Influence of the Commons on Early Legislation*, p. 96.
[3] Gray, p. 381.
[4] Cf. Gray, pp. 382, 383, 384. My statement does not seem to me invalidated by Prof. Gray's remarks that the "effort to define a statute as legislation which extended the common law and was to endure forever...was abandoned by the beginning of the fifteenth century" (p. 408) and that "the term statute came to be less and less used in the fifteenth century" (p. 386).

yet was valid only pending repeal,[1] it led minds towards the possibility of altering Law.

It was over local and peculiar law that statute decisively triumphed in Tudor times. The modern norm of one system of positive law possessing legal finality for all the persons and all the relations of a certain territory had been as far as possible from being the normal arrangement of the Middle Ages. By the end of the fifteenth century the legal competence of statute to control or destroy every legal autonomy or exception in England (leaving aside the question of the Church), its *legal* competence was by then no new claim: and the claim had no effective resistance to fear, because practically Henry VII was too powerful to be withstood by any feudal magnate or particularist corporation. Parliaments had developed a habit of specifying the application of their statutes *tam infra quam extra libertates*, as well inside as outside liberties:[2] other courts also had long been striving to circumscribe and retrench liberties and sanctuaries.[3] Commons and kings were well aware that in this process they were serving each others' interests and were doing together what neither could well have done alone. As far back as 1347 the commons had petitioned the king to refrain from granting liberties to the hindrance of the common law and oppression of the people, and had been promised that liberties should not in the future be granted unadvisedly.[4]

The king's supremacy over all liberties was fully asserted by Lancastrian lawyers, though its effectiveness in practice was not matter of course: "Every franchise commences by the grant of the king....If in

---

[1] Cf. p. 135, n. 4.
[2] Pollard, *Evolution of Parliament*, p. 145. And cf. pp. 66 ff. above.
[3] Cf. I. D. Thornley in *Tudor Studies* (ed. R. W. Seton-Watson), p. 197; and p. 54, above.
[4] *R.P.* II, p. 166: two generations later, when in a parliament called to regularise the revolution of 1399, the commons wished that Henry IV "be in as great Liberty Royal as his noble progenitors were before" (*R.P.* III, p. 434), no doubt they were wishing what the triumphant usurper wished, but there is no reason to suppose that they did not really wish it, did not see their advantage in the maintenance of the Liberty Royal, in the subordination of all private and peculiar franchises. They recalled that Richard had used the same Liberty to "turn the laws to his will" but declared their confidence that the new king "had no will to turn the Laws, Statutes, and good Customs".

any return, the bailiff of a liberty is mentioned, and it is not said whose franchise it is, he shall be intended to be the bailiff of the king, and the franchise to be in the hands of the king": and a little later (1429) it appears that the king can grant only by record, for "nothing passes from the king without matter of record".[1]

To make real the policy of subordinating privileges of locality and association was to be the pre-eminent feat of the Tudors. Henry VII in his parliament of 1495 "for very zeal and gracious favour that he beareth to the common weal of this his realm, not willing his true and faithful liege people and subjects to fail of remedy...by reason of such franchise as was used within" North and South Tynedale, enacted with the assent of the lords and commons that those lordships should lose their franchises and become part of the county of Northumberland.[2] The franchise of Tynedale had been in the king's hands for generations,[3] and Henry VII was able to emphasise and extend the control of king in parliament over local immunities at least as much because he was himself the great engrosser of feudality as because there were precedents for the competence of statute *infra libertates*. He used his resources so well that his son was able, on the assumption by then already long orthodox that wherever "prerogatives and authorities of Justice" were not attached to the crown they must have been "severed and taken from the same by sundry gifts", by one general act of parliament to resume them wholesale.[4]

The subordination of corporations was also made clear. In the year 1504 a statute[5] beginning with the words "Prayen the Commons", but doubtless originating in the policy of the king, recited the act of 15 H. VI c. 6[6] against the unlawful and unreasonable ordinances of

---

[1] H. A. Merewether and J. S. Stephens, *History of Boroughs*, p. 914, quoting from *Y.B.* 1422, fol. 6B and 1429, pl. 11, fol. 29A.
[2] *R.P.* VI, p. 575.　　　　　[3] I. D. Thornley, *Tudor Studies*, p. 200.
[4] 27 H. VIII c. 24: cf. Pollard, *Reign of Henry VII*, p. xxx; and below, p. 148.
[5] 19 H. VII c. 7: cf. p. 148 below. Cf. also Williams, p. 179, for the earl of Surrey's jurisdiction as Lieutenant in the North, 1492, and for the agreement between the freemen of York to forswear all but local jurisdiction; and I. S. Leadam, *Requests*, p. 7, for conciliar jurisdiction defending a royal patentee against the City of London authorities.
[6] 1467: this act directed all gilds to register their letters patent and charters before the justices of peace or the chief governors of towns: it was to stand during pleasure,

gilds, fraternities and other companies corporate, and after this recital proceeded to enact that

> no Masters, Wardens and fellowships of Crafts...nor any rulers of guilds or fraternities, take upon them to make any act or ordinances, nor to execute any acts or ordinances by them heretofore made...but if the same acts or ordinances be examined and approved by the Chancellor Treasurer of England and chief Justices of either Bench, or three of them; or before both the Justices of Assizes in their circuit...in that Shire....And over that it is enacted that none of the same bodies Corporate take upon them to make any acts or ordinances to restrain any person or persons to sue to the King's Highness or to any of his Courts....

By the end of the fifteenth century a good deal had been done towards making the idea of *corporation* explicit and technical. Lawyers were already of opinion, largely influenced by Roman Law and clearly contributing to the development of what was to become state sovereignty, that a corporation can be called into existence only by a definite[1] act of the prince. That is one technicality about corporations which was to have great importance for constitutional theory and practice: another is that there is a plain distinction between the corporation, that artificial person created by the law and therefore altogether subject to it, and the natural persons of whom it is composed. This was getting settled just about the time when the Tudor period began: in

and the act of 1504 alleged that it had expired: perhaps it had been held void by Henry VI's deposition, suggests I. S. Leadam, *Select Cases in Star Chamber*, I, p. cli. Apart from statute, it had been normal in the fifteenth century for a gild on incorporation to submit its by-laws for approval by the municipality, cf. I. S. Leadam, *Select Cases in the Star Chamber*, II, p. cv: and cf. below, p. 148.

[1] Cf. p. 137 above and see *Y.B.* 2 H. VII Hil. pl. 16, fol. 13, referred to by F. W. Maitland, *Collected Papers*, III, p. 215: Sjt. Fineux argued that it would be dangerous to admit that the king's charter could be construed to make a corporation by *implication:* and Sjt. Keble, "corporation is a thing which is proper to be made by the king himself and by his words and he cannot give licence to another to make a corporation"; yet in 1522 Fineux C.J. said that there were some corporations by the common law, as "the parliament of the king and the lords and the commons are a corporation". Quoted by Maitland, *Coll. Papers*, III, p. 247, from *Y.B.* 14 H. VIII Mich. pl. 2, fol. 3. But was Fineux right about parliament? and what other corporations at common law could he have cited? In any case he seems to have been clear that the normal corporation owed its existence either to the king or to the pope. Cf. *Henry VIII*, p. 285.

1481 it was still possible to cite in argument the case of a bond between the mayor and commonalty of Newcastle and the man who happened at the time to be mayor, which bond had been held invalid on the ground that a man cannot be bound to himself:[1] in 1488 the mayor and commonalty of York endeavoured to justify themselves as individuals against a writ of trespass, but it was ruled that the writ was against them as one corporate person and that therefore the justification was no plea.[2] To argue that the distinction between a corporation and its components was quite unknown at the end of Edward IV's reign and perfectly understood at the beginning of Henry VII's would be excessive, but certainly it was gaining clarity and effect at about that time.

Another development of the corporation idea[3] which is discernible in the fifteenth century, to become conspicuous in the sixteenth, is the corporation sole, consisting not of a combination of individuals but of one single individual regarded in a distinguishable official capacity. In the fifteenth century the conception was being evolved to suit chantry priests:[4] as late as 1522 it was still neither very clear nor very familiar,[5] but by then one thing at any rate was clear and familiar, the distinction between the two capacities of the head of a corporation, the capacity in which he takes to his own use and the capacity in which he

---

[1] Vavisour's citation is referred to by Maitland, *Coll. Papers*, III, p. 308. It is at *Y.B.* 21 E. IV Mich. pl. 57, fol. 68, and the case to which Vavisour referred appears to have been *Y.B.* 17 E. III (Rolls Society edition by I. S. Leadam), p. 70, though the reference does not appear to bear out his argument. Cf. also Holdsworth, III, p. 482.

[2] Quoted from *Y.B.* 1488, 4 H. VII, fol. 13 B., Trin. Term, pl. 11, by H. A. Merewether and J. A. Stephens, *History of Boroughs*, vol. II, p. 1069.

[3] Cf. Holdsworth, III, pp. 469 ff.

[4] Maitland, *Coll. Papers*, III, p. 214.

[5] Maitland, *Coll. Papers*, says that "Fineux C.J. B. R., was, if I catch the sense of his words, declaring that a corporation sole would be an absurdity, a nonentity": but it may be doubted, with great respect, whether he has caught the sense of the chief justice, who said (if I translate him rightly) "...for although the king wish to make a corporation to J. S. that is not good, because reason says, that is not a permanent thing, and cannot have successor...": is not the characteristic of corporations to which Fineux is here referring rather their immortality than their compositeness? so that he might have seen no objection to the king's making a corporation of an office-holder and his successors, though he thought it impossible for a private individual specified only by his personal name?

takes to the use of his house, and the distinction was being applied to the king,[1] as, for instance, to distinguish between the things he does as the head of parliament and the things he can do without parliament.[2]

Edward III had had to distinguish between his two kingships, of England and of France, and to promise his English subjects that they should not at any time to come be put into subjection "nor in obeisance of us nor of our heirs and successors as kings of France".[3] Distinctions of this sort were not new, and they had already long since contained the embryo of a distinction between king and crown: that was bound to be so as soon as there was an ordered expectable course of administration, especially as soon as there was a seal whose keeper might use it in the king's absence, more especially as soon as there was more than one such seal: as when Edward I died at Burgh-on-Sands on 7 January 1307 but his chancellor continued to issue writs of course till the 25th;[4] or when Richard II after declaring formally that he had resigned the throne took from his finger "annulum auri de signeto suo patentium", and placed it on the finger of Henry IV;[5] or when the king himself found it necessary to request his chancellor to present particular persons to benefices which were nominally in his own gift;[6] or when in 1454 the council substituted the Privy Seal, which was in their control, for the Signet of the Eagle as the mainspring of the duchy of Lancaster;[7] or as when attempts were made to restrict the king's power of issuing immediate warrants for the application of his seals, attempts none of

[1] Cf. Fortescue (ed. Clermont), *On the Law of Nature*, p. 154, how there is no right to reign nor to transmit such a right in a king's daughter, "quo medio sanguis et *hereditas privata* avi transferri potest in nepotem (grandson); respectu tamen regni, quod *publicum dominium* est et quod ab avo filia recipere nequit nec transferre potest..." (my italics). Henry V could leave his property by will, but parliament decided that he could not bequeath the kingdom (*R.P.* IV, p. 326). T.r. Henry VII it was recognised that the king might be seised of land "in right of the crown or otherwise" (*R.P.* 7 H. VII, no. 5, VI, p. 444, quoted Holdsworth, III, p. 468). Cf. *Henry VIII*, p. 283, king cannot be feoffee to use, because corporations cannot and all gifts to him are to his corporate capacity; *Henry VIII*, p. 125, Wolsey persuaded to surrender York Place.

[2] Cf. Fineux again, in the same case 14 H. VIII, fol. ii, and Holdsworth, III, p. 468.

[3] Adams and Stephens, p. 105, referring to *S.R.* I, p. 292.

[4] H. C. M. Lyte, *The Great Seal*, p. 87.

[5] *Ibid.* p. 117.   [6] *Ibid.* p. 221.

[7] *Ibid.* p. 124.

which, however, went so far as to deny his right of giving orders to his chancellor without the intervention of signet or privy seal.[1]

All this about distinctions between various royal capacities is a digression from considering the supremacy of central authority over local and particular corporations: boroughs were not less than other associations subject to statute, as may be seen in the acts regulating the governments of Northampton, Leicester, and Exeter.[2] In short, it is clear that statute was already supreme (even sovereign, if the word must be used, but it had better be kept waiting a little longer), in this sense, that it pronounced the last word, from which there was no appeal, on what was lawful and unlawful in all secular transactions within the realm of England. To any question which English law or government could properly raise statute could give a decisive answer,[3] and the answer would generally be effective in practice as well as decisive in law, now that statutes were established by a king stronger than any of his lords or even all of them, and in sympathy with his commons or at least the preponderance of them. This looks so much like what the nineteenth century has called legislative sovereignty and was in fact so different from it, that it needs further explanation.

One difference, perhaps the greatest of all, lay in the unconsciousness with which legislation was accomplished still at the beginning of the sixteenth century. This unconsciousness was not absolute and can be exaggerated, but almost any degree of exaggeration would be less misleading than understatement. For it is only when legislation is completely conscious that it can grasp sovereignty or omnicompetence.

[1] *Ibid.* p. 159 and neighbouring pages. Cf. T. F. Tout, *Chapters in Medieval Administrative History*, v, pp. 226–30—failure of Richard II's attempt to make the signet the special engine of prerogative: to the late seventeenth century it was regarded as appropriate to the king's private capacity but in practice was becoming another public seal, the *primum mobile* of an elaborate administrative process: similarly the secretary becoming a state officer with public responsibilities: fifteenth-century secretary often promoted to privy seal: T. Cromwell the first lay secretary: down to 1689 the secretaries, like clerks of signet and privy seal, were still attached to the chamber: the sign manual coming into the administrative stream above the signet: statutory stereotyping of the routine 27 H. VIII c. 11, cf. *Henry VIII*, p. 282: French parallels. "The office was greater than the man, and the strongest king could not successfully distinguish between the two", as was settled in 1399, after which date "no manifestation of the royal authority can be divested of its official character".
[2] Cf. the quotations in Pollard, *Reign of Henry VII*, II, pp. 181 ff.
[3] Cf. p. 90, above.

There were infinite gradations in the practice of parliament, from acts of great and general importance and, in modern categories, of legislative character, to acts of private interest and judicial character, acts all performed by the same authority and mainly along the same procedural lines.[1] An early Tudor parliament was never forced into consciousness that it was acting as a legislature by the use of words and forms which would have been plainly out of place had it been acting in any other capacity. Nor was this scarcely differentiated performance of all of its duties under forms which have since come to seem appropriate to only one class of them a peculiar practice, unlike anything to be found in other courts. Every court in England performed functions that were legislative and some that were administrative as well as those that were judicative, justices of peace and justices of assize no less truly, if less freely, than lords of parliament.[2] It was precisely as the activity of parliament became familiar and effective that justice and jury were confined, mainly in practice and almost exclusively in common opinion, to judicial work.[3] That their purpose had been executive as well as judicial made their action sometimes rather less than ideally arbitral: that their forms were always those of judicature preserved it at the worst from appearing nakedly arbitrary, and had something to do with the English trust in the courts and the English willingness to believe that a dispute is most likely to come right after public discussion, free exchange of evidence and argument.

Since, then, it was only very gradually that the other courts were becoming consciously peculiar as the judicature, it is not surprising that the high court of parliament, though consciously unique by virtue of supremacy, was not yet consciously peculiar as the legislature. Besides that great mass of its acts which came somewhere below the line dividing those which may be held to be legislative from those which

---

[1] Cf. p. 121 above.

[2] Cf. pp. 49, 61, 73 above. And cf. p. 161 below for the view that the king enjoyed taxation as a perquisite of his high court of parliament.

[3] Cf. Holdsworth, II, p. 441; IV, pp. 137 ff. The judges of assize were general governmental agents, and reported, e.g., who were suitable to be sheriffs or justices of the peace; M.P.s were utilised for making known new statutes, cf. Williams, p. 145 (and note also his reference to the official printing of statutes early in the next reign).

were certainly judicial, it served also purposes which were clearly administrative and political, clearly to any one aware of those categories even if ignorant of the words: as, for instance, the hearing of the lord chancellor's sermons declaring to the whole realm the king's policy and its duty: the general usefulness of parliament in collecting information and distributing instruction to the localities, and especially the usefulness of the presence there of local dignitaries and royal officers side by side: the employment of members to see that the taxes which they had voted were properly assessed and collected, or to take back to their constituencies the weights and measures which were to be the standard of uniformity:[1] combined with the fact that there was nowhere in England a court exclusively judicative, all these things tended to keep parliament from the belief that it was principally a maker of new rules, *novel ley*, or potentially a Maker of Law.

Nevertheless a court which is consciously supreme, beyond which there is no legal appeal, is compelled, whatever its theory, to do more than apply law, to extend, to develop, it on occasion: and indeed the judges of other English courts also were accustomed to doing so. The medieval idea of Law as an absolute, a good in itself, the voice of God heard by the ear of Reason, unalterable because eternal, that was lofty enough: but the technique stumbled as much as the idea soared. Whose ears were attuned to the divine utterance? whose reasons were right? These were great questions, and there was no unmistakable test between conflicting answers. The modern state has ceased to ask questions so difficult, perceiving that for the convenience of social life the great need is certainty. The beginnings of certainty came from the activity of a supreme court: it provided a test, a method of applying to every case the laws of England; the reinforcement of authority and the intensification of social relations led to the identification of the laws of England with Law. Responsibility for the rules of a society in conscious and even boasted movement enforced the lesson that rules might come into being or go out of force, introduced the notion that an authority supreme for the declaration of law might declare law that which had not been law and not law that which had been law. This was to

[1] Cf. p. 69, n. 1.

make law, and that state which had been law's creature thus become its creator.[1]

How far had this reversal gone in 1485? in what sense did parliament "make" law in Henry VII's time? The fullest sense possible is that in which all the law of the kingdom depends on each parliament, is valid at any given date because the last parliament explicitly or implicitly enacted it, and can be rendered invalid, all or any of it, as soon as the next parliament chooses to repeal it. A modern parliament does not go the whole distance because most of its members would think such extreme action unwise. No parliament at the end of the Middle Ages could have acted in this sense because none of its members could have thought in quite this way. The frequent affirmations of the statute-roll by fourteenth and fifteenth-century parliaments amounted not to an assertion of legislative capacity so much as to an assumption that the business of parliament was to assert, and most often to reassert, the law, and to a recognition of the great value, in the technical imperfection of the times, of every exemplification of rights.

Some first indication how nearly the full-blooded theory of legislation had been approached may be gathered from an examination of what Henry VII's statutes did actually purport to effect. There are a hundred and twenty-four public acts of Henry VII according to the table in the *Statutes at Large*: a few might be added if the subsidy bills, there classified as private, be counted, in accordance with later notions, as essentially public, but more would have to be deducted as essentially private. The great majority were certainly far from altering or instituting general rules. Statutes were to be construed (as they are still) as not intending in any way to change common law unless such an intention was expressed, and in most cases they were in affirmation of common law or by way of making it more available: that is, they were judicial and administrative rather than legislative. If the acts of Henry VII are examined they will be found, almost all of them, to be unquestionably designed for the enforcement of what no one doubted to be already law

[1] Cf. Fritz Kern, "Recht und Verfassung im Mittelalter", in the *Historische Zeitschrift*, vol. cxx, *passim*, especially pp. 13–15, 28, 37, 41. Cf. also p. 156 below.

(right, *jus*)—by fortifying or adapting procedure, by increasing penalties, by directing police administration, by applying admitted social principles to industrial and commercial occasions, as in customs or industrial regulation. Most of them fall easily under these headings and discussion is necessary only for those which have some appearance of being really legislative, really creative of new substantive law or destructive of old.

Those which have most of this appearance are those dealing with clergy and sanctuary, which will be considered in connection with ecclesiastical policy, the "Star Chamber" Act, the "Navigation" Acts, the Statutes of Fines and for the maintenance of husbandry, the "De Facto" Act, the acts for the subordination of local legislation, the act dispensing with indictment in certain cases, and the "shoring or under-propping act for the benevolence":[1] to which should perhaps be added Poynings' Act. Here, if anywhere, is Henry's law-making to be found, the justification for Bacon's eulogy, "his times for good commonwealth's laws did excel. So as he may justly be celebrated for the best lawgiver to this nation; after King Edward the first"[2] and again, "the laws that were made in this king's reign" formed his "preeminent virtue and merit".[3]

The Star Chamber Act[4] was certainly not regarded by its authors as in any way innovatory: rather it put above question one way of enforcing law: there were other statutes of the same sort before and since.[5] The Navigation Acts,[6] preserving certain import trades for English ships, were perhaps not so original as Bacon thought when he described them as "bowing the ancient policy of this estate, from consideration

---

[1] So called by Bacon, *Henry VII* (ed. J. R. Lumby, 1876), p. 134.
[2] Bacon, p. 69.
[3] Bacon, p. 74.
[4] 3 H. VII c. 1: cf. pp. 32–5, 39–42, 44–9, 64 above, 150 below.
[5] E.g. 11 H. VII c. 25, to deal with perjury, retainder, maintenance, embracery, champerty, corruption of officers: parties complained against to come before the chancellor and treasurer, the two chief justices, and the clerk of the rolls.
[6] 1 H. VII c. 8 and 4 H. VII c. 10: cf. W. Cunningham, *Growth of English Industry and Commerce*, I, pp. 394, 490, and Pollard, *Henry VII from Contemporary Sources*, II, last 100 pages. Henry was not always protectionist: cf. 1 H. VII c. 10, repealing, on the petition of Italian merchants, various statutes restricting foreign merchants.

of plenty to consideration of power", and even if they were something more than merely confirmatory, yet it is to be noted that it was *policy* they altered, not *law*: as yet no one doubted that the regulation of foreign trade was a mere matter of local and temporal expediency, for any government to regulate at its convenience: when the regulation was on a large scale it was best done, by an English government, in parliament. The act for the maintenance of husbandry [1] (whereby houses customably supported by arable farming were to be maintained so that arable farming might not decay) comes somewhat nearer to the making of law: but not very much, for it was an act for the continuance of things as they had been: that such and such a proportion of the land and the people should live by ploughing had been in the righteous nature of things: old custom, good right, true law wished that it should be so: if express enactment became necessary for keeping it so, the enactment may be called making a law, but hardly Law-making; it was law because prescription, legitimate expectation, the eternal principles of statecraft, all demanded it, and therefore it was enacted: only in a superficial and minor sense was it law because it was enacted.

The Statute of Fines [2] may perhaps be classed with the merely procedural, the adjective,[3] statutes whose purposes are outside themselves, and besides, it "did in effect but restore an ancient statute, which was itself also made but in affirmance of the common law":[4] but if it was procedural, it was so in a very high and pregnant manner, restoring efficacy to what had before the Statute of Non-claim[5] (1360) been the

---

[1] 4 H. VII c. 19: cf. 4 H. VII c. 16 (to keep up the population of the Isle of Wight); 11, c. 2 (vagabonds to the stocks, beggars back to place of abode, apprentices and servants to play unlawful games only at Christmas, justices of the peace to punish gaming houses and regulate ale houses, cf. 19, c. 12); 11, c. 22 (citing 23 H. VI c. 12 and others, fixing maximum wages, but was repealed by 12 H. VII c. 3). Weights and measures 7, c. 3; 11, c. 4; 12, c. 5. Rough lists of acts dealing with trade are 1, cc. 2, 9, 10; 3, cc. 5, 6 (usury), 7, 8, 9, 12; 4, c. 23; 7, c. 7; 11, cc. 6, 13, 14, 23; 19, cc. 2, 21, 23, 27; with industry 1, c. 5; 3, c. 11; 4, cc. 2, 3, 8, 9, 11, 21, 22; 11, cc. 5, 8 (usury), 11, 19, 27; 12, cc. 1, 4; 19, cc. 5 (coinage), 6, 17, 19. Cf. pp. 69 above, 171 below.
[2] 4 H. VII c. 24.
[3] Cf. *N.E.D.* "Relating to procedure, the subsidiary part of law; opposed to *substantive*, relating to the essential justice of law." And cf. p. 156 below.
[4] Bacon, p. 70: Henry's act re-enacted and improved 1 R. III c. 7.
[5] 24 Edward III c. 16.

most respected process for conveying land.[1] The Benevolence Act[2] need hardly detain us: if so-and-so had promised to give someone else so much money and had failed, there was no legal novelty in keeping him to his word: and though future generations might find constitutional vices in this sanctioning of royal exactions whose origin was unparliamentary, yet the men who did it found obvious personal and political advantage in what they did. Poynings' Law too needs no discussion here: it was for three centuries the guiding document for constitutional relations between England and Ireland, but the direction it gave was rather by declaration than by institution. English laws in force in 1495 were asserted to be binding in Ireland, as had already been decided by the judges ten years before:[3] later English statutes were to extend to Ireland only if adopted by the Irish parliament, which, however, was precluded from sitting or from passing statutes without the previous assent of the king in council. This was in fact no more than had always been matter of course with the English parliament,[4] and the whole purpose of the statute (which contained other provisions here omitted) was not to make law but to extend its operation and increase its efficiency, in particular to keep the lord deputy in due subjection to the king. The statutes regulating sanctuary and benefit of clergy must be treated later:[5] they did not create substantive law, they were a use of the parliament for regulating the enforcement of law on the borderland of the two great jurisdictions, realm and church: and in this reign that borderland was at peace, so that the regulating of it resembled treaty-making more than law-making. The statutes

---

[1] Cf. Holdsworth, III, pp. 236–45; IV, p. 483: and cf. p. 165 below.

[2] 11 H. VII c. 10.

[3] *Y.B.* 1 H. VI Mich. pl. 2, overruling a decision to the contrary 2 R. III Mich. pl. 26, referred to by Holdsworth, IV, p. 28: "It had been common to extend the operation of English statutes to Ireland, even when not particularly named, if the judges thought that the subject was sufficiently general to require it": H. Hallam, *Constitutional History*, III, p. 357 n., where some instances are given. And cf. Agnes Conway, *Henry VII's Relations with Scotland and Ireland*, ch. VII (by Edm. Curtis).

[4] But of course there was the immense difference that in Ireland Henry was an absentee whose comfort and greatness depended not at all on the Irish, not considerably on the Anglo-Irish, but on the English.

[5] Cf. pp. 178 ff. below.

about local legislation[1] were in at least one way more absolutely legislative, being without qualification or disguise a dealing of a superior
power with an inferior: and Bacon, writing a century later and con-
demning corporations as "fraternities in evil", leaves the impression on
many readers[2] that he disliked them more because they might seem a
deduction from the complete sovereignty of the central government
than truly because their ordinances "were against the prerogative of the
King, the common law of the realm, and the liberty of the subject",
in short, were against the law. Henry VII's motives for desiring the
statute of 19 H. VII c. 7 may have been the same as those attributed to
Bacon, but the form of his act was compliance with the request of the
commons to revive a statute made against corporations which "often
times by colour of rule and governance to them granted and confirmed
by Charters and letters patents of divers Kings, made among themselves many unlawful and unreasonable ordinances".[3] It need not be
doubted that the parliament which passed this statute conceived of
itself as enforcing law and not making it.[4]

The most novel of Henry's statutes, to judge the first by modern
theorisings and the second by contemporary resentment, were two that
come very close together, 11 H. VII c. 1, the "De Facto Act", and
11 H. VII c. 3, that "Punishment of certain Offences (being) prevented
by Corruption &c. of Jurors, Justices of Assize and of the Peace (be)
empowered to hear and determine and to punish" unlawful assembly,
maintenance, etc. "upon Information without Indictment".[5] It might
be argued that this dispensation with indictment was a matter of mere
adjective law, a mere alteration of ways and means. But this argument
is unfair. The main lines of the methods of enforcing law are themselves

---

[1] Cf. p. 137 above: 3 H. VII c. 9 (a city ordinance forbidding its freemen to go to
fairs and markets annulled); 19, c. 7 cited on p. 137 above (no local ordinances or
by-laws without central approval).
[2] Pollard, *Reign of Henry VII*, vol. I, p. xliv, seems to me to have this impression
excessively. For fifteenth-century notions of corporation, cf. pp. 138–41 above.
[3] Preamble to 19 H. VII c. 7: cf. p. 137 above: the preamble to 15 H. VI c. 6 has
a phrase almost identical.
[4] For ideas about corporations and for their subordination cf. pp. 137–9 above.
[5] *S.R.* II, p. 570: cf. pp. 85–7 above, esp. 85 n. 2, attempt of a statute of 1468 to
institute common informers.

law in the fullest sense: to us, that both sides shall be heard, that criminal trials shall be by jury, for instance, that judges shall be irremovable,[1] and so on, these are matters of direct and general human importance, and in their own right; they differ not only in degree from questions of the legal necessity of a seal or the invariability of a formula, they differ in degree so very much that they are different in kind.

The dispensing with indictment was to fifteenth-century minds (at any rate to politically active ones) a matter of this sort, or nearly, an interference with the machinery of law so profound that it was very like an interference with law itself: here there was legislation in a wider sense than in any of the statutes mentioned above, and therefore the act authorising procedure on information offers some support to the theory that the idea and practice of legislation in the full sense were within the compass of Henry VII's parliaments. It is no objection that the device of dispensing with indictment was not new, that already in 1468 Edward IV's parliament had authorised prosecution for livery on information alone:[2] the device was not new, but the making it effective was, and the argument for making it effective was no doubt that its effect was needed against a law-defeating force, that is, it was not making law but removing an obstacle to law. The significance of 11 H. VII c. 3 is not reduced because it was repealed by 1 H. VIII c. 6. The main motive of repeal was certainly not a sense of outrage in a public mind saturated with jurisprudence, jealously tenacious of Law above statute, but rather a determination of the propertied to be done with the exactions of Empson and Dudley: the manner of repeal was by way of declaring not that the act had been improper or impertinent but that

---

[1] And that legal procedure shall be in our own language.
[2] And cf. p. 49 above. Holdsworth, IX, p. 238, writes "It seems to be quite clear that, in Edward III's reign, the king could, by information to his court, put a man on his trial for treason or felony. But, probably before the close of the medieval period, this right to put a man on his trial by information, without the process of presentment and indictment, had been restricted to offences under the degree of felony, that is to misdemeanours. . . . There seems to be no doubt that the Council habitually proceeded criminally against persons, on the information, not only of the king and his counsel, but also of any private person": and besides the Edward IV statute in the text he refers to 3 H. VI c. 3 (a third of the penalty to the informer in cases of embezzlement of customs) and the "Star Chamber Act" with its procedure "upon bill or information".

"By force of the same act...sinister and craftily feigned and forged informations have been pursued against divers of the King's Subjects".[1] Here is law made and unmade. But it is law only just on the border line of the full sense,[2] and if it is above the dividing line in effect it could still well be below it in appearance. It was not like saying that murder should cease to be punishable or land to be heritable. The men who passed 11 H. VII c. 3 and 1 H. VIII c. 6 need not have been conscious that they were *making law* in the fullest sense: and certainly one of the most qualified of later commentators (a century later, indeed, but in the full and direct stream of tradition) thought that the statute-makers of 1495 had acted outrageously: the act, Coke said, "had a fair flattering preamble", but "tended in the execution...to the high displeasure of Almighty God, the great let, nay the utter subversion of the common law, and the great let of the wealth of this land"; and the repeal, he thought, was "a good caveat to Parliaments to leave all causes to be measured by the golden and straight metwand of the law, and not to the incertain and crooked cord of discretion".[3]

It was well enough for Coke to write like that, living in a time when he might be forgiven for thinking that Law needed no special arming against livery, maintenance, retainder, unlawful assembly, untrue demeanings of sheriffs, and so on. For essentially that special arming was what the dispensing with indictment was, and the Star Chamber Act and the Household Offences Act,[4] and the Collusions Act,[5] the Riot and Unlawful Assemblies Act,[6] the acts of 1495 regulating juries,[7] another Riot Act,[8] and another Retainder Act.[9] Henry VII, and the

---

[1] *S.R.* III, p. 3.
[2] Cf. p. 144 above.
[3] *Inst.* IV, pp. 39–41.
[4] 3 H. VII c. 14, the steward to enquire, by a jury of the Household, into conspiracy against officers or ministers, even where there was no overt act.
[5] 4 H. VII c. 20.
[6] 11, c. 7, any one against whom there was complaint or indictment for unlawful assembly should be proclaimed by the justices of the peace and appear at the next quarter sessions.
[7] 11, cc. 24, 25, 26: the acts of 11 H. VII against riot, perjury, etc. were continued by 12 H. VII c. 2: see also 19 H. VII c. 3.
[8] 19, c. 13, reinforcing 13 H. IV c. 3 and other riot acts.
[9] C. 14, reinforcing early statutes and especially conciliar jurisdiction.

bulk of his subjects, knew that in their time Law sorely needed some extraordinary sword to wield against the many-headed monster that obstructed justice, and if the most effective sword might prove two-edged they thought that a risk quite worth running. All these statutes were parts of a campaign[1] against the crying evil of the fifteenth century, the lack of governance, and were designed not to make Law but to make a reality of law and order. The object, and on the whole the effect, was to make it possible for the wheels of the legal machine to go round.

Lastly, the De Facto Act:

from henceforth no manner of person or persons, whatsoever he or they be, that attend upon the King and Sovereign Lord of this land for the time being, in his person, and do him true and faithful service of allegiance in the same, or be in other places by commandment in his Wars, within this land or without, that for the same deed and true Service, of allegiance he or they be in no wise convict or attaint of high treason, nor of other offences for that cause, by act of parliament, or otherwise by any process of law...".[2]

Here is the most legislative claim made by any fifteenth-century parliament. Law made kings, kings called parliament to help them realise the behests of law; it were a strange reversal if parliaments made laws to make kings;[3] but here was a parliament that came very near it, if it be construed as assuming the possibility that there might be simultaneously two men, one king in fact the other in right, and as claiming for statute competence to attribute to the mere possessor, to him who in Law was nothing and less than nothing, the essential right of kingship, the allegiance and service of his subjects. This looks new and legislative: legislative in a very high degree, for Law had few tasks more lofty than the attribution of kingly functions: and legislative in a

---

[1] Cf. the Irish Coercion Acts of the nineteenth century (and of the twentieth): and cf. pp. 65, 69, 85, 86 above.

[2] 11 H. VII c. 1, printed in *S.R.* II, p. 568.

[3] Cf. the opinion of the judges in 1485: "that he (Henry VII) was not attainted, but disabled of his crown, reign, dignity, lands, and tenements; and say that, by the very fact that he took on him the royal dignity and was king, all that was void": cf. p. 16 above. *Y.B.* 1 H. VII (edn. 1679), p. 4. Cf. Pollard, *Henry VII from Contemporary Sources*, II, p. 10.

very significant direction, in the direction of separating the man and the office, of distinguishing the rights and duties of the King from those of the Crown, distinctions without which it would have been impossible to develop the fifteenth-century parliament into a legislature independent of the monarch or the fifteenth-century monarchy into an executive that could be called to account without revolution. But the purposes for which the De Facto Act was passed were not the same as the effects with which in the course of a century or so it came to be credited.

The general purpose is plain enough—to quiet disturbed minds. For generations now Englishmen had been habituated to the difficulty of guessing whether the man who was on the throne would stay there till his removal by the act of God from which no king escapes, or whether he might not by a mere trick of fortune or stroke of politics be degraded and become as if he had never been, not a dethroned king but a convicted usurper. This uncertainty was one of the assets of every pretender who began to look as if he had the least chance of success, for as soon as that happened allegiance slipped away from the actual king, lest the eventual victory of the challenger should prove it to have been all the time not allegiance but treason: as the preamble put it, "subjects...are bound to serve their Prince and Sovereign Lord for the time being in his Wars....And that for the same service what fortune ever fall by chance in the same battle against the mind and will of the Prince (as in this land some time past hath been seen), that it is not reasonable but against all laws reason and good conscience that the said subjects going with their sovereign Lord in Wars...anything should lose or forfeit for doing their true duty and service of allegiance".[1] It was an argument whose reality came home to every Englishman of the time, and agreed especially with the interest of Henry, the man in possession, threatened by the competition of Warbeck.[2]

Bacon comments at length:[3] this "strange" law was "rather just

[1] 11 H. VII c. 1, *S.R.* II, p. 568.

[2] The parliament that passed this act sat from 14 Oct. to 21 Dec. 1495: Wm. Stanley had been condemned on 6 and beheaded on 16 Feb., Perkin Warbeck had appeared off Deal (backed by the emperor Maximilian and by Margaret of Burgundy) on 5 July: though he had failed in Kent and Scotland he was received by James IV at Stirling in Nov. (Pollard, *Inst. Hist. Res. Bul.* VII, p. 4).

[3] Bacon, p. 133.

than legal; and more magnanimous than provident" (a queer arrogance of Bacon's, to think he could estimate the chances more precisely than Henry; and an evident[1] miscalculation, for the act could not begin to benefit a pretender's supporters until after two turns of the wheel, until he had first climbed the throne and then had been himself supplanted, and not even then, unless the pretender's conqueror would waive the proviso "that no person nor persons shall take any benefit or advantage by this act which shall hereafter decline from his or their said allegiance").

Bacon adds to the reasons alleged in the preamble another, "for that it was agreeable to reason of estate, that the subject should not enquire of the justice of the king's title, or quarrel": and upon the provision that "if any act or acts, or other process of law...happen to be made, contrary to this ordinance, that then that act or acts, or other processes of the law, whatsoever they shall be, stand and be utterly void", upon this fourth clause of 11 H. VII c. 1 Bacon is quite Diceyan:[2] "the force and obligation of the law was in itself illusory...by a precedent act of parliament to bind or frustrate a future. For a supreme and absolute power cannot conclude itself,[3] neither can that which is in nature revocable be made fixed, no more than if a man should appoint or declare by his will, that if he made any later will it should be void": and he goes on to quote a much stronger case for his general argument, but from a generation nearer to his own than to Henry's.

Coke's comment[4] is much more unreal: with a logic much more

---

[1] If the writer is not more arrogant than Bacon.

[2] Cf. A. V. Dicey, *Law of the Constitution*, especially ch. 1.

[3] Already long before Bacon's time this lesson could be read in the history of the Church: cf. e.g. p. 164, n. 2 below, and Z. N. Brooke, *The English Church and the Papacy*, p. 28, on the Hildebrandine development, "It is a monarchical constitution that replaces the former almost feudal headship of the Church....The Pope is supreme legislator, not merely an authority on doubtful points, and his decrees are binding on the whole Church. He is supreme judge, to whom not only the greater cases have to be referred. His court is a court of first instance, to which he can summon any offender. It is also a court of appeal, not only for the bishops but for any of the clergy; and it is something more than a final court of appeal, for any one can appeal at any stage, and appeal to Rome interrupts at once the proceedings in a court of first instance. Finally, the Pope is the representative of St Peter with supreme power over the souls of all men...". Cf. also below, pp. 164, n. 2, 166; and *Henry VIII*, pp. 110, 144, 211.

[4] *Inst.* III, 7 (edn. 1648).

legal than human he remarks that the statute not merely gives protection to the *de facto* king, but even takes it from the *de jure* king, who if he does later come to the throne must punish all treasons done to his *de facto* predecessor, and must expect his courts to disregard any pardons granted by himself during his merely *de jure* period.

It is clear that these paradoxical results could never have arisen in any human society: Coke was treating a rule of law as if it were a rule of mathematics, and if all or most other men could by any means have been persuaded to be of the same mind as he, the act would have become ineffective from superfluity, because there could never more have been any question of deposing a *de facto* king: revolution would have become unthinkable. Bacon kept much nearer to political facts and probabilities. No words on paper, or even parchment, were likely to prevent for all time competition for the royal title: and a successful pretender could be trusted to find means for destroying such champions of the wrong side as might still seem dangerous: yet to accept Bacon's view uncritically and without explanation would be to misunderstand the period of which he wrote, and, hardly less, the period in which he was writing. His conception of the power of statute-making as "supreme and absolute", limited only by the still subsisting supremacy of later statute, which was in his own day very far from commonplace, had in early Tudor days been nowhere explicit. The change that had taken place in the interval is a cardinal part of sixteenth-century constitutional history, and indeed is one of the hinges of the whole history of English government; for that reason it has seemed worth while to draw attention here to the two leading Jacobean comments on Henry VII's De Facto Act.

How little that act was itself intended to make any Diceyan claim of absolute supremacy for the statute-making organ can be shown without much difficulty. The act expresses its intention to be the removal of a hardship which "is not reasonable, but against all laws, reason, and good conscience"; nothing could be less like purporting to *make* law. And the very fact that the last clauses pronounced all future contrary acts to be invalid, and excluded from any benefit of the act anyone "which shall hereafter decline from his...allegiance", might by itself be sufficient evidence of an intention to declare what was and always had been the true meaning of law and dictate of reason. To put it shortly, the act was possible and useful not because of any parliamentary omnipotence implicit or explicit, but on the contrary just because of the technical difficulties in which government was from time to time entangled precisely for want of any organ whose omnipotence could be assumed. No one but God could make a king: God did not always make unmistakably clear who was king: in such cases the law could not mean to penalise subjects who treated as king the man who issued the writs on which parliament and every other court depended, who in fact acted as king and in appearance was king: so the high court of parliament, though it did not mention such ambiguous cases, ordained that there should be no punishment in the current case or similar cases (which might seem to the pusillanimous to be or to become ambiguous), and if in future punishment were nevertheless inflicted, then it would be in the future as in the past against law and reason: though clearly courts would still have to decide whether the person mistakenly adhered to had been king and sovereign lord for the time being and whether the adherent had not declined from allegiance. Coke was right, in the light of a rigid and systematised legality, in the conclusions he drew, but the conclusions meant nothing because the courts (parliament or other) could always have found reason enough why any special case was outside the statute. Bacon was right; in practice for the same reason for which Coke's conclusions were meaningless; in theory, he was right for his own time as the most perspicacious saw it and for the future as the well-informed were to see it, but wrong for the end of the fifteenth century as any one had at that time seen it. At that time the institutions of the realm of England were still so technically imperfect that they had no sure way of recognising their own head, the king: it was not strange that they should assert the injustice of punishing subjects for the same incapacity.

But the textbook title of the statute, De Facto Act, must not be allowed to mislead: the statute does not contain the expressions *de facto*, *de jure*, or English equivalents, nor does it mention the possible existence at one time of two kings. It may be said that without some such distinction the act does nothing but make a series of statements of the obvious. Part of the answer is that such was often the main business of statutes in days when laws were more commonly reiterated than instituted: but no doubt also the distinction was implicit: Henry's subjects who were disturbed in their minds about Yorkist enterprises and Scottish invasions were reassured that they could not legally suffer for following the king and sovereign lord of this land for the time being, just as by 11 H. VII c. 18 they were reminded that it was their duty so to serve, and neglect of that duty would forfeit any offices, fees or annuities held of the king.[1] Perhaps also the statute guaranteed Yorkists who had so far escaped attainder or forfeiture against any future proceedings on the ground of what they had done before Henry came to the throne.[2] It did not at the time, it seems clear, appear very novel or striking in effect: no chronicler mentioned it, nor was it ever invoked till the time of Oliver Cromwell.[3]

Henry VII's statutes in general and the De Facto Act in particular were not, still less were meant to be, assertions of the comprehensiveness and irresistibility of parliament's legislative potentiality; yet it is not to be doubted that they were an important stage in the process by which those qualities were acquired. If statute could deprive subjects of one of their main guarantees against oppression, could treat corporations as the merest underlings, could grant wholesale dispensation for negligence of God's royal vicegerent, if statute could do, could even seem to do, such things, then it became hard to know what things statute could not do. And if that had been easy to know there would have been a great difference in the conduct of Henry VIII and in all our later history.

In the expression *making law*, "law" may mean all the general rules about human relations, at least all such rules as it is either the right or the duty of the government to use the power of the community towards enforcing. Similarly, "making" may mean "absolutely controlling the existence of", so that the legislature is continuously and

---

[1] Cf. Pollard, in *Inst. Hist. Res. Bul.* VII, p. 5.
[2] *Ibid.* p. 12.
[3] *Ibid.* p. 11.

absolutely causing law to be or not to be, either actively by issuing or revoking edicts or passively by refraining from doing so. Or *"making"* may much more nearly mean pronouncing or defining: and, with a like lowering of sense, it was law that a bill must be on parchment, and is law that a cheque must have a two-penny stamp: it was law that a stranger arriving in a town must have a host, and is law that wheeled traffic must keep to the left. But such laws subsist not for the sake of the purposes at which they explicitly aim but for the sake of *law*, the law that really matters, the community's conception of what human relations should be or at least that part of the conception which the community will use its organised forces to realise. Law in this high sense came later to be thought of as the command of the state, existing by the state's choice: once it had been the sanction of the state, in right of which the state existed, a state precisely in so far as that was its principle of existence, otherwise a great thievery. In Henry VII's time it had neither of these simplicities.

At that time there had been a long development, and there was still going on in ways that have been indicated a noticeable development, in the practical technique of modifying the rules applied by the courts. How near that developed technique had come to the fullest Making of Law, how much nearer to what in retrospect might easily be mistaken for it, the last few pages have endeavoured to show: but especially to show that when fifteenth-century judges said that parliament "may make law, and that that is law it may make no law",[1] they were not attributing to a representative assembly legislative omnicompetence, authority to create, alter or destroy all law at discretion.

In the course of that demonstration an allusion was made to the development of the notion of a possible contrast between Crown and King, between two jurisprudential aspects of the same natural person, a development not unconnected with the development of the notion of legislation. The particular stage of this development round about the time when the sixteenth century was succeeding the fifteenth was one of the principal factors at the origin of modern constitutional history.

Though the idea of distinguishing between different capacities of the

[1] Cf. p. 133 above, and p. 166 below.

king was at the end of the century very far from universal acceptance or complete elaboration, yet it was by then almost equally far from novelty. The suggestion of it, in the terms which were to have most ultimate importance, was already nearly two centuries old. In 1313 a defendant was claiming that the writ he was being put to answer was invalidated by a provision of the Statute of Westminster II: the court contended that it ought to receive the writ in spite of its defect, because it had special instruction from the king to do so. The argument reported went like this:

Staunton J.—We have a later warrant from the king, and that is as high as the statute. *Stonore (for the defendant)*—The answer we put forward is fully warranted by the statute and no one can go against the statute. *Spigurnel J.*—You would be correct if the sheriff had taken the writ after the proclamation, but we have received it by the king's command and by a new authority that is as high as the statute.[1] *Passeley (for the defendant)*—Sir, the statute is given by common counsel of the realm and that cannot be defeated by the king's simple (counsel and)[2] command: wherefore it seems that such a command ought not to exceed the bounds[3] of the statute. *Ormesby J.*—When the king commands, one must suppose that it is by common counsel, and besides, no one may counterplead the king's deed.[4]

Accordingly the writ was held to stand, and the defendant was told he might sue error afterwards.

It may be that Spigurnel was already in danger of being old-fashioned, with his "authority that is as high as the statute", and by the time of Henry VII it was matter of course that the king's seals were of graduated potency,[5] his acts of varying authority, his acts in parliament highest of all. Yet even then Passeley would have been a century and a half before his time, with his argument from which it needed but a step to distinguish a natural will of the king subject to the constraint of his parliamentary will. The really characteristic sentence in the conver-

---

[1] Literally "as high etc.": Plucknett translates "as high as *a* statute".
[2] These words are not in all the manuscripts.
[3] "passer les poynts": ? out-point, over-trump.
[4] T. F. T. Plucknett, *Statutes and their Interpretation*, p. 140, translating from W. C. Bolland, *Eyre of Kent* (Selden Society, vol. 24), p. 174.
[5] Cf. p. 140 above, and p. 162, n. 2 below.

sation is Ormesby's, "no one may counterplead the king's deed". There was no public law, no political rights. The right of the king, with all the claims and duties therein contained, had in law and thought the same essence, the same reason to exist, was of the same kind, as the right of the bishop, the earl, the knight, or the villein. What was the right of each might be difficult to decide, to enforce even more difficult; but all existed on the same plane and for the same reason. All rights were fundamental rights, among them the procedural advantages of the person who wore the crown. If one sort of right was not only more respectable but more respected than another it was rights over land,[1] and arguments on the analogy of the land law were very strong arguments.[2] At the beginning of the Tudor period this had not ceased to be the natural assumption in any controversy about what we should call public rights, and there was not yet any habituation to the idea of public rights, constitutional law, nor any philosophical notion of a sovereignty in parliament, nor any clear and established distinction between the will of the Crown and what the King wants. This is illustrated by "the one flash of new thought"[3] which the latest student of fifteenth-century law and constitution can find there.

In 1481 the abbot of Waltham pleaded that royal letters patent which he held should exempt him from collecting a clerical subsidy, although Convocation had explicitly provided that for the occasion such exemptions should be void. The arguments which arose on this plea came almost all from the realm of private law, especially of land law: even when it was said that "among the clergy Convocation is as powerful as Parliament among the temporality, and every Act of Parliament binds everyone to whom it extends, forasmuch as every man is party and privy to the Parliament.... By the same reasoning every Abbot, Prior, and beneficed clerk is privy and party to the Convocation", it was added, "and so it is reasonable that he should be estopped[4] by the acts made in the Convocation": that is, he ought to

---

[1] Cf. p. 162, n. 2 below, and p. 163, n. 4 below.
[2] Cf. e.g. *Y.B.* 7 H. VII Trin. pl. 1.
[3] T. F. T. Plucknett, *The Lancastrian Constitution*, p. 176 in *Tudor Studies* (ed. R. W. Seton-Watson).
[4] For the meaning of estoppel, cf. Holdsworth, IX, pp. 144 ff.

have made his protest in Convocation, and as he did not he could not later claim the privilege which Convocation had then purported to suspend, he must be taken as having admitted Convocation's authority. And both the tax and the appointment of collectors were treated like heritable rights over land, incorporeal hereditaments. But Serjeant Starkey, for the abbot, struck a more modern note: "the charter should be allowed: otherwise you will have to affirm that the authority and jurisdiction of Convocation is higher and greater than the authority of the King in his prerogative, of which the contrary is true".

The truth and the strength of Starkey's argument were admitted. Its importance here is as an indication of what were at the end of the fifteenth century the prevalent modes of thinking about questions which we should call constitutional, of what were the prevalent modes and what other modes were becoming possible. The prevalent modes were still those of private, especially of land, law: but it was beginning to be possible to regard a clash of privileges as a conflict of powers, a matter of constitutional law: the man who put this view assumed, without contradiction, that the King's authority was superior to Convocation's, it being common ground that Convocation was to the clergy what parliament was to the laity. And it appears probable that in so doing he gave a new twist to the meaning of prerogative: what had meant the specific privileges of the king under feudal arrangements was being used as if it might mean a superiority which was above definition.[1] For this and all that might be developed from this it was a very light payment to admit such distinctions between Crown and King as that if a judgment has been given in court the king cannot undo it unless by due process at law, or that the king cannot himself like any of his subjects arrest a man on suspicion, because there would be no remedy against him if he were wrong.[2] Nor, with regard to what most mattered practically, the taxing power, had theory yet deprived the kingship of the advantages of that "scheme of private law where it had been placed by the feudal age":[3] for when in 1441 one chief

[1] Cf. Plucknett in *Tudor Studies*, p. 174.
[2] Cf. Vinogradoff in *L.Q.R.* cxv, pp. 276, 277: and cf. p. 51 above.
[3] Plucknett in *Tudor Studies*, p. 165.

justice argued that taxation was part of the profit of the king's court[1] of parliament and therefore grantable even before it accrued, he was answered by the other chief justice that "this fifteenth is a grant by the spontaneous will of the people. This proves that it is not a right in him before grant is made, in virtue of his inheritance of the courts": and then the chief baron of the exchequer came to the support of the chief justice, and asserted that tenths and fifteenths were rightly to be considered as part of the king's inheritance in his courts, "for the law which binds the King to defend his people, also binds the people to grant of their goods to him in aid of that defence—which proves the inheritance".[2]

This last argument long retained reality and importance:[3] but the main point to notice here is that by the end of the fifteenth century two things had happened without which the history of the sixteenth and seventeenth centuries would have been very different. The distinction between the king's person and his official capacity, in later terms between the king and the crown, was recognisable and, to lawyers at least, familiar: allusions might be made to it now without danger of suggesting a charge of treason as they had done in Edward II's time.[4] It was a distinction[5] which could hardly be hid when a duke of Lancaster became king and when two whole generations were filled with royal minorities, royal idiocy, and dynastic revolutions. These changes and chances and the growing recognition of the necessity of legal

---

[1] Cf. p. 142 above.
[2] Plucknett in *Tudor Studies*, p. 165. Cf. Fortescue, *Governance of England* (ed. Plummer), p. 127: Fortescue thought also, ch. vi (ed. Plummer, p. 121), that the king was bound or ought to be bound not to alienate any of the "livelihood" which ought to be used to meet his ordinary charges, and that this was no restraint on the king's power, "For it is no poiar to mowe alien & put away; but it is power to mowe haue & kepe...". Cf. *Henry VIII*, p. 373.
[3] It was used in the financial controversy between Charles I and parliament.
[4] Holdsworth, III, pp. 290, 466.
[5] One rudiment of it, the national and the feudal aspects of the king, was already centuries old, cf. pp. 5, 6 above: and another was the council's developed capacity of being in two places at once, and of enjoying the constructive presence of the king, cf. pp. 30, 39: remember also the corporation sole, graduated seals and documents, pp. 139, 158, 160, and perhaps the implied contrast between a king *de jure* and a king *de facto*, p. 155; and regnal dates, pp. 8, 14; and personal and public inheritances, p. 140, n. 1.

continuity had recently led to formal stabilisation of royal acts emanating from men whose kingship was denied, as when in 1461 the acts of all Lancastrian courts except parliament were validated and when in 1469 it was held necessary "that the Realm should have a king under whom the laws should be held and upheld, and though the said Henry was in power by usurpation, any judicial act done by him and touching Royal jurisdiction would be valid and will bind the rightful king when the latter returns to power".[1] It was a distinction not necessarily and by no means always disadvantageous to the king: in time it was to submerge the king's wishes under the intentions of the state, but when Henry VII came to the throne there was a long century and a half still to run before it was to make claims of that sort, and meanwhile it might be used to extricate the king from feudality and to recognise in him capacities of which his fathers had not dreamed. The principle that the king cannot commit a wrong had been very recently[2] asserted with especial completeness: in the sixteenth century "with the growth of the idea of the dual capacity of the king, it became acclimatised in the law"; later, indeed, it was progressively to diminish the power of the man who wore the crown: but the Tudors had no reason to fear that the application of the principle to the distinction was having that effect, certainly not Henry VII when his De Facto Act made what two high authorities have called "perhaps the earliest recognition to be found in English Law of a possible difference between the person and the office of the king".[3]

So much for the dual capacity of the king. The second of the two developments to which the beginning of the last paragraph referred as conditioning sixteenth and seventeenth century history was the accumu-

[1] *R.P.* v, p. 489 and *Y.B.* 9 E. IV Pasch. pl. 2, both referred to by Vinogradoff, *L.Q.R.* xxix, p. 279.

[2] 1483, *Y.B.* 1 E. V Trin. pl. 13, referred to by Holdsworth, iii, p. 466: "Note that it was said the same day [on which Richard of Gloucester claimed to be king] in the Chancery and agreed by all the judges and serjeants there present, that the king cannot be said to do wrong (dit un que fist tort) for if one wish to disseize another to the use of the king, where the king has no right, that cannot be called disseisin" (my translation).

[3] Stephen, *H.C.L.* ii, p. 254 n., quoted approvingly by Holdsworth, iii, p. 468, n. 5, "the earliest *statutory* recognition" would be, I think, nearer the truth; and even then, cf. the previous page, esp. n. 8: and cf. p. 151 above.

lation of considerations likely to suggest the immense technical convenience of some unmistakable criterion to which all questions of
jurisdiction or competence could be referred: though the desirability
of public law and constitutional definition was not yet generally recognised or anywhere specified, still lawyers at least were having forced
on their attention the possibility of conflicts between different political
organs,[1] the necessity of regulating the legitimacy and capacity of bodies
politic,[2] the need of some shibboleth for recognising the king and of
some device for keeping the law alive over a period when he had been
unrecognised:[3] these problems were being forced on their attention,
and so was the difficulty of settling them by mere application of the
rules of private and feudal law. Fortescue[4] was aware of the difficulty,
and could solve it no better than by admitting that even in a *dominium
politicum et regale*, a limited monarchy like the English, something must
be left to the king's discretion: and serjeant Starkey seems to have been
of the same opinion.[5]

---

[1] Cf. p. 80 above. [2] Cf. p. 138 above.
[3] Cf. p. 162 above.
[4] Cf. p. 134 above and *Works* (ed. Clermont), e.g. *On the Law of Nature*, p. 205,
how St Thomas commended "dominium politice et regale"—"For in the kingdom
of England the kings make not laws, nor impose subsidies. . .,without the consent of
the Three Estates of the Realm. Nay, even the judges of that kingdom are all
bound by their oaths not to render judgement against the laws of the land, although
they should have the commands of the sovereign to the contrary". P. 214, "Again,
O King, who governest politickly, govern thy people royally also, when occasion
demands it. For it is not all cases which will admit of being embraced in the
statutes & customs of thy kingdom; wherefore, such as remain are left to thy
discretion; for thou dost deal with all criminal matters according to thy will and
pleasure, & dost mitigate or remit all punishments, provided only thou canst do
so without damage to thy subjects or offence against the customs and statutes of
thy kingdom. Equity also is left to thy sagacity. . .for ofttimes the written law lies
as it were dead under a covering of words, though not wholly lifeless. . . .Wherefore
in such case the office of a good prince, who is called a living law, supplies the
defect of the written law. . . .Whence the Philosopher says, not without cause, that a
kingdom is better governed by the best king than the best law. . .".—"As a piece
of land which is given to me is called my right (jus) so power which is given to the
king is rightly named the king's right. . . .And although an unjust king may un-
justly use that power, power itself is always good, nor can it be defiled by the use
made of it. . .[but] no edict or action of a king, even if it hath risen politickly, hath
ever escaped the vengeance of divine punishment, if it hath proceeded from him
against the rule of nature's law."
[5] P. 160 above.

It would be very misleading to exaggerate the degree to which these ideas were defined or elaborated, or the extent to which they were dispersed. But at least the persons most interested and most influential in such things had gone a long way towards using, and sometimes even towards noticing and naming, conceptions which even in isolation and in embryo were hardly medieval, and which in combination and development were to make, almost to be, that most modern invention—the Constitution: not merely the English constitution but in general the constitution of all white men's states.

Those conceptions and the relations between them were closely connected with contemporary notions of the competence of statute[1] and of the sense in which Law could be made. The old distinctions between various kinds of Law were endangered both by the desire for technical precision and by the economic and social changes[2] which were compelling alterations of Law in the most practical sense of the words, that is, the rules accepted by the courts and enforced by the organised power of the community about what were generally assumed to be most important affairs. The distinction between law natural and law positive (or rather the assumption that there ought to be such a distinction, for to make it was more difficult) was part of the medieval equipment. In fifteenth-century England it was a commonplace of jurisprudence, and was becoming familiar to the public mind, as when Edward IV's chancellor[3] in 1468 told lords and commons "that Justice was grounde well and rote of all prosperite, peas and pollityke rule of every Reame, wheruppon all the Lawes of the world been grounde and sette, which resteth in thre; that is to say, the Lawe of God, Lawe of nature, and

---

[1] Cf. pp. 133–7, 157 above.

[2] Cf. p. 166, and *Henry VIII*, pp. 110, 144, 211. And by the sweeping purport of papal decree, e.g. the general dispensation of 1501, *L. and P.* II, p. 96, "Also our said holy father hath disannulled and suspended all manner of pardons and grants granted *or to be granted* notwithstanding any special clause that they should not be revoked without special mention made *de verbo in verbo*". The fifteenth century had experienced the extreme need and the extreme difficulty of a technique for recognising with certainty what was Law, Law of the Church and Law of God: it had not completely developed such a technique and the development so far as it had gone had been away from the representative deliberative assembly: cf. the history of the conciliar movement. Cf. p. 153, n. 3 above.

[3] *R.P.* V, p. 622: cf. p. 134 above.

posytyfe Lawe". *The Doctor and Student*, in discussing the grounds of the laws of England, mentions only as the sixth and last "divers statutes...in such cases where the law of reason, the law of God, customs, maxims and other grounds of the law seemed not to be sufficient to punish evil men and to reward good men".[1] And it is not irrelevant here to look ahead and to notice that as late as 1604 the Speaker was still orthodox, even if not beyond dispute, when he said, "The Laws whereby the ark of this government hath ever been steered are of three kinds: the 1st the Common Law, grounded or drawn from the Law of God, the Law of Reason, and the Law of Nature, *not mutable*; the second the positive law, founded, changed and altered by and through the occasions and policies of times; the third Customs and Usages practised and allowed with times approbation without known beginnings".[2]

But some of the Speaker's listeners must have been conscious that his analysis left a good deal of the last century's history rather difficult to explain: and it has been shown above[3] that even in a fifteenth-century parliament there could be talk of making and unmaking law, and it has been suggested in what sense: nor was there any adequate technique for telling what law was susceptible of change and what not. It could not be without effect in this connection that the very sort of law which was generally assumed to be most important and most conclusive had, to the eye of common sense, suffered great changes; the law about property in land. Men who were conscious of the Statutes of *Mortmain*[4] (1279), *de Donis Conditionalibus*[5] (1285) and *Quia Emptores*[6] (1290), conscious of the development of a whole system of rules about trusts, of Taltarum's Case[7] (1472) which made or marked the inefficacy of *de Donis*—men who were conscious of all this, as was every Englishman with the least education or with the least interest in landed property (which meant every Englishman individually considerable in

---

[1] Dialogue I, ch. 12, quoted by McIlwain, p. 72. Published 1523–31.
[2] *Parl. Hist.* I, p. 1046, quoted by McIlwain, p. 63: the italics are mine.
[3] Pp. 111, 133 above.
[4] Cf. Holdsworth, III, pp. 36, 86.
[5] Cf. Holdsworth, II, pp. 350, 381, 547; III, pp. 17, 18.
[6] Cf. the index of Holdsworth, II, III, and V.
[7] Cf. Holdsworth, III, pp. 119, 137.

any sort of politics), men so conscious could not be very far from the capacity of conceiving (even though they might not yet begin to conceive) not only that law could be changed but even that there was more than one way of changing it: and if law about land were not Law, what was? nor were the early Tudor generations allowed to forget the land law and its pliability: the Statutes of Fines¹ (1489), of Uses (1536), and of Wills (1540) kept the subject fresh. This is not to say that those generations had either the idea or the practice of omnicompetent legislation:² but they had already materials out of which could be constructed a bridge to go a long way towards the idea of omnicompetent legislation³ and all but the first of Tudor generations were to do things most easily (if not most truly) explained as the beginning of the practice.

¹ Holdsworth, III, p. 244: cf. p. 146 above.
² Cf. p. 133 above: and note that as late as Chudleigh's Case (1589–95) the judges spoke of the Statute of Uses as a "judgement given by the whole Parliament": Holdsworth, IV, p. 183, n. 3.
³ Cf. pp. 133, 157 above.

CHAPTER VI

VILLEINS AND CLERICS

So far the principal task has been to suggest how different from our experience were both names and institutions which appear at first sight perfectly familiar: it is necessary now to say something about two institutions to the understanding of which the main obstacle is not any delusive appearance of familiarity, but on the contrary the very completeness of their passing away, their utter remoteness: serfdom and the Church. People may still be found, no doubt, to maintain that neither has passed away: but such people are using *serfdom* metaphorically, and *the Church* esoterically, and it is not here to be enquired whether they may not be using either or both truly.

It cannot be much of an exaggeration to say that at the end of the fifteenth century the first of these institutions had only just ceased to be among the two or three which most affected most of the people most of the time, and that the other was still in that position. Serfdom is the one that was passing, and it may be dealt with first, for the position of the Church was to be the cardinal problem of ensuing generations and the settlement of that problem the link which connected up all the other factors hitherto mentioned, and made out of them a constitution.

The main importance of villeinage was that the mass of the population had only just emerged or was only just emerging from a condition in which social and economic positions and activities were fixed and imposed, a condition in which the individual did the work allotted to him, at the place allotted, at the times allotted. It was true that the allotment was mostly matter of right founded upon custom and the common conscience, but by no means sufficiently so to give security to all tenures or to set bounds to all dues. It was true also that if for ordinary Englishmen there was little free choice of economic ends or means, yet on the whole the economic arrangements were customary and were administered by ordinary Englishmen, with very little that would be resented as arbitrary or external interference. On all this side of life freedom was rather to seek, but government also was un-obtrusive: there was plenty of compulsion, but it was mostly compulsion of the accustomed and it was mostly exercised by neighbours and equals on each other. Yet, at any rate, there remained a good deal of personal and economic unfreedom and the memory of a great deal more: just how much and where and how and why are questions not yet solved, but at least it is certain that the society nowadays generally assumed to be normal, a society in which all men have legally equal rights over their persons and their labour, had at the end of the fifteenth century never existed in England, and was only just beginning to come into existence. It is to be remembered always in thinking of the sixteenth century (and even the seventeenth, and even the eighteenth) that a section of the population can hardly be confident and active in claiming a share of the highest political power till its members are (and take it as a matter of course that they are) in possession of complete civil liberty. What degree and what amount of servitude lasted into the sixteenth century it is not easy to say, but it is necessary to insist that it still remained an habitual reality not only to memory but even to experience, so that an intelligent and well-informed foreign observer could report that "the people are held in little more esteem than if they were slaves".[1]

At the end of the thirteenth century most Englishmen were unfree: by the middle of the sixteenth, the mass of them were free.[2] There had been varieties and fluctuations of unfreedom: into these it is not necessary here to make any particular enquiry, although it should be said that if the villein had no rights against his lord, relatively to everyone else he was free: it is enough to remember the distinction between unfree tenure[3] and unfree status, between the holding of land under obligation to do uncertain services and the condition of being personally unfree, with one's property and even one's person unpro-tected by the law of the land against one's lord. In almost all the agitations after 1450 questions of tenure, not of personal servitude, were

[1] *Italian Relation*, p. 54.
[2] E. P. Cheyney on "The Disappearance of English Serfdom", in *E.H.R.* xv, p. 20.
[3] Cf. W. S. Holdsworth, *History of English Law*, III, pp. 29, 199 ff., 206–13.

raised, though the rebels led by Ket in 1549 demanded "that all bondmen be made free".[1]

Unfree status was already at the beginning of the Tudor period proportionally rare and at the end rarer still; nevertheless a modern historian of that century can find bondmen in twenty-six counties, and eighty manors, and believes that they existed in many more; he thinks that "they were not an important class in the life of the country",[2] but they were important in this way at least, that they kept alive the acceptance of unfreedom as a part of normal arrangement and the memory of it as constituting the normal arrangement. At least three Tudor statutes spoke of villeins as of a class still in being, and law treatises almost all assumed their existence.

Nor was personal unfreedom a merely nominal survival. A lord might still assert his right to his bondman's realty and personalty,[3] and as late as 1586 Lord Stafford was claiming as his villeins the inhabitants of Thornbury, one of whom was mayor of Bristol.

To be a bondman's child was a disadvantage in the marriage market, and probably the position of villeins was more difficult from the social point of view in Elizabeth's time than in Edward I's, just because there were fewer of them.[4] Even in 1617 a plea of villeinage was raised in court, and in the same year Norden (who a little earlier had spoken of "a tenure called villeinage" as "almost out of use") himself detected three bondmen; so that Elizabethan patriots like William Harrison and Sir Thomas Smith, boasting that "As for slaves and bondmen, we have none", or "I never knew any in the Realm in my time", must be taken with a grain of salt: they meant, "We wish there weren't any, and there aren't many left, and with luck there will soon be none".[5]

---

[1] F. W. Russell, *Kett's Rebellion in Norfolk*, p. 51.
[2] A. Savine, "Bondmen under the Tudors", *R.H.S.* n.s. XVII, pp. 243, 247, 261, 267: cf. also I. S. Leadam, "Last Days of Bondage", *L.Q.R.* vol. IX, who speaks of the great number of bondmen on monastic lands at the Dissolution.
[3] *L.Q.R.* IX, p. 355.
[4] References in *R.H.S.* n.s. XVII, p. 241.
[5] Both these quotations are cited by E. P. Cheyney, *E.H.R.* XV, p. 24: other sixteenth-century comments are cited and discussed by I. S. Leadam, *L.Q.R.* IX, p. 348: and A. Savine in *R.H.S.* n.s. XVII, p. 235.

There were various reasons[1] for the diminution—manumission,[2] migration, the inclination of the royal courts to freedom, and economic changes, especially the obsolescence of demesne farming, that is, the direct exploitation of large estates by lords. An important instance of the third of these reasons was the judicial dictum of 1496 that a lease for years to a villein operated as an enfranchisement.[3] The fourth reason may lead back to the consideration of unfree tenures; for if unfree status was already rare in Henry VII's time and was dwindling almost out of sight in the time of his dynasty, so that its importance for us is almost exclusively as an element in the minds of sixteenth-century men, a fact decayed almost to nothing but an idea still powerful in the thinking and feeling of most men about state and society, unfree tenure is a different matter: it and its results were by no means reduced to theoretical or indirect interest but were very directly and practically important.

First it will be convenient to speak of some results which descended partly from villein tenure and partly from villein status, and which were already operative at the beginning of the sixteenth century. Along with the economic reasons which made it both less profitable and less easy for the lords to maintain villeinage, went the decay of their jurisdiction and the replacement of customary jurisdiction by that of the justices of the peace, which had a similar effect.[4] And along with the diminution both of the main purpose of villeinage and of its incidents,[5] along with the depression of landowners, along with the change of ideas about the value of land and the means of exploiting it, along with these things went the beginnings of interference by the central government with the common man's pursuit of a living—his relation to the land, his wages, hours, food prices, poor relief. This process of substituting national for manorial regulation of economic arrangements was as old as the middle of the fourteenth century, when there began the series of

---

[1] *E.H.R.* xv, pp. 29 ff.
[2] E.g. by the king (Campbell, I, p. 166, Nov. 1465), or by a bishop (Williams, p. 247, referring to *Reg. Bp Fox*, p. 54, Apr. 1493).
[3] *Y.B.* 11 H. VII Hil. pl. 6, quoted by Holdsworth, III, p. 501 n.
[4] Cf. *American Economic Association*, series III, vol. I, p. 93, article by T. W. Page.
[5] Cf. *E.H.R.* xv, p. 37.

statutes[1] enjoining agricultural labour on those who could show no other means of subsistence, forbidding migration, fixing wages, prohibiting alms to the able-bodied, and authorising enforcement by justices of the peace. As early as 1362[2] this statutory nationalisation was doing something, although something only microscopic, to help the relief of destitution, and as early as 1388 it was admitting the right to relief of those who were unable to work.

Clearly there was a close connection between the decay of villeinage and this gradual taking over of economic compulsion and paternalism by parliamentary regulation and the king's courts instead of customary regulation and the lords' courts. Some sort of social control of the aims and methods of production and distribution was already immemorial when the Tudors began to reign, and the control was beginning to be a royal and national sort. For the workers emerging from villeinage, the fixing of the kind, place, conditions, and remuneration of their labour by superior authority was nothing new: for landlords it was a very different matter, and there might be much better chances of successful resistance, passive or active,[3] by them, the more since the decay of villeinage had been accompanied by the survival of some insecurity of tenure.

Henry VII's statutes about employment and destitution were part of the series. 11 H. VII c. 2[4] threatened rather less severity than earlier legislation to beggars and vagabonds, but still enacted that vagabonds were after three days in the stocks to be expelled from the townships where they were found and that beggars were to return to their own hundreds and stay in them. 11 H. VII c. 22, in a quite traditional way, fixed maximum wages, forbade the withholding of labour, and authorised justices of the peace to punish disobedience: but next year such of it as concerned wages was repealed.[5] The most novel part of Henry's

[1] E.g. Ordinance of Labourers 1349, Statute of Labourers 1351, 34 E. III cc. 9, 10, 11; 12 R. III cc. 3 and 7; 13 R. II c. 8; 6 H. VI c. 3; 8 H. VI c. 8. Cf. p. 146 above, and p. 172.
[2] 36 E. III c. 8, referred to by E. M. Leonard, *Early History of English Poor Relief,* p. 4.
[3] Cf. p. 69 above, for the practical weakness of Henry's enclosure policy.
[4] Cf. Leonard, p. 5, and W. Hasbach, *English Agricultural Labourer,* p. 24: and p. 148 above.   [5] 12 H. VII c. 3.

economic policy was, prophetically enough, the first legislation against enclosure and eviction, 4 H. VII cc. 16 and 19.[1]

The essence of a villein tenement was that it was held by the performance of villein services, that is, speaking generally, indeterminate services towards the cultivation of the lord's demesne. The time had been when from any such tenement the holder could be ejected as the lord pleased without having remedy in the royal courts:[2] how much he had been protected by custom, the lord's interest, and the manorial court need not be enquired here; nor the manner in which he began to acquire protection from the king's courts; but it is to be noted that a decisive stage in this later process has usually been marked by reference to a paragraph[3] in Littleton's *Tenures*: "And although that some such have an inheritance according to the custom of the manor, yet they have but an estate but at the will of the lord according to the course of the common law....But Brian chief justice said, that his opinion hath always been, and ever shall be, that if such tenant by custom paying his services be ejected by the lord, he shall have an action of trespass against him: 21 E. IV. And so was the opinion of Danby chief justice in 7 E. IV".

This was in the generation which saw the beginning of the Tudor dynasty. The old economic basis of tenure in villeinage was obsolescent. One authority believes "that when the first third of the fifteenth century ended the abolition of predial services...was approaching completion", and that "after 1450...it became very rare to find a manor still cultivated by the compulsory labour of villeins".[4] The usual

[1] Cf. pp. 69, 146 above. And his patronage of explorers (cf. A. F. Pollard, *Henry VII from Contemporary Sources*, II, pp. 325–47).

[2] Pollock and Maitland, *History of English Law*, I, pp. 359, 362, 414.

[3] Paragraph 77: cf. Pollock and Maitland, I, p. 359 n. for the doubt whether Littleton wrote this passage. And cf. Holdsworth, III, pp. 198 ff., esp. pp. 207–9: the paragraph was incorporated into Littleton's text in 1530, but its dicta appear in *Y.B.* 21 E. IV Mich. pl. 27 and 7 E. IV Mich. pl. 16. The beginning of royal protection for copyhold seems to be a chancery case in 1439: cf. A. Savine in *E.H.R.* XVII, pp. 298–303: he adds "under Henry VII we have in the Year Books very clear instances proving that copyhold cases became determinable at the common law". How far the dicta in the text had been acted upon is uncertain. "On the whole," concludes Holdsworth, III, p. 209, "having regard to the action of the Chancery and to the relations between the Chancery and the common law, it is not improbable that there were many judges prepared to act upon them".

[4] *American Economic Association*, series III, vol. I, p. 77, article by T. W. Page.

name for the holdings also had changed, from tenement in villeinage to copyhold. At the same time, land had begun to be valuable more for the number of sheep than for the number of men on it, so that men were likely to be turned off unless they had strong protection. Land and their relation to it meant then to ordinary Englishmen all that industry and their relation to it mean now, so that this problem had then the interest and urgency of the problems of unemployment, hours, and housing now. All the time that attention is fixed on Tudor dealings with the problems of church government, national independence, finance, parliament, local administration, the back of the mind must remember that they were trying to deal with this economic problem also, and that it was in a real sense not less truly constitutional than economic. As it is highly relevant to the political problems that a free and equal status was not yet an English commonplace, so to the economic problem it is relevant that the protection of copyhold by the king's courts was not of immemorial antiquity and perhaps not of universal and undoubted efficacy. Mr Leadam may be right, that there was "ample and efficient protection afforded to copyholders between 1450 and 1550", but probably he is a little too optimistic; at any rate "under Henry VII[1] we have in the Year Books very clear instances proving that copyhold cases became determinable at the common law", and common law courts, chancery,[2] star chamber, court of requests,[3] administrative action, were all used for the purpose in Tudor times.[4] This at least is certain, and is to be remembered when approaching Tudor constitutional history, that in those days not every Englishman was born with an ancestral assurance or grew up with an unchallengeable assumption that he was as free, and the law could not doubt he

[1] Cf. p. 172, n. 3 above.
[2] Cf. I. S. Leadam on "Security of Copyholders in the Fifteenth and Sixteenth Centuries", *E.H.R.* VIII, pp. 676, 684, 686. He thinks also, on the other hand (*Requests*, p. xvi, referring to *T.R.H.S.* 1892, p. 229, *E.H.R.* Oct. 1893), that the relation of tenants to manorial courts and their own functions therein declined very much, so that in the sixteenth century their verdicts were limited to matters of fact and the law handed over entirely to the lords' stewards: cf. also pp. lii, liv, lxvi, lxxi.
[3] Cf. p. 37.above.
[4] A. Savine, "Copyhold Cases in the Early Chancery Proceedings", *E.H.R.* VIII, p. 303.

was as free, as his master, and that his land was as safe, and the law would see it was as safe, as his neighbour's. Such were the vestiges, neither rare nor obscure, of villein blood and villein tenure; and the ideas and practices of governing and being governed could not be unaffected by them.

About every branch of English government, such as it was when the Tudors began to reign, something has now been said—about every branch except one, church government. Though here mentioned last in order it is not last, perhaps even it is first, in interest and importance— most clearly illuminating the mind of the age which was just breaking into the beginnings of modernity, entitled to an exclusive supervision of the highest and most intimate concerns of men, quite indispensable even to those jurisdictions with which it was not directly concerned, raising by its very existence all the great questions of political theory, destined shortly by its changes to revolutionise political theory and practice—all these eminences might be claimed for the ecclesiastical organisation. Something of its nature and situation at the beginning of the sixteenth century may be illustrated from some incidents of Henry VII's dealings with it.

Henry was well disposed by dynastic tradition, and apparently by personal inclination, to the Church. The policy which made of an exiled pretender the monarch who ended the civil wars and united the Roses he owed very largely to John Morton bishop of Ely, whom he made archbishop of Canterbury. Not only did he take great care that there should be no doubt about the Church's approval of his marriage to a distant relative,[1] but he was also at pains to obtain and make known the papal recognition of his title to the throne,[2] publishing an English version of Innocent VIII's bull on what was perhaps the first of all printed broadsides and is at any rate the oldest extant.[3] He liked to choose his ministers from among churchmen, and all his chancellors, beginning with Morton, were bishops. He burnt heretics, and once at least by his royal exhortation converted one from his errors, though he

[1] Cf. W. Busch, *England under the Tudors*, I, p. 29.
[2] Wm. Campbell, *Materials Illustrative of the Reign of Henry VII*, I, p. 392.
[3] Cf. Camden Miscellany (1847), vol. I.

burnt him all the same.[1] He was a builder of churches and a patron of ecclesiastical foundations.

With regard to the pope's cherished project of a crusade against the Turks, Henry was; if not gushingly sympathetic nor rashly profuse, at least courteous and respectful.[2] In 1501 he admitted the nuncio who was sent to distribute the indulgences; these were to be sold to the faithful who had been unable to attend the previous year's jubilee at Rome, the payments to be on a sliding scale according to the incomes of the purchasers and to be applied towards the crusade.[3] Henry did not, like his brother-monarchs, keep half the proceeds,[4] but forwarded £4000 to Rome, in spite of a hint from Ferdinand the Catholic of the advisability of a more direct use of the money, "for if they should send it to the Pope it is certain that he would expend it for some other purpose and not on account of the said expedition".[5] To the pope's suggestion that he should himself be a crusader Henry replied with a polite excuse, not concealing his conviction that the Turks, even if they should reach Italy, were hardly a menace to England. He seems however to have had some interest in their repulse, for the Knights of Rhodes made him protector of their Order, and towards the end of his reign he positively urged the project upon Julius II.[6]

---

[1] C. L. Kingsford, *Chronicles of London*, p. 222, quoted A. F. Pollard, *Contemporary Sources*, III, p. 239: for other heresy cases, and ecclesiastical information generally, see pp. 150–255, and C. H. Williams, *England under the Early Tudors*, pp. 182–209.
[2] Cf. J. O. Halliwell-Phillipps, *Letters of the Kings*, I, pp. 185–94; part of his excuse was that English sailors were not accustomed to sailing beyond Pisa: he had discussed the matter with the nobles of this land, as well spiritual as temporal, being of his council in this behalf. Note that in the fifteenth century "Crusades aroused little interest, although Catholic Europe was more seriously menaced by Islam than it had been for centuries", W. T. Waugh, *Europe from 1378 to 1494*, p. 2.
[3] *L. and P. Henry VII*, p. 93.   [4] J. Gairdner, *Henry VII*, p. 177.
[5] Letter from Ferdinand and Isabella to their ambassador in England in 1502, printed by J. Gairdner in an appendix to his *Memorials of King Henry VII*, p. 414.
[6] J. Gairdner, *Henry VII*, pp. 177, 178. On the other hand, earlier attempts (1487, 1489, 1497) at raising money for crusading purposes had not been very successful; the English government did not scandalously obstruct, but was not more than decently helpful: on one occasion, when the collecting box had been passed round at court, "the contributions of the royal family and the assembled dukes, earls, and high officials only amounted to eleven pounds and as many shillings", Wm. Busch, *England under the Tudors*, I, p. 232; Busch adds that "On one occasion it was pointed out to the Pope as a special merit of Henry's that he, unlike other monarchs, had himself made over to the Roman chair two subsidies for the crusade", but I am not sure what this means.

In matters that came nearer home the English monarchy got on very well with the papacy. In July 1487[1] Henry wrote to Innocent VIII to describe to him the appalling fate of a contemner of papal sanctions, who on false news of the king's defeat harangued a group of sanctuary-men to this effect: "Do you not perceive that interdicts of that sort are of no weight whatever, since you see with your own eyes that those very men who obtained such in their own favour are routed...?" On pronouncing which words "he instantly fell dead upon the ground, and his face and body immediately became blacker than soot".[2] Henry went on to suggest the excommunication of the Irish bishops who had favoured Simnel, and the pope replied favourably.[3] The Milanese envoy told his master ten years later what advantage the king derived from the ease with which he obtained "ecclesiastical censures, so that at all times rebels are excommunicated. The efficacy of these censures is now felt by the Cornishmen, for all who eat grain garnered since the rebellion, or drink beer brewed with this year's crops, die as if they had taken poison, and hence it is publicly reported that the King is under the protection of God eternal".[4] Henry had also the prestige o high honours conferred by the pope, from whom no less than three times he received the sword and cap of maintenance;[5] but he failed to secure the canonisation of Henry VI.[6] How close was the connection in political minds between the secular and the spiritual is shown again by a letter from Somerset and Warham to the king, warning him that he must expect no security of the Emperor Maximilian's observing the treaty they were making unless he would submit to be bound by ecclesiastical censures.[7]

[1] *L. and P. Henry VII*, I, p. 95: at about the same time Innocent VIII declared that sanctuary should not be available for fraudulent debtors, cf. p. 179 below. In 1442 and 1462 the pope had issued mandates for enquiring into abuse of sanctuary.
[2] *L. and P. Henry VII*, I, p. 95.
[3] Pollard, *Contemporary Sources*, III, p. 158, quoting from Wilkins' *Concilia*, III, p. 623.
[4] Pollard, *Contemporary Sources*, I, p. 160, referring to *Venetian Calender*, no. 1 (ed. Rawdon Brown), p. 751, *Milanese Calendar* (ed. A. B. Hinds), no. 1, p. 323 (these two references are to the same letter).
[5] Pollard, *Contemporary Sources*, I, pp. lxiii, 251; II, p. 231.
[6] Busch, p. 229.
[7] *L. and P. Henry VII*, I, p. 172.

More continuously and materially important, and indeed essential at that time to satisfactory administration, was the control of clerical appointments. In this matter Henry found no difficulty: chapters were always willing to elect, and popes to provide, his nominees, who were his ministers whenever that suited him and foreigners only when he chose. The pope made only one English cardinal when five had been suggested, but the one was Morton, and perhaps Henry did not really feel very strongly about getting more. He did not attack ecclesiastical wealth but contented himself with the indirect exploitation of ecclesiastical revenues as an endowment for his service.[1] Indeed, a highly competent observer, Edmund Dudley, treated the king's influence on episcopal appointments as exclusive. After explaining that the love of God was the chief root of the tree of commonwealth, he went on to say that this might be supposed to be the clergy's business, but "verily the Prince is the ground out of the which this root must chiefly grow, for that it is he that doth appoint and make the Bishops", and provide them with force when necessary, whereby "he assisteth his maker and redeemer, of whom he hath all his power and authority".[2]

The beginning of the Tudor period was medieval in this sense, that an established and almost unquestioned orthodoxy still taught the existence of a wide area[3] of human thought and action which belonged properly to the ecclesiastical government headed by the pope, and in which any competition by secular authority would offend the highest of all laws. The Middle Ages had been accustomed to frequent frontier wars[4] about the line to be drawn between this

[1] Cf. Busch, pp. 231, 383, and Pollard, *Contemporary Sources*, I, p. lxi.
[2] E. Dudley, *Tree of Commonwealth*, p. 9.
[3] What the Middle Ages called a "liberty": Edward IV (1462) took much money from the Church, and in return confirmed its liberties, prerogatives and customs, especially the privilege of trial in the ecclesiastical courts: cf. Rymer, XI, p. 493; Wilkins, III, pp. 583 and 616 (endorsement by Richard III); and the comments of C. L. Scofield, *Life and Reign of Edward IV*, I, p. 282 and II, p. 391.
[4] A bishop would then be in the position of someone with citizenship and properties and duties in each of two belligerent states: how could he obey the Statutes of Provisors and Praemunire and keep the oath of papal fealty which, e.g., Warham took on promotion to Canterbury in 1503 (Wilkins, III, p. 697; Pollard, *Contemporary Sources*, III, p. 182)?

"spiritual" area and that which should be the undoubted province of the royal government. Henry VII's reign was troubled by no such disputes.

As has been seen, the *regnum* assisted the *sacerdotium* in the correction of heresy, not uncommon at the time;[1] the *sacerdotium* facilitated the business of the *regnum* by complacence in the matter of appointments. Convocations were summoned by royal writs and gave no anxiety to the royal mind. The hands of the bishops were strengthened for dealing with monastic and other clerical disorders by statute empowering them to inflict secular punishments;[2] and the king found the pope friendly and helpful about two border-line cases of a very debatable kind—benefit of clergy, and sanctuary.[3]

Sanctuaries were places, usually consecrated, in which fugitives from justice could find refuge and from which they could leave the realm. There were various restrictions: some places could give permanent protection, but in most sanctuaries the refugee could be starved into surrender after forty days; clerks could not take sanctuary but must be surrendered to the spiritual arm; men who had been condemned, or taken with stolen property on them, or who had committed felonies in church, could not take sanctuary; it was doubtful whether the privilege extended to treason, and efforts had been made to restrict its abuse by debtors.[4]

It was with this object that the matter was again taken up in Henry VII's reign. On 6 February 1486[5] the abbot of Westminster with his counsel came into the parliament chamber and showed the

---

[1] Cf. Pollard, *Contemporary Sources*, III, pp. 234 ff. Complaints by laymen of the behaviour of priests (cf. e.g. proceedings in Convocation 1487, Wilkins, III, pp. 618, 619) were of course quite a different thing.

[2] 1 H. VII c. 4.

[3] Cf. above, pp. 137, 147.

[4] Holdsworth, III, pp. 304–6: cf. also I. D. Thornley on *The Destruction of Sanctuary* in *Tudor Studies* (ed. R. W. Seton-Watson), p. 183, especially where she argues for the essentially un-ecclesiastical nature of the privilege and shows how it was protected on ecclesiastical estates by Becket's martyrdom: and p. 197, where she shows how the judges ruled out "by the time of Henry VIII" any claim to sanctuary where there was not a royal grant supported by usage and by allowance in general eyre.

[5] *Y.B.* 1 H. VII Hil. pl. 11, fol. 10: there is a version in Pollard, *Contemporary Sources*, III, p. 196.

privileges of his place, and so on. And he was advised by the lords spiritual and the judges that it was not well done of him to have his franchises and liberties argued, but that it would be better to see that the safeguards of them were well and duly kept. And that he himself would not think otherwise, but only those would disagree who cloaked evil-doers and rascals under cover of the liberties. And further, that the king had enlarged the statutes 50 E. III and 7 R. II against sanctuary-men defrauding their creditors. And opinion was given that he would go further in this matter by way of amending the said statutes.

The opinion proved correct: a few weeks later the judges showed their earnestness in the matter (and indeed they had by nature always disliked exceptions to jurisdiction) by the decision in Humphrey Stafford's case,[1] holding that not merely usage but also express warrant by charter and allowance in eyre were necessary to establish sanctuary rights, a decision which deprived almost every sanctuary of any claim to protect treason; and in 1487 not only did Innocent VIII[2] declare that sanctuary should not be available for fraudulent debtors, but also parliament[3] prohibited the practice of debtors assigning their goods to third parties so that they might live in sanctuary on the income, to the rage and loss of their creditors.

The papacy helped the regulation of sanctuary in other respects besides this of debt. A bull of Innocent VIII's in 1487, confirmed by Alexander VI in 1493,[4] deprived sanctuary-men of the privilege if they committed a second offence, and ordered traitors in sanctuary to be

[1] Referred to by Thornley, p. 199: *Y.B.* 1 H. VII Pasch. pl. 15, and Trin. pl. 1. Miss Thornley comments: "The King took a special interest in the case, perhaps because Henry VI in similar circumstances had failed in his object (in Cayme's Case, 1451, Thornley, p. 191). He desired the judges' opinion before the case came on, and was angry at the week's delay granted to Stafford to prepare his defence". The standard which the judges took was the charter of Westminster; this was a forgery, so that sanctuary had undone itself by doing too well for itself.
[2] Holdsworth, III, p. 307. It was in this year that the Westminster sanctuary-men "upon the false news that Henry VII had been defeated by the rebels,...mustered in a body to rob the houses of those whom they knew to be with the King in the field", Thornley, p. 186.
[3] 3 H. VII c. 4 (*S.R.* II, p. 513).
[4] Julius II in 1504: Thornley, p. 200, n. 90.

guarded by royal officers.[1] Clearly government well understood the evils of sanctuary.

"In another way, also, the priests are the occasion of crimes", wrote an Italian who visited England, probably in 1496–7: his "other way" was by benefit of clergy. Here also Rome did not hinder Henry's efforts to cut down abuses.

Benefit of clergy (originally exemption of clerics from punishment by secular courts) had been extended to all men who could read. On the other hand, high treason and some great offences, as well as all that minor class called *transgressiones*, misdemeanours, had been excluded from it, clergy could be pleaded only after conviction (so that the offender's goods would be forfeited to the crown), and the royal courts had usurped the right of deciding when the privilege was claimable; but the privilege still extended to petty treason and to most felonies.[2] 4 H. VII c. 13 distinguished between those actually in orders, who were to keep their privilege intact, and others, who on a first conviction were to be branded and disabled from pleading clergy again; 7 H. VII c. 1 withdrew the benefit from military deserters, and 12 H. VII c. 7[3] withdrew it from laymen in cases of petty treason, "slaying their master or their immediate sovereign".

These amendments are none of them very drastic, but they are further evidence how important the ecclesiastical organisation still was to the administration of the state, and how well the two got on together in Henry VII's time. It would be a mistake, however, to conclude that either was in a position of absolute dominance over the other or that their respective competences had been finally delimited. The Italian observer was certainly wrong when he wrote that "the clergy are they

[1] And see Pollard, *Contemporary Sources*, III, p. 184, for a bull transferring the spiritual jurisdiction of the Channel Islands from Coutances to Winchester, and another suppressing various priories: and Le Neve, *Fasti Eccl. Angl.* I, pp. 24, 142, 248, 300, 340, 376, 466, 554, for bulls providing and translating bishops.

[2] Holdsworth, III, pp. 294–9. Cf. L. C. Gabel, *Benefit of Clergy in England*: according to Miss Gabel, p. 122, Edward IV (cf. p. 177, n. 3 above) gave up almost all that secular jurisdiction had gained since Bracton, though practice does not seem to have been affected.

[3] It may be noted that this act was given retrospective force, so as to punish James Grame who had killed his master. This is to be remembered in considering the development of the Legislature.

who have the supreme sway over the country, both in peace and war".

There was a case early in the reign of a confusion of spiritual and secular interests, a clash of the royal and papal authorities. On the Sabbath after the Purification in the first year of Henry's reign[1] "the Chancellor asked of the *Judges* what should be done with the alum that was taken by Englishmen from the Florentines here in England, because the holy Father the Pope had sent to excommunicate all who attached the said alum from the Florentines, etc." The judges thought "that when merchandise came into the land by the safe-conduct of the king, that the king must be safeguard to the merchants, that they shall not be despoiled in his land, and especially by his lieges". But they, and at least one bishop, were reminded by this problem of earlier cases where papal authority had seemed too exigent and had been firmly dealt with: and "my lord *Hussey* said, that in the time of king Edward IV a Legate was at Calais, and sent to the king to have his safe-conduct to come in his land, and then in full council before the lords and Judges was asked, what shall be done: Who said that [a message] should be sent to the Legate, and if he would swear that he had brought nothing with him that should be in derogation of the king and of his crown, that he should have licence, or otherwise not", and so was done. "And the *chief Justice* said, that in the time of king Edward I" the pope sent him directions about his dealings with Scotland, and "the king by the advice of his council wrote to the Pope that he had not in the temporalty any persons above him, but that he is immediate to God....And the bishop of London said that he saw in the time of King Henry VI that when the Pope sent letters that were in derogation of the king, etc. And the spirituals dare not speak of that, that Humfrey Duke of Gloucester took the letters and put them in the fire...."

Yet not even the lawyers denied that there was an area of government[2] in which ecclesiastical authority was supreme: "It seems that the King cannot be called parson by Act of Parliament, for no temporal act can

---

[1] *Y.B.* 1 H. VII Hil. pl. 10: my translation. For other references about the alum dispute, see Busch, p. 383.
[2] Cf. p. 178 above.

cause a temporal act to make a temporal man have spiritual jurisdiction. For if it was ordained by act, etc., that such a one should not tender tithes to his curate, the act would be void, for concerning such a thing as touches merely the spirituality, such temporal act cannot make any ordinance": so argued a learned serjeant, and the chief justice agreed: "a temporal act without the assent of the Supreme Head [i.e. the pope] cannot make the King a Parson".[1]

There were other stories that might have been revived of how kings had thought popes arrogant and of the means they had employed to resist them; and controversies of more ambiguous import had not been forgotten, as when the northern rebels of 1489 proclaimed their intention "to withstand such persons as is aboutward for to destroy our sovereign Lord the King and the Commons of England for such unlawful points as Saint Thomas of Canterbury died for".[2]

Clearly, then, as the fifteenth century was being succeeded by the sixteenth, and the seventh Henry by the eighth, the political and ecclesiastical governments had the habit of amicable co-operation, but causes of conflict between them were not defunct nor methods of controversy forgotten.

---

[1] *Y.B.* 21 H. VII pl. 1 (p. 2), quoted from C. H. McIlwain, *High Court of Parliament*, p. 277.
[2] *Paston Letters*, III, no. 916 (ed. J. Gairdner, 1896): the proclamation was in the name of "Mayster Hobbe Hyrste, Robyn Godfelaws brodyr he is, as I trow".

LIST OF AUTHORITIES

ANDRÉ, BERNARD. *Vita Henrici Septimi* (ed. Jas. Gairdner, Rolls Series, vol. 10, 1858) *or* ANDREAS, BERNARDUS, *Historia Regis Henrici VII.*

BACON, F. *Works* (ed. W. Spedding); *Henry VII* (ed. J. R. Lumby).

BALDWIN, J. F. *The King's Council in England during the Middle Ages* (1913).

BEARD, C. A. *Justice of the Peace.*

BENHAM, W. G. (ed.). *Red Paper Book of Colchester.*

BERGENROTH, G. A. (ed.). *Calendar of the Simancas Papers.*

BLOCH, MARC. *Les Rois Thaumaturges.*

BOLLAND, W. C. *Eyre of Kent* (Selden Society).

BROOKE, Z. N. *The English Church and the Papacy.*

BUSCH, WM. *England under the Tudors.*

CAESAR, J. *Ancient State Authoritie and Proceedings of the Court of Requests* (1597).

CAMPBELL, WM. *Materials Illustrative of the Reign of Henry VII* (Rolls Series, 60, i, ii, 1873).

CHEYNEY, E. P. "The Disappearance of English Serfdom", in *English Historical Review*, vol. XV.

CHURCHILL, E. F. "The Crown and its Servants", in *Law Quarterly Review*, vol. XLII.

COKE, E. *Institutes.*

CONWAY, AGNES. *Henry VII's Relations with Scotland and Ireland.*

COX, HOMERSHAM. *Antient Parliamentary Elections.*

CRAIES, W. F. *Statute Law.*

CUNNINGHAM, W. *Growth of English Industry and Commerce.*

DAVIES, R. *Extracts from Municipal Records of the City of York, 1461–85* (1843).

DICEY, A. V. *Law of the Constitution* (edn. 1923).

DIETZ, F. C. *English Government Finance, 1485–1558* (Univ. of Illinois, Studies in Social Science, vol. IX, 1920).

DOWELL, S. *History of Taxation* (1888).

DRAKE, F. *Eboracum* (1736).

DUDLEY, E. *Tree of Commonwealth.*

ELSYNGE, HY. *Manner of Holding Parliaments.*

FINLASON, W. F. *The Judicial Committee of the Privy Council.*

FIRTH, C. H. *The House of Lords during the Civil War.*

FORTESCUE, J. *Works* (ed. Lord Clermont).

—— *Governance of England.*

FORTESCUE, J. W. *History of the British Army.*

GABEL, L. C. *Benefit of Clergy in England* (1929).

GAIRDNER, JAS. *Henry VII.*

—— (ed.). *Paston Letters* (library edition, 1904).

—— *Letters and Papers Illustrative of the Reigns of Richard III and Henry VII* (Rolls Series, no. 24, 1861 and 1863).

GAIRDNER, JAS. (ed.). *Letters and Papers, Foreign and Domestic, of the Reign of Henry VIII* (some vols. ed. J. S. Brewer and some R. H. Brodie).

GLADISH, D. M. *The Tudor Privy Council* (1915).

GNEIST, H. R. *Self-government in England.*

GRAS, N. W. B. "Tudor 'Books of Rates'", in *Quarterly Journal of Economics*, vol. XXVI.

GRAY, H. L. *Influence of the Commons on Early Legislation* (Harvard Historical Studies, vol. XXXIV, 1932).

HALE, M. *Jurisdiction of the Lords House.*

—— *Pleas of the Crown; Historia Placitorum Coronae.*

HALLIWELL (or HALLIWELL-PHILLIPPS), J. O. *Letters of the Kings of England.*

HARCOURT, L. W. V. *His Grace the Steward and Trial of Peers.*

HASBACH, W. *English Agricultural Labourer.*

HATSELL, JOHN. *Cases of Privilege of Parliament.*

HOLDSWORTH, W. S. *History of English Law* (3rd edn., 1922 and later).

HOLINSHED, RAPHAEL. *Chronicles* (1587).

HUDSON, WM. *A Treatise on the Court of Star Chamber.*

JERDAN, WM. (ed.). *Rutland Papers* (Camden Society, 1st series, vol. 21), (1842).

KERLY, D. M. *Historical Sketch of the Equitable Jurisdiction of Chancery.*

KERN, FRITZ. "Recht und Verfassung im Mittelalter", in *Historische Zeitschrift*, 3te Folge, 24 Bd., 1 Heft.

KINGSFORD, C. L. (ed.). *Chronicles of London* (1905).

KIPLING, R. *Rewards and Fairies.*

LAMBARD, WM. *Eirenarcha* (edn. 1610).

LAPSLEY, G. T. *County Palatine of Durham.*

LEADAM, I. S. "Security of Copyholders in the Fifteenth and Sixteenth Centuries", in *English Historical Review*, vol. VIII.

—— "Last Days of Bondage", in *Law Quarterly Review*, vol. IX.

—— (ed.). *Select Cases in the Court of Requests* (Selden Society, vol. 12), (1898).

—— (ed.). *Select Cases before the King's Council in the Star Chamber* (Selden Society, vols. 16 and 25), (1903 and 1911).

LEADAM, I. S. and BALDWIN, J. F. (eds.). *Select Cases before the King's Council* (Selden Society, vol. 35), (1918).

LE NEVE, J. *Fasti Ecclesiae Anglicanae.*

LEONARD, E. M. *Early History of English Poor Relief.*

Letters and Papers, Foreign and Domestic, of the Reign of Henry VIII (some vols. ed. J. S. Brewer and some R. H. Brodie). Ed. by Jas. Gairdner.

LODGE, E. *Illustrations of British History.*

LUMBY, J. R. (ed.). F. Bacon's *Henry VII.*

MCILWAIN, C. H. *High Court of Parliament.*

MCKISACK, M. "Borough Representation in Richard II's Reign", printed in *English Historical Review*, vol. XXXIX.

MAITLAND, F. W. *Collected Papers* (1911).

MAITLAND, F. W. *Justice and Police.*

—— (ed.). *Memoranda de Parliamento,* or *Records of The Parliament Holden at Westminster,* A.D. 1305 (Rolls Series, no. 98, 1893).

MANNING, JAS. and GRANGER, T. C. *Cases in the Court of Common Pleas.*

MAXWELL-LYTE, H. C. *The Great Seal* (1926).

MAY, THOS. ERSKINE. *Laws, Privileges, Proceedings, and Usages of Parliament.*

MEREWETHER, H. A. and STEPHENS, J. S. *History of Boroughs.*

MOUNTMORRES, H. R. M. 2nd Visct. *History of the Principal Transactions of the Irish Parliament.*

NEWTON, A. P. "The King's Chamber under the Early Tudors", in *English Historical Review,* vol. XXXII.

PAGE, T. W. "The End of Villeinage in England", in *American Economic Association,* Series III, vol. I, no. 2.

PALGRAVE, FRANCIS. Evidence in *Report on Public Petitions* (Parl. Papers, 1833, XII, 2nd pagination, p. 19).

PARRY, C. H. *Parliaments and Councils of England* (1839).

Patent Rolls, Calendar of, 1485–94.

PIKE, L. O. *Constitutional History of the House of Lords.*

PLUCKNETT, T. F. T. *Statutes and their Interpretation.*

—— *The Lancastrian Constitution,* in *Tudor Studies* (ed. R. W. Seton-Watson).

POLLARD, A. F. *Reign of Henry VII from Contemporary Sources.*

—— *Evolution of Parliament.*

—— "On the De Facto Act", in *Inst. Hist. Res. Bul.* VII.

POLLOCK, F. and MAITLAND, F. W. *History of English Law.*

POLYDORE VERGIL *or* POLYDORUS VERGILIUS (edn. 1603), *Anglicae Historiae Libri,* bk. XXXI.

PORRITT, E. and A. G. *The Unreformed House of Commons.*

PRYNNE, WM. *Brevia Parliamentaria Rediviva.*

REDLICH, J. *Procedure of the House of Commons.*

REEVES, J. *History of the English Law.*

REID, R. R. *The King's Council in the North.*

RIESS, L. *Geschichte des Wahlrechts zum englischen Parlament* (Leipzig, 1885).

ROPER, WM. *Life of More* (ed. J. R. Lumby).

Rotuli Parliamentorum... or *Rolls of Parliament.*

RYMER, T. *Foedera, Conventiones, Litterae,* etc.

RUSSELL, F. W. *Kett's Rebellion in Norfolk.*

SAINT-GERMAN, CHR. *Doctor and Student.*

SALZMANN, L. F. *English Trade in the Middle Ages.*

SAVINE, A. "Bondmen under the Tudors", in *Royal Historical Society,* new series, vol. XVII.

—— "Copyhold Cases in the Early Chancery Proceedings", in *English Historical Review,* vol. VIII.

SCOFIELD, C. L. *The Court of Star Chamber.*

—— *Edward IV.*

SHEPPARD, J. B. (ed.). *Christchurch Letters* (Camden Society, new series, vol. 19), (1877).

SKEEL, C. A. J. *The Council in the Marches of Wales.*

SKOTTOWE, B. G. *Short History of Parliament.*

SMITH, SIR T. *De Republica Anglorum* (ed. L. Alston).

SNEYD, C. A. (ed.). *Italian Relation* (Camden Society, 1st series, vol. 37), (1847).

Spanish Calendar, or *Simancas Papers,* ed. P. Gayangos and G. A. Bergenroth.

SPELMAN, H. *Larger Treatise concerning Tithes* (1646), in *English Works* (1727).

STAPLETON, T. (ed.). *Plumpton Correspondence* (Camden Society, old series, vol. 4), (1839).

Statutes of the Realm.

STEELE, ROBERT R. *Tudor and Stuart Proclamations.*

STEPHEN, J. F. *History of the Criminal Law.*

STUBBS, WM. *Constitutional History of England.*

—— *Seventeen Lectures on the Study of Medieval and Modern History.*

TAIT, JAS. *Taxation in the Salford Hundred* (Cheetham Society, vol. LXXXIII).

TANNER, J. R. *Tudor Constitutional Documents* (2nd edn. 1930).

THAYER, J. B. *Preliminary Treatise on Evidence at the Common Law.*

THOMSON, G. SCOTT. *Lords Lieutenants in the Sixteenth Century.*

THORNLEY, I. D. *The Destruction of Sanctuary,* in *Tudor Studies* (ed. R. W. Seton-Watson).

TOUT, T. F. *Chapters in Medieval Administrative History.*

TROKELOWE, JOANNES DE. *Annales Henrici IV.*

TURNER, E. R. *The Privy Council.*

UNWIN, G. *Industrial Organisation in the Sixteenth and Seventeenth Centuries.*

VINOGRADOFF, P. "Constitutional History and the Year Books", in *Law Quarterly Review,* vol. XXIX, p. 281.

WALLIS, JOHN E. W. *English Regnal Years and Titles.*

WAUGH, W. T. *Europe from 1378 to 1494.*

WHITELOCKE, B. *Notes on the King's Writ* (or *Whitelocke on Parlements*), 1766.

WILLIAMS, C. H. *England under the Early Tudors.*

WINFIELD, P. H. *History of Conspiracy and Abuse of Legal Procedure.*

WITTKE, CARL. *English Parliamentary Privilege.*

Year Books.

INDEX

Alexander VI, and efficacy of interdict, 176; bull about sanctuary, 1493, 179

Appeal, private accusation at common law, 41; before parliament abolished, 1 H. IV c. 14, 116; in modern sense non-existent, 117

Arthur, Prince, death, 1502, 23; grant in lieu of aid for knighting, 1504, 23

Attainder, its effect, 118

Attaint, check on juries, 82 f.

Auditors, or triers of petitions, 122; some commons among, by 1509, 123; judges among them, 132

Bacon, Francis, on Henry's title, and Elizabeth of York, 10, 12; on parliamentary approval of benevolence, 22; on Henry VII's law-making, 145; on corporations, 148; on the De Facto Act, 152

Beauforts, doubtful legitimacy of, 4, 5

Becket, Thomas, presented with sacred oil by the Virgin, 7; invoked by the rebels of 1489, 182

Benefit of clergy, nature and regulation, 180

Benevolence, in 1491 and 1495, and Bacon's comment, 22; Benevolence Act, 11 H. VII c. 10, 147

Bill (cf. Petition), kinds of parliamentary, 121, 123; readings in either house, 124; amendments, 126; and petition, 128 (and earlier); "containing the form of an act", 129

Boroughs, York expecting a vacancy of the crown after 1485, 14; Leicester to frequent the king's ovens, 17; officers and by-law supervised by justices of the peace, 61; some of their officers justices of the peace *ex officio*, 62; and parliament, 97 f.; subordination to statute, 141, 148

Brittany, Henry's debts in, in 1485, 20; preventing absorption of, by France, 1489, 20, 22; duchess's marriage with Charles VIII, 22

Canterbury, archbishop of, his petition in the house of commons, 1401, 123

Certiorari, used by council to procure records of other courts, 46

Chamber, King's, balance held by Treasurer of, 24; and Court of General Surveyors, as royal instruments for controlling finance, 26

Church (cf. Clergy), t.r. Henry VII, 174 ff.; Henry's relations with Rome, 175; appointments, 177; and state, 177 ff.; royal control of emissaries and documents, 181

Clergy (cf. Church), and Benefit: grants by, in 1489 and 1496, 21, 23; clerical character not conferable by temporal authority, 181

Coke, E., on trial without indictment, 150; on the De Facto Act, 155

Commissions, judicial, 56 ff.; regularity of circuits since t.r. Edward I, 57; commissions of the peace, 67; commissions of array, 75

Commons, house of, 90; relation to parliament, 96; superiority of knights to burgesses, 97; composition of house: franchise, 98 f.; quality of election, 101; contests, 103; re-election, 104, 108; royal influence, 105; procedure, 107; and privilege, 109 f.; officers, 114; and attainder, 119; and statute, 125

Constables, and right of arrest, 60; appointment, remuneration, etc., 73 ff.

Constitution, comparative absence of, 1, 5; supremacy of law, 55; and the judges, 58; and juries, 87; increasing recognition of necessity, 163

Convocation (cf. Clergy), grants by, 23; *Y.B.* argument about Convocation being equivalent to Parliament, 159 f.

Cornwall, rebellion defeated at Blackheath, June 1497, 9; fined after the rebellion, 23